GENRE ACROSS THE CURRICULUM

GENRE ACROSS THE CURRICULUM

edited by
ANNE HERRINGTON
CHARLES MORAN

UTAH STATE UNIVERSITY PRESS
Logan, Utah

Utah State University Press
Logan, Utah 84322-7800

Manufactured in the United States of America
Cover design by Barbara Yale-Read

Library of Congress Cataloging-in-Publication Data

Genre across the curriculum / edited by Anne Herrington, Charles Moran.
    p. cm.
 Includes bibliographical references and index.
 ISBN 0-87421-600-1 (alk. paper)
 1. English language–Rhetoric–Study and teaching. 2. Interdisciplinary approach in education. 3.
Academic writing–Study and teaching.
 I. Herrington, Anne, 1948- II. Moran, Charles, 1936-
 PE1404.G398 2005
 808'.042'071–dc22
                        2004022132

CONTENTS

1

THE IDEA OF GENRE IN THEORY AND PRACTICE
An Overview of the Work in Genre in the Fields
of Composition and Rhetoric and New Genre Studies

Anne Herrington and Charles Moran

GENRE IN CLASSICAL RHETORIC

Genre is an idea with a history perhaps as long as that of thought itself. Early creation myths often speak of a creator who brings form out of a formless chaos—in Scandinavian mythology, a cow licks the form of the first human out of a shapeless ice block; in Judeo-Christian mythology, a creator brings order out of a universe "without form and void," and then in the next six days populates it with the "kinds" of animal and plant life. But for our limited purposes here, an inquiry into the value of explicit attention to genre in the teaching of writing, we begin with Plato and Aristotle, both of whom have, in different ways, framed the issues the teachers and students in subsequent chapters will struggle with. What are genres in writing? Do they exist as ideal forms in an empyrean, or in the structures of the brain? Or are these forms to be found in the language that participates in recurring social action? And how are these genres, once described and understood, best taught and learned? In the *Phaedrus*, Socrates argues that advice about form in the existing handbooks is misguided because it ignores the organic relation between form and content. He outlines advice about the form of a speech allegedly drawn from contemporary handbooks:

Socrates: "First, I believe, there is the Preamble with which the speech must begin. This is what you mean, isn't it—the fine points of the art?

Phaedrus: Yes.

Socrates: Second come the Statement of Facts and the Evidence of Witnesses concerning it; third, Indirect Evidence; fourth Claims to Plausibility. And I believe at least that that excellent

	Byzantine word-wizard adds Confirmation and Supplementary Confirmation.
Phaedrus:	You mean the worthy Theodorus?
Socrates:	Quite. And he also adds Refutation and Supplementary Refutation, to be used both in prosecution and defense. Nor must we forget the most excellent Evenus of Paros, who was the first to discover Covert Implication and Indirect Praise. (Plato 1995, 266d–276a)

Socrates' point is that form is not fixed but organic: that the parts must relate organically to the whole, and that form cannot be abstracted from content and practice, then codified, then taught. "Every speech must be put together like a living creature, with a body of its own; it must be neither without head nor without legs; and it must have a middle and extremities that are fitting both to one another and to the whole work" (264c). For Socrates, and by inference Plato, handbook rules will not guide you to this organic unity; the true guide is not the rhetorician's prescriptions but the soul's memory of its experience of the "heaven" of the true and the beautiful.

Aristotle, as Plato's pupil, echoes the language of organic form, particularly in the *Poetics,* where he divides poetry into kinds or categories: "I propose to speak not only of the art in general, but also of its species and their respective capacities; of the structure of the plot required for a good poem; of the number and nature of the constituent parts of a poem . . . Epic poetry and Tragedy, as also Comedy, Dithyrambic poetry—and flute and lyre-playing—are all . . . modes of imitation" (1954, 1447a).

The emphasis in the *Poetics* is most steadily on its description of the structure of the "species"—which we want to begin to consider *genres:* the epic, the tragedy, the comedy. True, for Aristotle the study of drama is valuable because of its social use: the function of tragedy, for example, is famously the *catharsis,* a process by which the performance leaves the audience better than it was through the "proper purgation of the emotions." But the emphasis in the *Poetics* is upon the formal properties of the performance, an emphasis that has carried into the idea of genre in contemporary literary criticism.

Shakespeare's plays, for example, are most often considered tragedies, comedies, or history plays. Those plays—such as *Much Ado about Nothing*—that do not fit these genres have been considered Shakespeare's "problem plays." Until the arrival of the postmodern and the (perhaps) attendant move of English toward cultural studies, literature courses were typically organized around a genre: Nineteenth-Century British Poetry, Elizabethan Drama, The Eighteenth-Century Novel. Literary genres were seen to have origins and trajectories, as in Wellek and Warren's *Theory of Literature* (1942, 235) and Ian Watt's landmark study, *The Rise of the Novel* (1957). Northrop Frye, in his *Anatomy of Criticism*, developed a taxonomy of literary genres in terms of both transcendent aesthetic forms and rhetoric, "the conditions established between the poet and his public" (1957, 247). And, far from dead today, genres survive in MLA job descriptions, where we find advertisements for those qualified to teach these kinds of literature. Literary genres survive as well outside the academy, in the cottage industry that is "genre writing," where aspiring writers can find contemporary handbooks that will instruct them in the writing of "Young Adult Fiction" or "Romance" or "Science Fiction and Fantasy."

In the *Rhetoric*, as in the *Poetics*, Aristotle observes and classifies, discovering and making manifest the forms that are there to be seen. He finds these forms, however, not in an empyrean of pure forms but manifest in the world about him—in actual arguments made in actual and recurring social situations. In his derivation of genre through observation of actual rhetorical performance he anticipates the approach of the functional structural linguists, such as Michael Halliday, who have developed outlines for the study of units of language longer than the sentence—the generic features of extended texts—and linked these genres to recurring social situations. Aristotle lines out the kinds of oratory: forensic, political, epideictic; the kinds of persuasion: logos, ethos, and pathos; and the kinds of argument: the topoi. Yet to a greater degree than in the *Poetics*, these divisions are all keyed to communication/performance in particular and recurrent social situations. As Kenneth Burke noted, "Though Aristotle rigorously divided knowledge into compartments whenever possible, his *Art of Rhetoric* includes much that falls under the headings of psychology, ethics, politics, poetics, logic, and history" (1969, 51). We might add to this list "anthropology," so long as we understand Aristotle as describing the recurring social situations, and their attendant forums, of ancient Greece, and not of all societies in all times. Aristotle instructs us in audience analysis, in the presented persona of the speaker, in appeals to reason and to emotion—all located in social settings, in public forums.

We fast-forward here, through the development and sophistication of Aristotle's *Rhetoric* by Cicero and Quintilian, through the dispersion and loss of the Middle Ages, through the recoveries of the Renaissance, to the redefinition and reduction of genre in nineteenth-century American writing handbooks to the "modes of discourse": exposition, persuasion, description, and narration. These "modes" were based not upon the discourse used in recurring social situations but upon the faculty psychology of Hume and Locke as understood by the eighteenth-century rhetorician George Campbell, whose *Philosophy of Rhetoric* defined the four functions of mind—understanding, imagination, emotion, and will—that corresponded to the four ends of discourse: to inform, to please, to arouse emotion, or to influence action. Robert Connors finds the first American appearance of the "modes of discourse" in Samuel Newman's *A Practical System of Rhetoric*, published in 1827 and reprinted some sixty times by 1856 (Connors, 1981, 445). Connors traces the history of the modes—exposition, persuasion, description, and narration—through Alexander Bain's 1866 *English Composition and Rhetoric* and Genung's *The Practical Elements of Rhetoric* to universal adoption in the rhetoric texts of the early twentieth century. In Connors's words, "From the middle of the last decade of the nineteenth century, through the Great War, and into the middle of the disillusioned decade following it, the modes controlled the teaching of composition through complete control of textbooks" (449).

THE REACTION TO THE MODES: THE WRITING PROCESS MOVEMENT

The importance of the "modes" to the story of genre in composition studies is the hostile reaction to the modes, and to the forms of school writing in general, that begins in the 1960s with what Maxine Hairston has called the "paradigm shift" of the writing process movement (1982, 76). The process movement defined itself against the "other" of "current-traditional" teaching, which was characterized by the prescription of traditional forms of school writing—resulting in what Ken Macrorie would call "Engfish". The attack on the modes, and the concurrent establishment of the "five-paragraph theme" as the antagonist, began with Albert Kitzhaber and continues even today in the strand of pedagogical theory that James Berlin has labeled the "expressionist" school (1987, 145) Kitzhaber's attack on the modes was uncompromising. In his frequently cited doctoral dissertation, written in 1953 but just recently published, he wrote, "The effect of the forms of discourse on rhetorical theory and practice has been bad. They represent an unrealistic view of the writing process, a view that assumes that writing is done by formula and in a social vacuum. They turn the attention of both student and teacher toward an academic exercise instead of toward a meaningful act of communication in a social context" (1990, 139).

From Kitzhaber on, the reaction to the "modes," and to writing taught by formula, has characterized a powerful strand in the teaching of writing, one in which the teaching of genres has been forced into the background. The documents that issued from the 1966 Dartmouth Conference defined the principal aim of instruction in English as personal growth (e.g., Dixon 1967) and paid scant attention to the teaching of forms. James Britton's influential *Language and Learning* (1970) established a set of "kinds" of writing based not on form but on function, upon what the writing did for the author. "Transactional" writing helped the writer participate in the work of the world; it was "language to get things done" (125). "Expressive" writing helped the writer make sense of her world; and "poetic" writing was expressive in its function but included as well an element of "formal arrangement" (177). The function of poetic writing was "to be an object that pleases or satisfies the writer" (1975, 91). In *The Development of Writing Abilities (11–18)* (Britton et al. 1975), Britton explicitly attacked the teaching of the "modes," which, he wrote, "have shown a remarkable capacity for survival" and "survive unscathed in the most influential of contemporary manuals" (3). In Britton's view, school writing focused too intensely on the transactional, leaving little room in the curriculum for the expressive and its consequent participation in students' personal growth. In the writing classes that followed the "personal growth" model, transactional writing was devalued, and this closed off the possibility of explicit teaching of the kinds of writing we do to "get things done," including the genres of academic writing.

For classrooms based on the work of James Moffett (1981), genres emerged organically from the students' writing as it was composed, and could be reinforced and coached by the teacher as it emerged, but not explicitly assigned or pre-taught. In *Active Voice* (1981) Moffett writes, "Coming up with a subject, a reason for writing about it, and a form to write it in can often happen rather naturally for individuals in an integrated language arts program where writing is going on in close conjunction with dramatic activities, work in other media, and reading in literature and other areas" (18). In classrooms based on the work of Donald Graves (1983), the teacher was to "[s]urround the children with literature" (65) and let genres emerge from the reading and writing that the teacher orchestrates in the elementary classroom. Donald Murray's influential book, *A Writer Teaches Writing* (1968), deals only briefly with genres in his section on creating assignments. He echoes the "modes of discourse" when he suggests that "most students will probably learn best in the beginning through description" (134), and suggests that student writers be encouraged to increase the range of genres in which they are writing, but he says nothing beyond this brief mention of genre about if or how form should be understood and taught—perhaps the perspective of the journalist, for whom forms of writing become habitual and therefore transparent.

This reaction to the teaching of the "modes," with its concomitant understanding of genre as form, continues today in textbooks that follow an expressivist epistemology. In their *Community of Writers* (1995), Peter Elbow and Pat Belanoff describe the genre "essay" in these terms: "The essay is a slithery form; perhaps (notice we only say *perhaps*) we all recognize an essay when we see one, but few of us could actually define the form. This may well be its strength" (232). In Elbow and Belanoff, we ask our students to write essays, but we are not to try to be explicit about the formal properties of the genre. This approach, contemporary genre theorists would be quick to point out, excludes all who are not "we," which is a group of writers and readers steeped in the masterpieces of Western literature. A writer outside this "we" is left to figure it all out on his or her own. Elbow and Belanoff continue the long-standing attack on the teaching of the five-paragraph theme: "This is a school-invented genre, and unfortunately, it is the only genre that some students are taught" (132). "But it is a handy formula in certain conditions where you don't want to think an issue through—either for lack of time or because you've already worked it out. . . . Thus, it is a handy genre for timed exams: 'In twenty minutes, explain the importance of the Civil War.'" In recent editions of the textbook, there is more attention to genre, but this is genre understood as form and not as linked to recurring social action (126).

This reaction to the "modes" appears as well in Tom Romano's recent advocacy (2000) of the multigenre paper, a composition that might include prose, poetry, dance, music, and graphics. In the teacher testimonials that Romano includes in his first chapter, the teachers say again and again that the multigenre papers they get are "more interesting" than the research papers they used to assign and read. In their words we hear the echo of Ken Macrorie's attempts to root out "Engfish" from his students' writing. Romano shares with Macrorie, and with Moffett, the assumption that his students, given the freedom to draw on a number of forms, will discover the appropriate forms and order them appropriately. Nowhere in his book is there explicit teaching of genre, and nowhere in the book is an understanding that genre is connected to social action.

And the reaction to the modes appears as well in the exploration of alternative discourses that was such a powerful strand in the 2001 CCCC (Powell 2002, 11) and in the subsequent publication of *AltDis* (Schroeder, Fox, and Bizzell, 2002), in which the authors advocate subverting an assumed standard academic discourse with alternative discourses—at times (Bizzell 2002) to open up new ways of thinking, and at times to create a "contact zone" between a monolithic academic discourse and other, marginalized discourses (Long). This book feels revolutionary in its intent, with its dedication "to everyone who has the courage to experiment with alternatives." In the preface this radical motive becomes overt: "*Alternative* evokes a sort of counter-cultural image that bespeaks the political resistance to hegemonic discourse that these new forms express—thus we see that the old left-liberal, social-justice-oriented agenda that motivated 'The Students' Right to Their Own Language' resolution maybe reemerging in a new guise" (ix). If we can tie the writing process "paradigm shift" to the "old left-liberal, social-justice-oriented agenda," as James Marshall (1994) so fully does, then *AltDis* can be read as following the line that we began in this section with Albert Kitzhaber and the reaction to prescriptive, acontextual modes of discourse. Important for our genre studies as well is the assumption in the work of the *AltDis* authors and of Tom Romano that teachers, and their student writers, have some say in the definitions of the genres in which they will write.

GENRE AND WRITING ACROSS THE CURRICULUM

The rise in writing across the curriculum (WAC) programs and scholarship in the 1970s and 1980s has its roots both in the writing process movement and in the study of rhetoric. Reflecting these different emphases, WAC has been characterized as comprising two strands: writing to learn and writing in the disciplines. While these distinctions are overly simplistic, they do reflect different stances toward genre and its role in curricular planning and learning. The "writing to learn" strand focuses on having students use writing to engage in exploratory thinking and learning in ways assumed to be useful in any classroom, in any discipline. Inspired by the developmental theories and research of James Britton, Nancy Martin, and their colleagues in the United Kingdom, proponents of this approach in the United States championed the expressive function of writing, which Britton et al. claim "may be at any stage the kind of writing best adapted to exploration and discovery" (1975, 197). Extrapolated from this claim is a sense that transactional functions (e.g., report, analogic)—functions associated with public genres and their writer-audience relations—are not as conducive for learning. As Randall Freisinger has written, "Language for learning is different from language for informing" (1980, 155). This more dismissive view of the learning potential of transactional functions was also linked for Britton et al. with their research finding that this function, coupled with a "pupil to examiner" writer-audience relationship, predominated in British schools over poetic and expressive functions. Arthur Applebee (1974) reached the same finding in a study of writing in U.S. schools.

For writing to learn advocates in the United States, the approach of Britton and colleagues was compatible with the view of writing as personal growth that issues from the 1966 Dartmouth Conference and progressive, expressivist traditions that viewed genres as narrow forms that constrained creativity and exploration of one's own ideas and voice. In his history of WAC in the United States, David Russell notes the connection with expressivists of the 1920s and 1930s who "dismissed the established genres and styles of academic writing as too confining and encouraged students to find more creative approaches for writing about experience, whether studying English or other subjects" (1991, 207). Also influential to WAC at this time was the focus on the process of writing, specifically Janet Emig's claim in "Writing as a Mode of Learning" (1977) that the activity of writing has a unique cognitive value for thinking and learning for the *writer*. From these various influences, "writing to learn" pedagogy came to be characterized by a focus on the value of writing for the learner and less so for its social function for readers, which meant a de-emphasis on genres and an emphasis on exploratory writing to a teacher in an assumed audience role as participant in a "teacher-learner dialogue." Journals—a genre themselves, although not presented as such—were advocated as a tool for learning, because they were assumed to invite expressive writing and were assumed to be free of the formal constraints of public genres. They were valued above transactional writing, which was represented as aiming to display knowledge (Fulwiler1987, 1979).

While we see this limited conception of the learning potential of transactional writing as mistaken, we also acknowledge the valuable work accomplished by advocates of this approach: by working directly with faculty from a range of disciplines to urge them to incorporate into their courses more expressive writing, through journals and other informal writing, they were working to broaden the types and functions of writing practiced in specific learning contexts across the curriculum.

The other strand of writing across the curriculum scholarship, characterized as "writing in the disciplines," focused on having students learn the ways of writing and reasoning assumed to be characteristic of academic contexts. The pedagogical focus of this approach is seen in such texts as Maimon et al.'s *Writing in the Arts and Sciences* (1981) and Bazerman's *The Informed Writer* (1981). Both conceptualize writing in terms of types—for example, the research paper, book review, laboratory report, journal—that entail particular kinds of thinking (e.g., interpretation, synthesis) and forms (e.g., types of documentation). For this group, genre represents an important concept for planning curriculum and writing assignments and for learning. This approach was influenced more by rhetorical theory than by developmental theory. The basic assumption was that by learning the genres of a given discipline or cluster of disciplines (e.g., humanities, natural sciences), one learned ways of thinking and problem solving. In other words, by learning and writing in public, transactional genres, students were *learning*. With this approach, audience is more of a focus, particularly the conventionalized assumptions of academic audiences. Using the metaphor of an informed conversation, Bazerman tells students that they will be learning to participate as "informed writers" in an academic conversation, learning "the issues, the level of the conversation, the typical ways of speaking, and the rules of proof and audience" (5). While these texts are conceptually sound, a practical limitation is that they were designed for composition courses taught most often by teachers trained in English. Thus, the informed conversation was with an audience not necessarily knowledgeable of the issues and lines of reasoning of particular disciplines. A more general critique is that this approach lends itself to a master-apprentice model where students are to be socialized into disciplines in uncritical ways, accepting the genres—and thus, the practices and ideologies of specific disciplines and the academy in general—as authoritative (Malinowitz 1998).

Research linked with this approach included both studies of professional contexts and texts (e.g., Bazerman's historical study of the evolution of the genre of the scientific research report, *Shaping Written Knowledge: The Genre and Activity of the Experimental Article in Science* [1988]) and classroom-based studies, including my (Anne's) own study of the functions of writing in two chemical engineering classes (Herrington 1985). What is striking to me now as I look back at that study is that although I examine two distinct genres (laboratory report and process design report) and associate them with forensic and deliberative forums, I never mention the term *genre* or invoke genre theory explicitly. In hindsight, I see that omission as reflecting the intermingling of the writing to learn approach with its focus on functions and negative construction of genres. Thus, while I drew heavily on argumentation theory (e.g., Toulmin, 1958) and Aristotle's *Rhetoric*, I focused less on genre and text features and more on function, writer and audience roles, and lines of reasoning.

Within the still relatively small community of WAC scholars and practitioners, the complementarity of these two strands has increasingly been recognized, leading to a dual focus on both exploratory thinking and writing (that is, invention), and genres as potentially flexible guides for that invention and social action within a given discourse community. If genre is an aspect of social action, manifest in the creation and reception of texts in specific situations, then it becomes important to consider not only conventions of typified texts, but how texts function in specific situations and what writer and audience roles are taken up in specific situations. In classrooms, this means attending to typified texts that teachers assign—whether it be a research paper, an argument, a journal—and the functions those texts serve for students and teachers in specific situations. That is a goal of this collection.

CONTEMPORARY APPROACHES TO GENRE

Although genre was forced into the background in the writing process movement, and although it was not at the center of the writing across the curriculum movement, elsewhere it was the focus of substantial theoretical and practical work. Aviva Freedman (1994) has divided this work on genre into two schools, the North American, which derived chiefly from a line of rhetorical theory, and the Australian, or "Sydney School," which derived chiefly from M.A.K. Halliday's theory of functional linguistics, the fundamental assumption of which is that how language is used determines how it is organized (1985, 191). While Halliday's book, *An Introduction to Functional Grammar*, focused on the sentence level, theorists and educators associated with the Sydney School applied his theories to the text level, viewing genre as texts with conventionalized features as linked to recurring social purposes and contexts of use. One of the more influential pedagogical approaches associated with the Sydney School is that of J. R. Martin (1993), as implemented in the LERN project for the Disadvantaged Schools Program in Sydney. This approach begins by analyzing and describing texts in their functional contexts. The result of this analytic process is a set of text types, or genres, which, once defined and codified, can be taught explicitly to student writers. The motive, which we admire, is to make explicit the "rules of the game" and by doing so, to give students access to the "games" played by those with power and status. The curriculum typically begins with the analysis of examples of the genre with discussion of function as well as form, followed by scaffolded performance (Cope and Kalantzis 1993a; Martin 1993; Macken and Slade 1993). The work of the Sydney School has had an importance influence on the movements called English for Academic Purposes (EAP) and English for Special Purposes (ESP), which form the context for the work of Kapp and Bangeni, chapter 6 of this volume.

We have to admit that we feel uncomfortable with the prescriptiveness of the curricula that derive from this approach. Yet it is important to recognize the context from which the work of the theorists and practitioners of the Sydney School, and, to a degree, the work of the EAP and ESP movements as well, has emerged: a school or college system in which many of the students have had little or no prior exposure to academic discourse. In this situation, it can seem cruel not to teach the forms of academic discourse. Mary Macken-Horarik, a researcher studying a class in the Disadvantaged Schools Program in Sydney, argues that "students at risk of failure fare better within a visible curriculum" (2002, 17). This argument is similar to ones made by Mina Shaughnessy in the 1970s and more recently Lisa Delpit, both focusing on the analogous situation of students in U.S. schools who have had little exposure to Standardized American English and academic discourse. The attractiveness of the explicit teaching of genre, or of teaching the rules of classical grammar, is that both teachers and students can feel that the rules have been made visible and they do have "something to shoot for." The risk is that this visible curriculum can too easily be reduced to a focus on form, where what is taught is a reduction of the complex social interactions that constitute the situations for writing.

We are not, ourselves, convinced that genres are stable entities that can so easily be classified, defined, and taught, at least in the form-first manner of approaches associated with Martin and colleagues. Instead, we find ourselves, geographically and pedagogically, in what Freedman and Medway have termed the "North American" school of genre studies (1994c, 3), drawing on the work of Carolyn Miller (1984, 1994), Freedman (1994, 1995), and Freedman and Medway (1994a, 1994b, 1994c, 1994d), and through them Bakhtin (1986), for our favored approach to the teaching of genre. In 1984, Carolyn Miller published a seminal article in the

Quarterly Journal of Speech in which she argued that genre was not a closed form but a "recurrent, significant action" that "embodies an aspect of cultural rationality" (165). Genres are, in her definition, "typified rhetorical actions based in recurrent situations" (159). Drawing on Aristotle, Burke, and Bitzer, she grounds her work with genre firmly in the rhetorical tradition. "The understanding of rhetorical genre that I am advocating is based in rhetorical practice, in the conventions of discourse that a society establishes as ways of 'acting together.'" Because these ways of "acting together" are not fixed but change over time, genre "does not lend itself to taxonomy, for genres change, evolve, and decay; the number of genres current in any society is indeterminate and depends upon the complexity and diversity of the society" (163). Catherine Schryer makes the same point in slightly different words: she holds that "the concept of genre can help researchers describe a 'stabilized-for-now or stabilized enough site of social and ideological action'" (1994, 107). In a later piece, Carolyn Miller defines genre as a "cultural artefact," which she takes to be "an invitation to see it much as an anthropologist sees a material artefact from an ancient civilization, as a product that has particular functions, that fits into a system of functions and other artefacts" (1994, 69).

Just to complicate this transcontinental division we have implied between Australia and North America, we want to include Gunther Kress, another linguist associated with the Sydney School and systemic functional linguistics. (Indeed, he was involved with the LERN project cited above.) Diverging somewhat from J. R. Martin and similar to those associated with rhetorical approaches, Kress takes a more social/rhetorical view of genre. As Cope and Kalantzis (1993a) characterize his approach, he is "less interested in classifying textual forms than he is in the generative capacities and potentials of using certain kinds of text for certain social purposes" (13–14). In a 1999 article in *Language Arts,* Kress looks at such kinds of texts as "Rules and Regulations" and, in a fascinating analysis, finds in different examples of the genre expressions of different social worlds. For Kress, and for us, "the important point is to be aware of a fundamental tension around genre, between regularity and repeatability, on the one hand—the effect of social stabilities and of regulations erected around text to keep them close to 'convention'—and the dynamic of constant flux and change on the other—the effect both of inevitable social change . . . and of the constantly transformative action of people acting in ever changing circumstances" (1999b, 466). He concludes, "[A] newer way of thinking may be that, within a general awareness of the range of genres, of their shapes, their contexts, speakers and writers newly make the generic forms out of available resources" (468). This sounds very much like the situation of Aristotle's rhetor. Unlike Aristotle, however, other contemporary theorists of genre argue for a critical approach to our understanding of genre, asking us to consider how genres relate to the distribution of power in society and, in particular, how a particular genre approach to teaching might impact learners. Literacy scholars such as Allan Luke, and composition scholars such as Harriet Malinowitz (1998), have questioned genre approaches that aim to socialize students to conventionalized dominant genres without engaging them in a critique of the ideologies and social roles embedded in those genres. Luke would argue that a focus on the generative potentials for any writer needs to be couched within a critical literacy approach where consideration of "available resources" includes "power relations in particular *institutional sites* and *cultural fields*" (1996, 333). One such site is a classroom.

CONTEMPORARY TEXTBOOKS BASED ON GENRE THEORY

Bill Cope and Mary Kalantzis (1993a), in describing the application to genre theory in the curricula of Australia, write that this move "means a new role for textbooks in literacy learning" (1). Insofar as the writing process movement, and its companion, the whole language movement, devalued textbooks, they are right. Explicit teaching of genre can be facilitated by a text that provides materials: prose models for analysis and explanations of the relationship of the genre to the social situation that it arises from. Not surprisingly, there have been a number of American texts based on genre theory that are designed for first-year college writing courses. We choose two popular texts from major presses as our examples.

Rise Axelrod and Charles Cooper, in the sixth edition of *The St. Martin's Guide to Writing* (2001), show their grounding in genre movement as they write, "We have tried to emphasize that writing is both a social act and a way of knowing. We try to teach students that form emerges from context as well as content, that knowledge of writing comes not from analyzing genres alone but also from participating in a community of writers" (vii). In their introduction they present an approach very similar to that associated with the Sydney School: "reading texts that work well for their readers," "writing the kinds of essays you are reading," and "think critically about your learning" in order to "become self-reflective as a reader and writer" (4–5).

Each chapter in their textbook follows the same approach. At the beginning, Axelrod and Cooper name specific genres and present models that they explicate, identifying purpose, audience, text, and other features. While they stress variation and creativity, the process is to analyze prose models and then to write following the features of the models. Recurring form is expected by particular groups of readers, they argue, yet there is room for the writer's agency: "Each genre's basic features, strategies, and kinds of content represent broad frameworks within which writers are free to be creative" (2001, 6). A key term is here is *within*: not *writing against* or *bringing in new features*, but writing *within* the form—not a critical stance, but a conservative approach that permits existing genres to reproduce themselves and thereby to reproduce existing power relations.

The title of John Trimbur's *The Call to Write* (2002) suggests its relationship to genre theory: we write because we are called to write by social situations. For Trimbur, as for Carolyn Miller, genres are rhetorical action and reflect "recurring writing situations." Addressing the student user of the textbook, Trimbur forecasts, "You'll see how writers' choice of genre takes into account the occasion that calls for writing, the writer's purpose, and the relationship the writer seeks to establish with readers." Under the boldfaced heading "Understanding Genres of Writing," Trimbur includes letters, memoirs, public documents, profiles, fact sheets/FAQs, brochures, Web sites, commentaries, proposals, reviews (and not the college essay!). And he argues, with Bakhtin and Freedman, that genres are not fixed, but evolve: "This, of course, is by no means a comprehensive list of all genres of writing. Nor are the genres of writing fixed once and for all. New genres are always emerging in response to new conditions. . . . In the following chapters, we have selected some of the most common genres to illustrate how writers respond to the call to write—genres you will find helpful when you are called on to write in college, in the workplace, and in public life" (109).

Yet as the book and the argument progress, the focus is less on the recurring social situation and more on the form of the writing, what we might think of as "text type." For instance, Trimbur writes, "Letters are easy to recognize . . . have a predictable format that usually includes the date of writing, a salutation" (111). But he also includes the social situation: "[T]he letter is the genre that comes closest in feeling to conversations between people." And, referring to an example of a letter, he writes, "Notice how the occasions that seem to be calling on the two individuals to write their letters come from their involvement in the larger social context" (115). Each genre-focused chapter begins with a section, "Thinking about the Genre." The "Public Documents" section feels to us especially fine: "Public documents speak on behalf of a group of people to articulate the principles and procedures that organize their purposes and guide their way of life" (183).

Both the Axelrod/Cooper and the Trimbur texts, despite their attempt to construe genre as rhetorical action, too often slide toward a representation of genre as decontextualized form. As Alan Luke has noted, "The danger lies in going too far towards analysing and reproducing genres, in effect freeze-drying them in a way that would obscure the dynamic cultural, economic and political forces vying for airspace and airtime, image and voice" (1994, viii). We see this "freeze-drying" as an inevitable outcome of the first-year college writing textbook, in part because of the "frozen" nature of text itself (that was one of Plato's concerns about writing) but in part, too, because American first-year college writing courses seemingly operate without a powerful context: they are designed to teach academic writing, but what *kind* of academic writing? Which of the many particular discourses, and, within those discourses, which recurring social situations? Lacking a clear context to refer to, textbook authors inevitably privilege form. We believe that the chapters that follow will function as a "good" textbook, one not for the student, but for the teacher. Here the teacher will find models of practice, descriptions of the practice of other teachers who have integrated the teaching of genre into their pedagogy in ways that both support and empower the student writer.

PREVIEW OF CHAPTERS

While the chapters that follow look at courses across disciplines and a range of genres, they are similar in presenting genre as situated within specific classrooms, disciplines, and institutions, the assignments embodying the pedagogy of a particular teacher, and students' responses embodying their prior experiences with writing. In each, the authors define a particular genre, define their learning goals for their students implicit in assigning that genre, explain how they help their students work through the assignment, and, finally, discuss how they evaluate the writing their students do in response to their teaching.

In some of these courses, a genre approach guided these teachers from the outset in designing their full curriculum (for instance, Kapp and Bangeni; Petroff); in others, the concept of genre is implicit in the design of particular assignments (e.g., Peagler and Yancey); and in others, the concept of genre is used to understand emerging and hybrid genres (e.g.,

Edwards and McKee; Palmquist). Some of the chapters illustrate teachers presenting an established genre for students to learn; one shows a teacher working against an established genre (Kynard); others illustrate teachers assigning writing for new situations where genres are still in flux (e.g., Edwards and McKee).

In the first section, "Genres across the Curriculum: General Education and Courses for Majors," the book takes the reader on a cross-curricular journey, looking at the ways genres are used and negotiated in courses in comparative literature, history, and biology. The first two chapters focus on teaching genres with substantial histories, although for different primary pedagogical aims: one more often associated with a general-education course and "writing to learn," the other more often associated with a course for majors and "writing in the disciplines." In chapter 2, "Reading and Writing, Teaching and Learning Spiritual Autobiography," Elizabeth Petroff writes of her course, Spiritual Autobiography, in which this genre structures the entire course in that students both read and write spiritual autobiographies. For this general-education course, Petroff's aims for students include not only development of writing and reading skills, but also personal growth. Chapter 3, "Writing History: Informed or Not by Genre Theory?" Anne Beaufort, a composition specialist, and John Williams, a historian, focus on teaching and learning the genre of "the historical argument," with Williams examining Beaufort's assignments and teaching approaches and Beaufort studying one history major's work to learn this genre over the course of three years. The aim that interests Beaufort and Williams is for students to learn to master a genre central to the work of a particular discipline. The next two chapters move into biology classrooms, and again, we pair a course for nonmajors with one for majors. In chapter 4, "Mapping Classroom Genres in a Science in Society Course," Mary Soliday, a composition scholar, examines the function of writing in a variety of genres—including journals, critical arguments, and public interest brochures—in biologist David Eastzer's general-education course for nonscience majors, Science in Society. Here, the professor's aims were for students both to learn the fundamentals of scientific research and to think critically about science in their own lives. Chapter 5, "'What's Cool Here?': Collaboratively Learning Genre in Biology," also the result of a project undertaken by a composition scholar and biologist—Anne Ellen Geller and David Hibbett—focuses on a biology seminar for majors in which Hibbett asked students to write mini–review essays for Nature, a magazine for educated nonspecialist readers. The focus of this chapter is on pedagogy, specifically how students and faculty can learn from explicit negotiation of genre in writing workshops.

In the second section, "Genres in First-Year Writing Courses," chapters 6 and 7 present new takes on genres often associated with first-year writing and general-education courses: argument and the research paper. Very likely reflecting the rhetorical training of the teachers, these chapters, in contrast to the chapters in "Genres across the Curriculum," emphasize not only the enabling power of genres but also their shaping and constraining power. In "'I Was Just Never Exposed to This Argument Thing': Using a Genre Approach to Teach Academic Writing to ESL Students in the Humanities," Rochelle Kapp and Bongi Bangeni focus on teaching academic argument in an ESL academic literacy course at the University of Cape Town, South Africa. Reflecting the direct approach to genre instruction often associated with ESL and the Sydney School, they call for explicit instruction in the genre, but accompanied with critical reflection on academic as well as home discourses. In "'Getting on the Right Side of It:' Problematizing and Rethinking the Research Paper in the College Composition Course," Carmen Kynard demonstrates a critical approach as well, in this case a challenge to the traditional construction of the research paper as an acontextual "encycolopedia-type form" with rigid formal conventions, accrued over time and enforced through departmental curricular guidelines. In both of the courses described in these chapters, a central aim of the teachers is to teach students to engage with other texts and authorities while also encouraging them to question conventions and establish their own authority, including the authority of their own knowledge. In chapter 8, "The Resumé as Genre: A Rhetorical Foundation for First-Year Composition," Shane Peagler and Kathleen Blake Yancey focus on a genre less often identified with first-year writing, the resumé, making a case for how it can be used—as could other genres—to teach key issues in writing, including the link of text to context, the representation of self, and the writer's understanding of audience.

The chapters in the final section, "Mixing Media, Evolving Genres," look at what happens when teachers include other media—speech, the Web—into the "writing" that their students do in their courses. In chapter 9, "Teaching and Learning a Multimodal Genre in a Psychology Course," Chris M. Anson, Deanna P. Dannels, and Karen St. Clair—a composition scholar, an oral communication scholar, and a psychologist—focus on the psychologist's course, Controversial Psychological Issues, to examine a hybrid-genre assignment where writing and reading are brought together in a common performative event. They consider the pedagogical rationale of the assignment, how students interpreted it, and the decisions they made regarding how to integrate the oral and written components. The next two chapters focus on Web-based texts and the questions that arise as teachers ask students to compose texts in a medium where genres are more in flux. In "The Teaching and Learning of Web Genres in First-Year Composition," Heidi McKee and Mike Edwards focus on how they and their students negotiated expectations and genres in the process of students' work to compose Web sites for their classes. In chapter 11, "Writing in Emerging Genres: Student Web Sites in Writing and Writing-Intensive Classes," Mike Palmquist explores the same question, but shifts the focus from a first-year writing course to a speech communications course taught by a colleague. To provide a frame for considering the challenges these teachers and students face, Palmquist also reviews recent work on the emergence of new genres.

In a closing chapter, we reflect on what we have learned as we have read, responded to, and edited the chapters as they came in. We approached this book project with certain assumptions about genre and with certain questions as well, particularly about how both teachers and students see the experience of writing in certain genres as relating to students' learning, and about the utility of genre as a concept for guiding course planning. The chapters that we have commissioned, read, and edited have pushed and complicated our understanding of genre and, to an even greater extent, our understanding of the place of genre in college and university teaching.

PART ONE

Genre Across the Curriculum:
General Education and Courses for Majors

2

READING AND WRITING, TEACHING AND LEARNING SPIRITUAL AUTOBIOGRAPHY

Elizabeth A. Petroff

I teach a general-education course at the University of Massachusetts entitled Spiritual Autobiography in which students read and write autobiography. The course is centered around the interrelationships between the act of reading autobiography and that of writing it: through reading autobiography students can discover how different writers express their own experiences, and as a result write in new ways, and through the act of writing their own life experiences students gain a new understanding of their own lives as well as coming to be better readers of autobiography. We focus on the experience of the artist reading her own autobiography as she writes it, along with the experience of the reader who composes his own autobiography as he reads another's autobiography. It is now a commonplace in studies of autobiography to assert that the self comes into existence only through writing or narrating; my task is to show what that means in practice.

I've been teaching in universities for over thirty years, and I've taught Spiritual Autobiography for twenty years, usually in the format of a large lecture for about 150 students and weekly discussion sections of 30 students. The course is usually elected by first- and second-year students, many of whom have not yet chosen a major and for whom this will be the only literature course in their college careers. It satisfies the general-education requirement of a Global Diversity arts and literature class, and most students say they chose the course to satisfy this requirement, not because they had a prior interest in autobiography.

The reading list varies from year to year, but for the sake of brevity I will be writing primarily about the course in fall 2002. We read seven books in a fourteen-week semester, which allowed us on the average two weeks of lectures and two discussion sections for each book. The syllabus includes *Incidents in the Life of a Slave Girl*, by Harriet Jacobs (2000); *A Narrative of the Life of Frederick Douglass,* the earliest of Douglass's three autobiographies

(2000); *Black Elk Speaks,* as told to John Neihardt (1932); *Obasan,* by Joy Kogawa (1994); *Dreams of My Russian Summers,* by Andrei Makine (1997); *Of Water and the Spirit,* by Malidoma Patrice Some (1995); and *The Far East Comes Near,* edited by Lucy Nguyen and Joel Halpern (1960). These texts come from many different parts of the globe and several historical periods, as is required for a course meeting the guidelines for Global Diversity. As autobiographies they share two important qualities: they are "spiritual" autobiographies in which the protagonist, even when denied agency and subjectivity, is engaged in a deep inward search for meaning, often in response to trauma; and they are autobiographies of young people the same age as the students.

While students are reading these books, hearing about them in lectures, and talking about them in discussion sections, they are also writing out their own experiences in the form of three short autobiographical papers on aspects or events of their lives suggested by a list of possible topics. In addition to writing autobiographical essays, students are asked to demonstrate their understanding of autobiography in take-home midterm and final exams. Since one of the goals of the class is understanding the connections between the reading and writing of creative texts, the midterm and final offer students several different ways to demonstrate their experience of these books. Some questions ask them to respond discursively by comparing and contrasting different authors and books; other questions ask them to engage with autobiographers and their autobiographies in more personal ways, such as interviewing Harriet Jacobs, or writing a letter to Andrei Makine. Several questions encourage students to compare the themes and styles of their own essays with some of the autobiographies we read. Another tool for self-reflection was provided in a survey I created to learn more about how students perceived their own learning experiences in the course and the connections they perceived between reading and writing autobiography.

My intention in offering this class to fulfill a general-education requirement is to give students an opportunity to enrich their knowledge of other times and other cultures; the readings are designed to give them a more personalized understanding of history and of the twentieth-century world by reading American slave narratives, Native American autobiographies, and accounts of wartime internment in North America, student life in the Soviet Union during the cold war, and the legacy of colonial occupation in traditional societies in Africa and Southeast Asia. Almost all the texts speak of the authors' experience of biculturalism in these coming-of-age stories, and in my lectures I explore the different modes of biculturalism all of us experience as the descendants of aboriginal peoples, immigrants, refugees, and colonists. I also try to give students access to the historical and cultural background they need to better participate in their reading, and to catalyze students' personal insights in the course of reading the life stories of writers the same age as they are. In my lectures, I try to weave together the themes of commonality and of difference, in our lives and in these books, while providing background material that helps place each book.

WHAT IS AUTOBIOGRAPHY?

Reading Autobiography

We read and write autobiography for similar reasons: a search for self-knowledge and a desire to place ourselves in the world. In reading, we communicate with a transpersonal world, learning what it feels like to live in other times or in other cultures. In another's autobiography an alienated young reader may discover a kindred soul or identify a role model to be followed. Reading autobiography allows us to find ourselves in others and to see our own experiences from a new perspective. It also teaches us how to shape our own experience in writing from the inside out. What I term "spiritual autobiography" is autobiography that explores the deepest parts of the self, the inner force that can keep us alive in the direst and most traumatic of circumstances, and at the same time reveals our place in the universe, our connections with other beings and other forms of consciousness.

All of these dimensions of reading center on the reader and his or her response to the autobiographical text, yet the life must be lived before the text is narrated or written. The autobiographical text is the mediator between the lived experience of the author and the reflective experience of the reader. The languages and styles of autobiography show us readers how our deepest experiences may be put into words. Reading autobiography is itself an autobiographical act, for there is a continual process of association, memory, and insight that takes place as we read, which leads to the construction of a reading self. You cannot read the autobiography of another person without remembering and understanding more of your own life.

Writing Autobiography

The self that comes into existence through reading is similar to the self that comes into existence through writing, through the process of reading one's own autobiography while writing it. We embark on the process of autobiography in order to remember and account for our experiences. Even though one might think that the narrative of an autobiography is already known, since it has been lived by the narrator, in actuality autobiography is the inscription of an inner life far deeper than a mere listing of events. We write autobiography, then, to discover our selves, often by tracing continuity and loss in our lives, or by examining where we've been and where we want to be. We also write to understand the others in our lives, to recapture certain moments that will not return, and to analyze our own motives. Sometimes we need autobiography to find healing, to confess, or to seek forgiveness, although this may not be the conscious justification for beginning to write. We may write autobiography when we feel we have reached the end of one phase of our lives and are embarking upon another phase. We may write in order to let go of the things that haunt us; it is a hedge against death, as well as a way to integrate our different selves and the memories they carry for us.

The Genre of Autobiography

We know that an autobiography (etymologically "self-life-writing") is the story of a lived life, containing narratives of moments the author finds meaningful for the purposes of self-representation and reflection. We can never write the whole truth of our whole lives (although some diarists may aim for such inclusiveness). An autobiography is always selective, always retrospective, and often unfinished; it calls into question the writer's identity, sincerity, honesty. In writing an autobiography, the writer uses the resources of prose and poetry and blurs the line between truth and fiction.

Autobiography, as a genre, is characterized by questioning one's experience. And as an object of critical study, autobiography raises questions about chronology and causality; how can someone tell his or her life story when the ending is not yet known? What aspects of a person's experience can an autobiography represent? Since the medium of autobiography is language, can language represent visual or nonverbal consciousness? To what extent does autobiography represent culture in revealing contemporary assumptions about race, class, and gender, and to what extent does it represent individual consciousness? What constraints are externally imposed on autobiography? How much of a life can be spoken publicly? And what about a dictated autobiography? Can a second person, no matter how sympathetic, represent to us the world of a person who does not write? How is it that the exploration of interiority may come to represent a universe, a cosmos that is home to the individual?

Fortunately for the many readers of autobiography, the complex issues involved in defining autobiography have little to do with the popularity of the form. Today, publishers, booksellers, and teachers know that autobiography has wide appeal to readers of all classes and backgrounds, that Western and non-Western readers enjoy reading autobiographies, that historically autobiography has been popular in the East as well as the West. Women writers and readers exhibit a preference for autobiography, and have done so for a millennium. Although popular autobiography in the West is thought to have arisen at the same time as the novel, in the late seventeenth and early eighteenth century in Europe, deriving from current notions of the individual, of religious or moral introspection, and social mobility, women were writing their spiritual or visionary autobiographies much earlier (see Petroff 1986). Consequently, the bibliography positioning the history and practice of autobiography is very large. Contemporary autobiography exhibits many different models of subjectivity, identity, and individuality, and at the same time, definitions of what constitutes an autobiographical text have become wider and more flexible; we now include diaries, memoirs, letters, and as-told-to narratives under the heading of autobiography. Many contemporary novels are autobiographical fiction, as are travel records, family chronicles, communal storytelling. Studies of autobiography have moved away from focusing on the individual narrative of a personality (which limited autobiography to those texts by Western, literate, and mostly male writers), and many scholars in the field now speak of autobiography as composed of collective voices, or position collaborative autobiographies, tribal and community representations, alongside autobiographies of individual identities.

Writing in 1971, one scholar defined autobiography as "the retrospective prose narrative that someone writes concerning his own existence, where the focus is his individual life, in particular the story of his personality" (Lejeune 1989, viii), a statement that applies to eighteenth-century as well as twentieth-century autobiography, but, as Lejeune himself notes, fails to distinguish between "autobiography and the autobiographical novel" (ix). Rather, a writer establishes a boundary between fact and fiction by the "autobiographical pact," the signs within a text of authorial intention (ix). Reading *On Autobiography*, which includes English translations of chapters from Lejeune's best-known studies of autobiography, one sees the evolution of notions of autobiography from individual and confessional to collective and historical. Recent studies by James Olney (*Memory and Narrative* [1998]) and John Eakins (*How Our Lives Become Stories* [1999]) are useful for their careful explication of this more inclusive view of the genre.

Those new to designing courses on autobiography in the West might begin with Jill Ker Conway's recent study, *When Memory Speaks* (1998); having written her own autobiography, Conway reports on the "history of self-narrative in modern and postmodern times" (4), observing that "virtually the only prose narratives which are accorded the suspension of disbelief today are the autobiographers' attempts to narrate the history of a real life" (5). Autobiography attracts us because it gives us the sensation of that rare experience of being allowed inside another person's experience and provides us with an alternative to our own perspective. An autobiography is also a window into a culture: "Whether we are aware of it or not," Conway says, "our culture gives us an inner script by which we live our lives . . . and the dynamics of that script come from what our world defines as success or achievement" (6).

Conway speculates on the difference gender makes in autobiography. She finds the shaping male narrative to come from the classical epic, and that sense of agency carries over into Christian autobiography, right up to frontier narratives and the quest for meaning in Joyce's *Portrait of the Artist as a Young Man*. For women, she says, the shaping narratives are different (they weren't citizens and were supposed to keep silent in church): "[I]t was within the special enclave of religious life that the tradition of Western European women's autobiography was first established, in narratives about the autobiographer's relationship with God. Such a tradition, involving a relationship with a first cause, did not permit the development of a sense of agency and acting on one's own behalf with which the Greek idea of the hero is fused. Instead, it promoted meditation about the nature of God and the recording of direct experience of divine revelation" (12). In my own work, I argue that there is a strong sense of agency to be found in religious women's autobiographies, an agency that results from a dialogue with God (Petroff 1986). Carolly Erickson (1998) also posits a different approach to narratives about one's relationship with a higher power, also crediting such narratives with an awareness of agency, in *Arc of the Arrow: Writing Your Spiritual Autobiography*. She further provides a number of models for creating writing assignments that will assist readers in writing their own spiritual autobiographies.

A text my teaching assistants and I have found useful in course design, *Reading Autobiography: A Guide for Interpreting Life Narratives,* by Sidonie Smith and Julia Watson (2001), sets out to "explore the building blocks and components of autobiographical acts, review the histories of autobiographies and autobiographical criticism, and offer a 'tool kit' of pertinent questions for twenty key concepts" (xi). In their chapter on autobiographical subjects they identify five elements that make up an author's representation of subjectivity: memory, experience, identity, embodiment, and agency (15–16), which constitute commonalities among all the books we read in my class. In preparing lectures for each book, we may address the meaning of these elements for each writer, and how they are contingent upon the culture and historical moment in which the author is presenting his or her life narrative. I'll give a few examples of how I utilize Smith and Watson's ideas.

For instance, memory for Black Elk is closely tied to his experience as he narrates his personal memories of his visions and of the major events of his search for healing for his people, contextualized by his understanding of the collective history of the Plains Indians up to the slaughter at Wounded Knee in 1887. His identity as a visionary is embedded in his awareness of race and gender as well as defined by the responsibility he feels for all Native Americans in his role as shaman and spiritual guide; his sense of agency is represented by his desire to learn how Wasichus think about their world, his attempts to find a common ground for cross-cultural communication, and his feelings of failure in his later life on the reservation. His sense of embodiment includes his out-of-body experiences.

Linda Brent (the pseudonym of Harriet Jacobs, the author of *Incidents in the Life of a Slave Girl*) begins with her memories of her early childhood, before she knew she was a slave. Her memories then become intertwined with her experiences in slavery, and are conditioned by her gender as well as her status as a house slave. Her sense of embodiment is represented by her awareness of her vulnerability to the sexual advances of her white master and white lover. The language she chooses to tell her life story is colored by her knowledge that as a woman in the domestic culture of the nineteenth century she ought not to speak of her sexual experiences, as well as by her conviction that she must communicate her sexual experience if she is to demonstrate the terrible fate of female slaves: deprived of any rights over their own bodies, helpless to protect the children they bear, and forbidden to marry and live faithfully with a black man they choose. "Linda Brent" vividly portrays the contradictions in asserting her own agency—she can be free only by surviving seven years hidden in a crawl space in her grandmother's house (located just around the corner from the home of her master) and by using her intelligence to defeat her master psychologically as she convinces him (by means of letters purportedly written by her safe in the north) that she has already escaped his grasp.

Smith and Watson demonstrate other ways of reading the affinities in autobiographies by asking their readers to look at the occasions that solicit a life narrative (John Neihardt interviewing Black Elk in old age, the women abolitionists in Massachusetts who encourage Linda Brent to write and publish her story, the abolitionists' meeting in Nantucket that provides the stage for Frederick Douglass to tell his story to a white male audience). Sites of narration are equally important and condition the audience in how to read a story: a southern plantation, the city of Baltimore, the Great Plains and the reservation, an internment camp for Japanese Americans, an African village and a French Catholic school. In "spiritual" autobiography, we find other sites of narration, ones not found in the physical world; one of Linda Brent's sites is the experience of expansion and freedom while cooped up in her hiding space. One of Black Elk's sites is the world of the Grandfathers in the sky, the true reality behind what we take as reality in the physical world. There are "characters" in our autobiographies: the autobiographical "I" testifies to the veracity of the story, and the "Others" reveal the narrator in relationship and dialogue with other people. The addressees, the audience selected by the narrator, affect the way a story is told and contribute to the readers' and auditors' complicity in the telling.

WHAT IS SPIRITUAL AUTOBIOGRAPHY?

This brings us to the nature of spiritual autobiography. We have noted in passing a number of identifying traits of spiritual autobiography: (1) it is the inscription of an inner life far deeper than a mere listing of events (2) in which the protagonist, denied agency and subjectivity, is engaged in a deep inward search for meaning, and (3) in which the exploration of interiority may come to represent a universe, a cosmos that is home to the individual. As in autobiography in general, spiritual autobiography is a retrospective, interrupted narrative, often written early in life. All autobiography is a search for truth, but the writers of spiritual autobiography seem to look for a demonstrable truth, repeatable truth, that they can carry with them into the future. They see their lives from the fulcrum of a radical change, a before and after, a deep rupture separating very different experiences, an epiphany that suddenly makes sense of previous experience. Seventeenth-century spiritual autobiography found this fulcrum in the search for inner proof of being saved or damned, as in John Bunyan's *Grace Abounding to the Chief of Sinners* (1962). Experiences such as emigration, catastrophic events, natural disasters, loss of family—all precipitators of spiritual autobiography—bring along with them a sense of isolation and abandonment and create a search for community. It is paradoxical that spiritual autobiography, perhaps the most inward turning of autobiographical forms, is at the same time the most community oriented of all, for in autobiography as well as real life, the individual experience of trauma may be healed in the return to community.

Such autobiographies reveal a process of healing to the writer and the reader. In writing spiritual autobiography, contemporary writers can reveal the deepest parts of themselves, their buried experience of trauma, of illness or abuse, of crimes of war. In the process of finding words for the buried fragments of experience, whether the autobiographers are survivors of childhood sexual abuse or life in a concentration camp, the language they discover on their written pages gives an objective, externalized shape to their experience, now an experience for readers as well, demonstrating to themselves and to their readers that the act of writing transforms their isolating experiences of pain into a bond with others.

Contemporary readers and writers believe that autobiographers are not limited by formal considerations: autobiographies may easily take the form of diaries narrating events day by day (like Carolina Maria de Jesus's *Child of the Dark* [1962] or Anne Frank's *Diary of a Young Girl* [1952]) or of life writing focusing on the experience of exile, or escape from slavery, or capture by the Indians. The memoir form, which develops a narrative on a significant part of a life rather than on a total life review, seems most appropriate to many spiritual autobiographers, where the central focus may be on the portrayal of a person important to the autobiographer's self-understanding (such as Andrei Makine's French grandmother in *Dreams of My Russian Summers*) or a moment in which the meaning of life for the autobiographer changed utterly. Resistance to war, or ideology, may be the cause of the rupture that initiates spiritual autobiography, as it is in Carlo Levi's narrative of his exile in *Christ Stopped at Eboli* (1970), in Primo Levi's recollections of his concentration camp experiences in *Survival in Auschwitz: The Nazi Assault on Humanity* (1993), and in Joy Kogawa's *Obasan*, detailing her search for understanding in the Canadian relocation camps for those of Japanese descent . Similarly, a memoir may single out for examination the rupture in a life caused by becoming a refugee, or emigrating to another country, by experiencing threatening or terminal illness, as in Marie Cardinal's *The Words to Say It* (1983), or undergoing great personal loss, as in Isabel Allende's *Paula* (1994), written on the illness and death of her daughter.

What *does* matter, what is essential if spiritual autobiography is to effect a change in the writer, is the actual writing (or speaking aloud) of the words, for the words that an autobiographer finds perform a kind of alchemy on hidden suffering, in which the leaden experiences of personal or collective pain are refined, transformed into gold, as it were, liberating the autobiographer from isolation and loneliness, able at last to forge links to other human beings. The density of inner pain becomes expansive, stony hearts melt, and the experience provides metaphors and structures for the perceived new life.

My hypothesis about how spiritual autobiography effects transformations in writers and their readers also derives from understanding the impact of trauma on the lives around me. Thanks to modern psychology, we all know something about how great pain (especially but not exclusively in childhood) creates fractures in the self, severing the person who undergoes pain from the person who remembers, often burying the pain in another self, leaving the dominant personality with a kind of amnesia in the deepest levels of the psyche. In writing an anatomy of the moments of suffering in his or her life, the autobiographer performs a kind of *anamnesis,* a recollection that reconstitutes the inner pain by standing outside it in order to record it. This remembering forges a dialogue in which the broken pieces of the self may communicate with the social or public self-representation. It is this dialogue that not only brings forth healing, but speaks to the audience to engage us, the readers, and to bring us to a higher understanding of what it means to be a human being. The act of writing the autobiography of the soul not only unifies the divided self, it creates a luminous space in which readers begin to re-create and understand the creative uses of their own suffering and its relation to their own survival.

And since pain often brings guilt with it, as one tries to justify one's suffering to oneself, the autobiographer must forgive him- or herself *and* forgive those that caused the suffering. This circle of forgiveness also embraces the reader, as the reader's own suffering comes to light. As Nakamura Sensei says to the family gathered for Uncle's funeral in Joy

Kogawa's *Obasan*, "We are powerless to forgive unless we first are forgiven" (1994, 287).

It seems that the art of experiencing spiritual autobiography, as writer or reader, is a delicate one to learn. Often we do not willingly explore our own pain or that of others. Something in our daily experience, some mystery in our sense of self, some glimpse of a new life, must compel us to go into those depths. If we are to gain from our reading, and share in an author's progression from dark to light, we need to write our own experiences as we read. We need to practice our own alchemy of suffering.

HELPING STUDENTS WRITE SPIRITUAL AUTOBIOGRAPHY

If one believes that the best way to learn to read spiritual autobiography is to try writing it, one needs to create assignments that will prompt students to examine their own lives. Such assignments will of course highlight many of the essentials of good expository writing: immediacy, vivid descriptions of remembered details, sense impressions and emotions, clarity of thought and sentence structure. Over years of teaching spiritual autobiography, I have learned some rules for creating effective assignments that students are ready to write. My first rule is to avoid large, generalized topics: no assignments on "My High School Years" or "My Parents' Divorce": no topics that ask for the meaning of life. I do not ask my students to begin their autobiographical writing by searching into the deepest parts of themselves. I learned, when I first began teaching this class, that nothing paralyzes a group of students faster than asking them to write about meaning in their own lives. My second rule is to create assignments that allow for individual experience to come forward: "My Earliest Memory," "A Recurring Dream or Nightmare," "My First Day of School." My third rule is to create a progression of assignments that will build confidence in one's ability to reflect on one's own life, beginning with short narratives in which the writer presents his or her perceived reality, moving on to more complex events involving others, often accompanied by ambivalent feelings.

So when I distribute assignments for the first paper (see appendix 1, "Paper Topics"), I simply encourage students to *remember*—to remember an early memory, a recurring dream or nightmare, a moment in their family history, the mood when a certain snapshot was taken. I ask them to make this memory as vivid as possible for the reader. Show, not tell, is the guideline here. Create the presentness of the remembered moment by physically inhabiting it with all your senses. To write out your physical sensations, you may need to describe colors, the scent in the air, the room in which something happened, the clothes you were wearing, the weather that day. Also observe your feelings, the movement of your emotions, the sensation of time slowing down or speeding up. If you wish, you may end your paper by speculating on why you think you remember this experience, how it speaks to the person you are today. Some students will think they don't have anything to remember that's big enough for a whole paper, and I encourage them by saying they will be surprised at what they remember once they get started. They may modify the suggestions any way they wish, or try a topic of their own choosing.

The first assignments don't ask students to identify "spiritual" experiences. I ask them to write out "personal" experience, the memories that are exclusively their own, so they can begin to see a self take form on paper. The paper is due within the first month of classes, when the lectures and discussions are exploring what "spiritual" means in broad terms, separate from religious worship or the expression of piety. I hope students will come to see "spirituality" as experience shared by all of us, contacting our deepest sources of strength and starting to reveal our place in the universe.

I give students ten to fourteen days to write this first paper; I point out similar passages in the book we're reading in class at the time; I encourage them to take risks and experiment with writing style. I ask them to give the paper a title that will direct the reader's attention, and bring the paper with them to their discussion section to turn in. If the discussion leader senses trust in the room, he or she can ask the students to form small groups and help each other proofread and edit their papers. The emphasis is on learning to be helpful in reading someone's writing, never to be judgmental.

A couple of weeks before the second or third paper is due, I remind students that they can choose another topic from the first list or select a new topic from a new list I pass out. Many of these topics are more complex: I may ask for a portrait of a person about whom you have strong feelings or a description of a relationship you have with such a person. I encourage them to create portraits of boyfriends or girlfriends, but the portraits should reveal the idiosyncrasies, the little revealing gestures, the personal differences that have to be bridged, rather than employing the language of Hallmark cards. Writing about a pet or the loss of a pet, about the first friend you made, or the first book you remember—all such topics will lead the writer to represent himself or herself in dialogue with something or someone, in relationship with something that matters. For the third paper, when we have explored the role of trauma in spirituality and analyzed ways in which writers deal with the ruptures in their lives, some of the suggested topics may seem quite abstract: write about an experience of loss, about a challenge you successfully met, about a "failure" that brought something good with it. Yet the process of writing on one of these topics is not abstract at all; the "experience of loss" must be remembered, relived, objectified so that a reader can experience it too, and these are the papers that at the end of the semester students find to be most revealing of themselves and most comforting to recall.

Sometimes students choose to link all three papers thematically or chronologically; more often they use the papers to explore very different aspects of their lives. Since this course, as I teach it, is directed primarily to first-year students, writing assignments don't ask students specifically to employ a particular kind of rhetoric, although we discuss rhetorical strategies used by our different writers. I don't ask students to write autobiography in the form of a diary, or a memoir, or in the second or third person, although we discuss how an author uses these modes. Many upperclassmen do choose to experiment with form and style; if a student chooses to write about a traumatic event, especially physical or sexual abuse, he or she will often choose to write in the third person.

STUDENTS' WRITING: HOW STUDENTS PERCEIVE AND DESCRIBE THEIR EXPERIENCE

Students enrolled in Spiritual Autobiography in fall 2002 were invited to complete a survey on their experience of the reading and writing dimensions of the course. This was the first time I had used such a survey to gather student assessments of how the class worked for them; in the past I had used the standard teaching evaluation forms supplied by the Department of Comparative Literature, but I felt that writing this essay necessitated a closer knowledge of students' perceptions of the course. In all, 86 of the 140 registered students completed the survey, and it is their responses to the survey questions from which I quote below. I asked them to share with me several kinds of information: (1) the topics they chose to write on; (2) how they now assess their writings, including whether they had a particular favorite; (3) what they learned about themselves through the process of writing; (4) what they learned from reading autobiographies that they could apply to writing their own stories; and (5) what they valued in the books they had read. The following themes were evident in their responses.

The Importance of Memory

In response to questions on their own writing experience, many students said that the assignments allowed them to remember more details of their lives and to treasure their memories. The act of writing allowed them to see into themselves and their families in greater depth. There was surprising breadth to their responses concerning their pleasure in writing and reading their memories. Some of their responses: "I liked reflecting on what I've done/accomplished. I liked writing about the Super Bowl because I spent it with my best friends, and now that we're all away at different schools, it brought back good memories"; "I learned that I could actually go back in time and remember what happened and write from my experiences"; "It's fun to remember your past, but also sometimes emotional and sad. Either way it is important to remember where you're from and remember memory, because I wrote about my mother and how my memories of her will never be forgotten"; "It was fun to reflect on my experiences. My writing showed me that I've overcome several obstacles."

Benefits of Choice of Topics

Students liked the variety of suggested topics and the freedom to write on a topic of their choice. "I enjoyed the freedom that was given to me regarding my papers"; "I liked the fact that we had a choice of topics, which made it easier to get into writing the paper."

The Importance of Feeling

There was a wide range of responses to questions about what they learned about themselves while writing and reading. Some focused on what they learned about expressing emotions and feelings: "I liked writing and exploring myself. I learned how to look at the inner part of me, underneath the surface"; "I learned that putting emotion in your writing can make a great deal of difference to holding a reader's attention"; " I learned that the feelings the writer uses can/does have a great effect on the reader understanding the intensity"; "I truly learned that I like reading autobiographies and until now, I did not know of any book type that I would enjoy reading."

Other students stressed what they learned about the complexity of emotion. "I learned that sometimes an experience can be more than happy or sad, there are many layers to the memory"; " I liked reading about details and emotions rather than just facts"; "I enjoyed the first autobiography the most because it was the one that I was the most emotionally vested in. It made me sad because I miss my relative a lot, but I was also happy while writing them because it brought back some fond memories."

Many students spoke of the difficulty they have had in the past with identifying and expressing their emotions. "I learned that I'm a person who doesn't easily decide what my emotions are, or maybe I try not to know what they are. Writing really helped me to evaluate certain situations and helped to figure out how I was really feeling"; "[I learned] that I don't really like to discuss my feelings, but with the encouragement of my TA, I went into deeper depths about how I felt and wrote more about myself as opposed to just telling a story"; "It gave me a chance to actually reflect deeply on topics I often don't get an opportunity to. I have a deeper sense of feelings on topics such as these that I didn't know I was aware of."

Many responses hinted at self-knowledge, and new writing strategies, that came from the experiences of both reading and writing: "From reading autobiographies I applied my feelings much more intensely, and I was able to clearly express myself from understanding the books"; "I learned about myself and realized what an amazing story I have. I learned about style—and intimacy. My writing became open, personal, and *very* intimate"; "While I was writing, I realized that I don't work well with change. Most of my papers were sad and discussed topics varying from a tragic breakup to a friend committing suicide"; "The styles of some of the autobiographies I took to write my own. It made me learn how to open up and not hold anything back"; "I've found that incorporating lots of emotion is more effective in telling your story."

The Importance of Description and Detail

Students seem to have discovered for themselves how important full description, with many sensory details, can be in expressing experience. "I . . . learned to show not tell and be more descriptive"; "I learned that each autobiography needs a lot of detail and description to be able to understand what someone is going through." Their insights about the importance of description were often connected to honesty about emotions. "I learned that telling the whole story, not holding back, would make my writing a lot more powerful"; " Be open, honest, and sincere. Also explain your surroundings and show your story to others"; "When reading autobiographies, I was able to picture the experiences in my mind. Therefore, when writing I learned that I had to be more descriptive so the reader can mentally envision my story."

Writing as Therapy

In class lectures and discussions, we rarely spoke directly about the idea of writing as therapy, yet the theme came up often in student responses about their own writing. "It gave me the opportunity to write about Sept. 11 which I witnessed—it was painful but I feel as though it helped"; "Writing about these instances was painful at times but therapeutic. I vented my anger through the language in the paper and tried to write (the first two especially) in the first person so I could put myself back in time"; "[T]he three exercises were therapeutic. It was admitting to past stupidities and looking them right in the eye. Why the hell did I do that? What was I thinking?"; "I got so much from simply writing about myself. From this class, the three autobiographies, I feel like I have transformed into a stronger, more enlightened person. Through writing, I have been able to see the beauty and the meaning in my life"; "I learned that writing down what I felt helped ease my soul. I felt so much better after I got it down on paper. To open up and leave nothing behind. Just let it all down on paper. Let your emotions run free." Many students would agree with the young person who said: "When I write an autobiography, I feel strong and proud. It gives me power to know that my life is on paper."

Wider Experience through Reading

Students often related that the deeper self-knowledge acquired from writing was connected to the wide range of life experiences they were reading about. "All of the autobiographies showed me a different world"; "This course . . . made me explore other cultures and it made me think. It made me think about myself as a person, and it made me think about others as individuals, all with a different story to tell"; "I liked the autobiographies because . . . I could feel their anxiety, pain, fear, or frustration. That they all continued on in times of despair"; "I learned that my life is more eventful than I realized and my experiences have affected me greatly"; "I liked reading these stories because I was able to look into their life and see their spiritual side. They were valuable because they offered knowledge." Students also noted that they absorbed different styles of autobiography and learned to improve their own writing by reflecting on their reading. Students observed: "I learned that even though not anything that drastic has happened, everyone has a story to tell"; "By reading these autobiographies I realized that an important key in writing my own was to try and make the memories as real as possible."

Students felt encouraged to be more direct and honest in their writing by their reading experiences: "Mainly, the honesty that I read has helped me be more honest with myself and look deeper into my real self." One of the most succinct statements noted: "Some of the best books are about extremely trying/difficult experiences. Don't block out the bad stuff, *use it.*"

Summary of Student Responses on Learning

In the process of writing autobiographical papers, students found they could remember more events and more details of their own lives than they expected; thanks to the fullness of their memories, they used the paper topics as opportunities for self-analysis and discovered themes in their own lives they'd never noticed before. They felt their writing was empowering for themselves and their families, that it allowed them to see their own lives as interesting and important and to recognize strengths they had not acknowledged earlier. Many students commented on their improved writing skills and appreciated the opportunity to experiment with different styles of narrative. Almost all students ended the course feeling they understood themselves more deeply and had found therapy or healing in both reading and writing.

After teaching Spiritual Autobiography each fall semester, I often questioned whether students had actually internalized the ideas and values that structure the course and had profited from the relationships between reading and writing autobiography. After reading dozens of student autobiographical essays for my discussion sections each semester, I had a pretty good idea of the issues students wrestle with and explore through writing, but I was less sure of what students gained from the books read, and how they related their reading to their writing. The answers to my student survey have reassured me that coordinating writing assignments with autobiographical reading has resulted in a deeper understanding of the books read, more ability to participate in reading as a creative experience, greater self-knowledge, and improved self-expression. The responses I have found particularly moving are those that comment on the pleasure and value of memory and the consolation found in writing through their own suffering. I feel that my hypothesis about the Alchemy of Suffering has been validated and merits further study.

APPENDIX 1

PAPER TOPICS: SPIRITUAL AUTOBIOGRAPHY

TOPICS FOR FIRST AUTOBIOGRAPHICAL PAPER

Choose one of the following topics, modifying it to suit your own particular circumstances. The idea is to write a part or scene from your own autobiography. Since you will write three autobiographical papers in this course, you might like to link them as you go along. You will have an opportunity to peer edit this paper and to rewrite it, so please be willing to take risks. Writing your own autobiography is not always easy or comfortable, and there is no one correct way to do it. Papers should be three to five pages in length, typed, double-spaced, and proofread. Make your writing as vivid as possible—don't talk *about* your experience. *Show* your experience to your reader.

1. An early memory. What is the first thing you remember? Describe it as fully as you can, keeping in mind that your consciousness was more limited then, and that you remember things differently now. Why do you think this memory stayed with you? What does it mean to you now?
2. A recurring dream or nightmare. What did you dream? Be as specific as you can. Why was it frightening or memorable? What does it reveal about you?
3. A challenge successfully met, a victory over difficult circumstances.
4. A portrait of a person important in your life, including positive and negative qualities. What does this person mean in your life?
5. Imagine that you are an old person, perhaps retired now, and looking back on your life. Write a letter to the person you are right now, sharing your knowledge of what is important in life. Give enough details of your life story for the reader to understand why your advice is important.

TOPICS FOR SECOND AUTOBIOGRAPHICAL PAPER

For your next paper, you may choose from one of these topics or use a topic from the previous handout, modifying it to suit your own particular circumstances. You will have an opportunity to peer edit this paper and to rewrite it, so please be willing to take risks. Writing your own autobiography is not always easy or comfortable, and there is no one correct way to do it. Remember to make your writing as vivid as possible—don't talk *about* your experience. *Show* your experience to your reader.

1. An experience with death or loss. (This could be the death of a pet, or a friend or relative, or the loss of an ideal or a hope.) Who or what did you lose? How did you learn about this loss? What feelings and sensations did you have? How did you deal with those feelings? What have you gained from the experience?

2. A fight and its outcome. Describe a fight you had with someone (it could be on the playground in first grade, or a struggle with a family member, or a breakup of an important relationship). What triggered the fight? How did you handle it? Why was this issue so important to you? What was the outcome? How do you feel about this event now?

3. Traveling to someone of spiritual authority in your life. Spiritual teachers often say that consulting your guru begins with the first step you take. Describe the steps of a journey to someone of authority in your own life; this could be a musical group or an audience with the pope or a visit to a college. What did you learn about yourself in each step of the journey? What happened when you finally arrived?

4. Describe an encounter or a relationship with someone who seemed totally unlike you. How did this encounter or relationship begin? In what ways were you and this person like? unlike? Did you or your ideas change because of this encounter? What was important in the experience?

5. An act of forgiveness. Describe the greatest act of forgiveness you have seen in your life. What needed to be forgiven? How did the forgiver find the strength to forgive? How did you know it was real forgiveness?

6. A relationship with an animal. This could be something like Black Elk's relationship with horses in his vision, or your personal bond with a pet, or rescuing an animal that needed help. Don't just describe the animal—describe the relationship, show what it meant to you at the time and what meaning it has for you now. How do you see human/animal relationships at this point in your life?

TOPICS FOR THIRD AUTOBIOGRAPHICAL PAPER

For your final paper, you may choose from one of these topics or use a topic from the previous handout, modifying it to suit your own particular circumstances. The idea behind these topics is to represent some of the complexity of your inner life: your relationships with others, dealing with painful events in your past, finding your place in the world, learning to trust. The topics are intended to get you to start thinking about the shape of your own life, and to assist you in reflecting about where you want to go. Remember to make your writing as vivid as possible—don't talk *about* your experience. *Show* your experience to your reader.

1. A new or unfamiliar culture. Describe how the new culture appeared to you, what was confusing about it, how you tried to adapt to it. This might be an experience of traveling, of changing schools or neighborhoods, or it could be more radical, such as the experiences of the Vietnamese refugees we read. Really examine the disorientation, the homesickness, the excitement of newness, the new language.

2. Misunderstanding difference. Tell about a time in which you did not understand a difference you were facing: a miscommunication between friends or family members, or a serious confrontation you got yourself into by not being able to read the (danger) signals, or even discomfort you felt because of different food you were served. What happened? What did you feel? What can you learn from this experience?

3. A paranormal experience such as precognition (knowing the phone will ring just before it does ring), or an out-of-the-body experience (such as floating on the ceiling looking down at your own body, known as "astral projection"), or a dream that foretold a future event. Describe what you felt, saw, or heard as carefully as possible. How did you interpret your experience at the time? How would you interpret it now? What importance does it have in your life?

4. Describe the most important event in your life so far. What was it, when did it happen, what was the context, what were the consequences? Analyze why you believe it is your most important event.

5. A powerful sense experience. Describe a moment in which you were overwhelmed by your sensations. The event might be felt by several senses at once or a single sense experience: a powerful visual image, a breathtaking melody, the scent of night-blooming jasmine, the song of a nightingale, a storm. Describe your sensations in this experience as fully as you can, both the physical sensations and emotional feelings.

6. An event in family history that has had an impact on your life. This could be something momentous that happened to your grandmother or grandfather, or the unexpected death of a relative, or the fact of immigration. Show how this family event was presented or revealed to you, and the difference it has meant in your life.

APPENDIX 2

MIDTERM AND FINAL TAKE-HOME EXAMS:
SPIRITUAL AUTOBIOGRAPHY

TAKE-HOME MIDTERM EXAM

This is an open-book exam in which you may use your books and class notes (but no other aids, online or in book form). The exam should take about three hours, if you budget your time carefully. Your answers must be typed, double-spaced, and proofread. Please follow instructions carefully. Write the name of your TA and the number of your discussion section on your exam.

Part One: Thematic Questions

Answer two questions from this section. Each answer should be at least two double-spaced pages (five hundred words). Be as thorough as you can in comparing and contrasting the texts, and use specific quotations in referring to particular incidents. No vague comparisons, please. Back up your assertions.

1. Human beings cannot grow unless they find others whom they can trust. Not very many opportunities for trust present themselves to our three protagonists, but there are a few instances, and they have a profound effect on their lives. Choose one example of experiencing trust from each book, and show the difference it makes in that person's life.

2. Compare and contrast all three books as collections of memories for posterity. What kinds of events and experiences do they contain? Is there anything they choose to leave out? What kind of posterity are they thinking of? Whom do they imagine as present and future readers? What does memory mean for them?

3. Compare and contrast the role spirituality plays in each life story we have read. Begin with showing how each author might define spirituality. Do you think the concept of spirituality changes or evolves for each writer? How so? Do you see any aspects of spirituality that all three writers share? To what extent does spirituality seem to be culturally defined?

4. Looking at the childhood of each of these figures, discuss *what* values each is taught, and *how* these values are communicated to each (e.g., ritual,

mentoring, parental instruction, divine guidance). Then assess the impact
these early teachings have on their adult life.

Part Two: Specific Questions on Individual Works

Choose two questions to answer in this part. Each answer should be at
least one page. You must write about two different books. Again, be specific and use quotations.

1. Discuss the importance of the Rough Lock Bill episode in Naomi's life
   and in the book *Obasan*. What does she learn from his behavior toward
   her? How does he help her? How is her life different after her encounter
   with him?
2. What is the meaning of the death of Crazy Horse to Black Elk and to his
   people? Look at the reputation he has, how he dies, and the community's
   response to his death, immediately and later. Why is he considered a mar-
   tyr by his people?
3. Why is Linda Brent so resentful when her friend says she will buy her freedom? In accepting this offer so that she may be legally free, what conclusions does she come to?
4. Choosing one of Naomi's dreams, show how it helps her to uncover the
   secret of her mother and her relationship to her. Describe the dream,
   show how it is related to the events in that part of the book, and what
   Naomi learns from it. Think about what we as readers also learn.
5. Why is it so difficult for Black Elk to reveal his vision to the elders in his
   tribe? How does he finally choose to do it? Why is the whole story only
   told late in his life, to John Neihardt?
6. If Dr. Flint is so determined to possess Linda, what do you think prevents
   him from raping her? Look at what characterizes their relationship, how
   each person expresses his or her feelings toward the other, and where the
   power lies in the relationship.

FINAL EXAM QUESTIONS FALL 2002

The purpose of this final is to demonstrate your understanding of the
books we've read by exploring your learning experiences with one or two
books that we've read since the midterm and with writing your three autobiographical papers. *Choose only one of the following questions*, and answer
it in a well-organized essay of approximately four double-spaced pages
(one thousand words). The books are *Obasan*, Joy Kogawa; *Dreams of My
Russian Summers*, Andrei Makine; *The Far East Comes Near*, ed. Nguyen and
Halpern; *Of Water and the Spirit*, Malidoma Patrice Some.

1. What was the book or books from which you learned the most, or which made you reflect upon your own life to the greatest extent? (These may not be the books you liked the most.) Discuss what you got out of that book or those books, your process of reading it. You might want to write a brief summary, then show what the contents meant to you. Then try to look at your autobiographical papers objectively, and show what you experienced and learned in the process of writing them. Then explore what your papers and your chosen book(s) have in common—fears, obsessions, grief, joy, hopes for the future.

2. Choose a book where you identify to some extent with the protagonist, and imagine what the story would be like if it were based on your experience, from your point of view, as if you were the protagonist. (You'll only be able to pick a few telling episodes.) What would you have done if faced with the challenges the protagonist met? What would your weak point be? What can you learn about yourself by inserting yourself into someone else's autobiography? What about your own autobiographies? What have you learned about yourself in writing them?

3. Write a dialogue between yourself and a protagonist of one of our books. (You can make it like a TV interview, or a two-character play, or a movie script.) The important thing is to have you and the author both speak and compare opinions. You do not have to agree on everything. You can take your author to task for his or her attitudes and behaviors: "Why on earth did you do that?" and then allow him or her to offer a defense. You will want to find out what your author wants to communicate to us. Then imagine this person reading your writing, your autobiographies, and questioning you about them. This exercise should show you what you have learned from reading and writing in this class, and it should give you a sense of your own progress.

3

WRITING HISTORY
Informed or Not by Genre Theory?

Anne Beaufort and John A. Williams

What is history writing? The answer to that question is complex. And equally complex is the question of how to help students become better writers of history. In this chapter, the two of us—a composition specialist and history professor—look from our respective vantage points at these questions. As we undertook this project, our aim was to further our collective thinking about what it means to teach and to learn the genres of a particular discipline, and in particular, what it means to try to design and execute effective writing assignments in undergraduate history classes to promote a deeper understanding of both the subject of history and the ways in which historians "write" that history.

We will begin with an overview of some of the particular challenges of defining, teaching, and learning the genres of history writing. Then we will briefly present two case studies—one of a history major's limited progress in writing history genres over a three-year period at an elite, private university, and the other, in one history class at a large public university, of an experiment to refine a writing assignment, situating it more completely within the genres and discourse community of history.

MATERIAL CONDITIONS IN TEACHING HISTORY WRITING

In spite of the centrality of writing to the "doing" of history, teaching writing in undergraduate history courses is challenging. Courses may be part of general-education requirements and enrollments may be high. The subject matter to be grasped is extensive. Anne collected data at a private, elite university. The history major she followed—Tim—received little direct instruction in writing for history. Each course Tim took required writing, yet only one professor wrote more than an end comment and a few marginal comments on Tim's essays. And the majority of comments focused on issues of content, an important aspect of writing, but not the sole aspect. The scarcity of teacher comments on Tim's writing suggests the multiple demands on history professors' time and the relatively low priority of teaching the genres of history writing to undergraduate history majors. And as the case study will demonstrate, Tim made few improvements in his history essays from his freshman through junior years, the point at which he completed his history requirements and began pursuing his double major in engineering.

At John's institution some of the circumstances are similar. For at least the last thirty-five years, virtually all history courses have required written work. Few courses have ever used machine-graded "objective" examinations; blue book essay examinations have been all but universal. Nearly all courses have required written work as well. The assignments have ranged from book reviews to conventional term papers to reaction papers on issues raised in the course. This has been true of introductory surveys and more specialized thematic lecture courses. For senior majors, the department offers colloquia, with a seminar format, in which the course requirement is one lengthy research paper. Graduating history majors have to submit one of their papers, of at least ten pages, to certify fulfillment of the "major writing requirement," a campus requirement administered by departments.

This emphasis on writing is rare in the social science division of this institution, and the history department takes pride in it. Yet how effectively the department is teaching the genres of history writing is a question. In spring semester 2003, the department had extensive discussions about the major writing requirement and ways in which the department could make it more rigorous, less perfunctory. After discussion, the undergraduate committee decided that "expository and analytic papers are equally acceptable. Extensive research is not intrinsic to the requirement." These statements reflect the variety of assignments given and the great diversity of approaches to writing in the faculty and the profession at large. The revised major writing requirement guidelines called for papers to be submitted "well before the end of the semester," to allow for comments, revisions, and improvements. They also encouraged the use of smaller lecture courses with intensive writing components to fulfill the requirement, and questioned but did not forbid the use of larger lecture courses for this purpose. They also recommended a stricter enforcement of standards: a grade of B- had been acceptable; now it was noted that this grade should reflect the quality of writing, not simply the content of the paper.

In John's view, and in his colleagues' view, whatever the size of the course, a difficulty arises from the nature of undergraduate lecture courses in history. In laboratory science courses, and even in many sociology and psychology courses, professors teach, say, what chemists do, or how to pursue the discipline. Yet history courses do not emphasize "what historians do" but rather the results of historical work, what conclusions historians have come to. Though this may be changing, the lectures typically offer an exposition or narrative of a historical field. Students receive, and expect to receive, a systematic survey, a body of information, about a field or theme of history. The greatest innovation of recent decades has been the introduction of new topics and themes, new bodies of synthesized information—women's history, histories of ethnic and racial minorities, "history from the bottom up," "the history of the inarticulate," and the like. Criticisms of existing work and emphasis on interpretive debate are, of course, at the center of "what historians do," but this aspect of historical work does not enter fully into undergraduate lecture courses.

What, then, of the "paper" assignments in courses defined by the historical material to be "covered"? Writing is "what historians do." But the paper tends to be attached to the lecture course more to provide part of the grade than to teach skills of writing or of historical analysis. A minimum goal of such assignments seems to be to assign some outside reading and to prove that students have done it. Often due at the very end of the term, papers are written and graded sometimes without any feedback or consultation, nor do students always get papers back before the end of the semester to see comments.

The burden of the course is to present the subject in lecture form, with textbook or other supporting readings. Students study this material and write midterm and final examinations based on these. There is often little time spent on teaching the students the skills needed to write the paper—for example, helping students to understand the genre requirements of the assignment through explicit instruction and use of models, and so on, and helping students to develop the analytical frameworks they need to do the task. Teachers tacitly assume that students bring those skills in with them and complain when they do not.

PROBLEMS OF DEFINING THE GENRES IN HISTORY

When asked at the end of his senior year to describe the genres of history writing, Tim, the history major Anne followed, replied, "There's so many different kinds of historical writing. . . . there's the textbook, there's the Shrewsbury type paper [referring to a particular primary source document], which just focuses on one little document and squeezes as much blood as it can out of that. . . . there's the kind of typical history assignment which would be something like one of the Islamic [papers] . . . take one of these writers or these books and discuss it in a certain context."

We see in Tim's reply a beginning understanding of varying purposes for writing in history and types of content in history writing, and with the mention of textbooks, an acknowledgement of length and structure of one type of history writing. When asked if he felt making an argument was essential to the success of a history essay, he said, "Yeah. Maybe not in those, umm, I guess I did here [referring to one of his assignments], but this [referring to another assignment] is more of a synthetic approach. This one doesn't seem to be very argumentative. Here I say, 'There lies a stark contrast.' Okay, well, so what? I guess you're kind of trying to make a point that your analysis is valid." His hedges—"I guess I did . . . I guess you're kind of trying to . . . yeah, maybe . . ."—suggest that Tim is not altogether certain what rhetorical purposes are common or expected in the discourse community.

But trying to define genres in history writing is difficult to do, as even experts in the field recognize. Tosh says: "Historical writing is character-ized by a wide range of literary forms. . . . [T]his lack of clear guidelines is partly a reflection of the great diversity of the historian's subject matter: there could not possibly be one literary form suited to the presentation of every aspect of the human past. But it is much more the result of the different and sometimes contradictory purposes behind historical writ-ing, and above all of the tension which lies at the heart of all historical enquiry between the desire to re-create the past and urge to interpret it" (1984, 94–95).

John's view of genres in history is similar to Tosh's. In John's view, the oldest model for the student history paper is the "term paper," and stu-dents know how to write these assignments. They have a topic, and a few days before the paper is due they get several books on this topic open in front of them. (Of course, nowadays, they may well use Internet sources.) They move from book to book, paraphrasing, following the sentence and paragraph sequences of their sources. At its worst, the term paper is an exercise in looking up some information but has little value as writing. Students imitate the models they have—readings assigned in this or other courses. In addition, professors often say they want students to have "criti-cal thinking" skills, but these are seldom defined or talked about. What historians mean by critical thinking is an awareness of historiographical issues, problems of interpretation, historical debates, and methods. But where will students get these skills? These matters are difficult to put across in a survey lecture course, with its own burden of presenting a synthesis of knowledge about, say, the history of the United States or some theme within that field.

To make matters more difficult, historical writing is varied and rapidly changing. Methods, topic selection, and style of presentation are vigorously debated within the historical profession, and no single definition is acceptable to all. Philosophers and sociologists, among others, often claim that the discourse of professional historians is loose, lacking in rigor, with great inferential leaps between evidence and conclusions. But the more scientific and quantitative historians are criticized for not successfully conveying, through narrative, how reality was experienced in past societies, how it felt to be there. According to Weinstein, historical novelists such as Mary Lee Settle claim that they can portray the subjectivity of historical personages with greater authenticity than historians have been capable of. After all, that inferential leap into the feelings of past times is the historical novelist's stock in trade (1990, 11–19). Thus, history is hung between the humanities and social sciences, and its procedures and its values are contested, within the discipline and without. Part of the difficulty history teachers have in explaining to students what historical writing is all about stems from the problems of the discipline itself.

DEVELOPMENTAL ISSUES IN LEARNING TO WRITE HISTORY

The problem of learning to write in history is not just a matter of appropriating a particular form. Consider Slevin's definition of genre: "Genre is a received form, part of a cultural code, that synthesizes discursive features (e.g. subject matter, meaning, organization, style, and relations between writer and implied/actual audience) in recognizable ways" (1988, 4). Issues of subject matter and meaning are embedded, as Slevin indicates, within cultural codes. Genres, or the individual texts a historian writes, do not exist alone, as single points of communication. Rather, genres are a part of a whole activity system, a discourse community of historians who pursue writing projects as part of ongoing conversations on the meaning of the past.

So an equally challenging task for history teachers, if they want to introduce students to the genres of history writing, is guiding students to tasks appropriate to the discourse community in which history genres are situated. Wineburg (1991a) has pointed out that the historian must find not only a subject, but a problem to be solved through the writing project. He states, "Historical inquiry differs considerably from problem solving in well-structured domains. . . . in history goals remain vague and indefinite, open to a great deal of personal interpretation" (73–74). The teacher who discusses these issues of what "counts" as a worthy topic in the discourse community of historians with his or her students will at the same time be furthering their chances of taking on a subject matter and an authentic rhetorical purpose in their essays that not only meets genre expectations in history, but also invites apprenticelike participation in the discourse community of historians (Lave and Wenger 1991).

How to structure a historical essay is not straightforward or formulaic, either. In one student guidebook for writing history, the author (Storey 1999) advises using one of two types of structure—either a narrative with analysis embedded, or an analysis with narrative embedded. Stockton (1995), a rhetorician, also found different expectations when she analyzed teachers' instructions and grading practices in history courses. One history teacher in Stockton's study stated her expectations—that students should write essays that made arguments—but in fact gave As to papers that were chronologically structured, with the argument embedded in the narrative, and lower grades to expository essays that make the explicit argument the top-level structure of the essay.

In addition to appropriate subject matter and structure, Slevin's definition of genre also highlights matters of style or linguistic features. What historical vocabulary should one use in order to speak with authority? And what person should be used in a historical essay—omniscient third person? Second person? On occasion, first person singular or first person plural? According to Stockton, historians establish the credibility of their reports, in part, by writing in an "autonomous voice capable of telling time . . . not subject to history, not entangled in self-doubt, self-reference, or the webs of discourse" (69). Can student writers be taught the appropriate vocabulary, and the appropriate authorial voice for history writing, not as a superficial overlay onto weak content, but as part of a multipronged approach to learning the genres of history writing? That is part of the challenge of mastering history genres.

In addition to being cognizant of genre knowledge students must gain, history teachers can benefit from an awareness of related developmental processes for history students in both reading and critical thinking. Reading skills are crucial to writing successful historical essays, as the primary rhetorical task is the interpretation of texts. A variety of critical thinking activities might be associated with reading-to-write tasks: for example, recall, synthesis, analysis, and/or classification. In addition, besides assimilating and manipulating information from source texts, the skilled reader/writer draws upon rhetorical and lexical knowledge to discern issues of bias, tone, and author credibility. Historians must deconstruct texts for their reliability (both internal validity and corroboration with other sources) and rhetorical features (Britt et al. 1994; Greene 1993; Paxton 1999). They must also synthesize texts, doing associative, comparative thinking to provide as multidimensional a perspective on events as possible (Bohan and Davis 1998; Greene 1993; Leinhardt and Young 1996; Wineburg 1991b).

Wineburg's (1991a) comparative study of students' (high school seniors) versus historians' reading of historical source documents points out the advantages of teaching students to read history texts through a genre lens: historians looked at source information, corroborated one text with another, and contextualized events in time and space—all part of understanding the inherent meanings of genres in history writing. Students, on the other hand, failed "to see text as a social instrument masterfully crafted to achieve a social end" (Wineburg 1991b, 502). Leinhardt and Young also studied key reading strategies of expert historians and found that historians "tended to maximize, uncovering the richest network of information available from the text, ever suspect of possible discrepancies or dualities." In contrast to these behaviors, they found "for the average reader, what happens in the text is normally seen as what happens in the story" (478). These differences in reading strategies—novice versus expert—are in part differences of understanding both the nature of historical texts in general (compared, say, to literary texts or scientific texts) and the understanding the genre features of a wide variety of historical records—letters, public documents, newspaper accounts, memoirs, oral histories, and so on.

Besides astute reading of historical texts and understanding the discourse community and genre conventions in history, to write history requires the critical thinking skills of synthesizing information and constructing historical arguments. Students transitioning from high school to college often find that college demands more than summarizing others' texts or reporting facts. The most typical type of historical reasoning is causal reasoning: "Because of X and Y, then Z." Such reasoning requires extensive background knowledge, close reading of source documents, the ability to see not isolated facts, but rather, institutional and structural factors that affect events (Hallden 1994; Wineburg 2001). Additionally, historical reasoning requires the ability to see multidimensional, complex perspectives (Bohan and Davis 1998) and to understand how these analyses are woven into the rhetorical purposes, forms, and so on of the genres of history writing. As Watts states, "[H]istory is a subject in which it is difficult to assemble all the evidence, difficult to have conclusive proof, and yet easy to find, from the vast range of material, rival evidence of a different argument" (1972, 38). Several studies of high school or college history students wrestling with the critical thinking skills involved in synthesizing evidence and constructing arguments have demonstrated this skill is not one college students necessarily have mastery of (Greene 1993; Hallden 1994; Langer 1984; Wineburg 1994, 2001; Young and Leinhardt 1998). Students frequently resort to easier cognitive tasks, such as summary, rather than analysis or argument.

But these learning goals are entirely attainable. Within a general framework of understanding genres' roles in the disciplinary field of history, the critical thinking and argumentative skills needed will likely become clearer to students as they see the genres' purposes within the discourse communities the genres are a part of.

A LONGITUDINAL CASE STUDY

A longitudinal study of Tim's undergraduate's work in six history courses, from freshman through junior years, demonstrates the importance of devoting at least a small portion of class time to explicit disciplinary writing instruction, ideally from a genre perspective. This was apparently not the case in Tim's experience, and as the analysis of his writing will show, Tim did not increase his writing skills in the genres of history in any consistent and significant ways over the course of his undergraduate history studies as far as I could see. I report here a small portion of the analysis of his work in history over a three-year period (Beaufort forthcoming).

The case study of Tim was part of a larger longitudinal study of five college writers across the fours years of undergraduate work. Tim volunteered to be part of the study, as he had a keen interest in writing. I did not have a complete data set: Tim brought me only the written work he could readily lay his hands on. Time constraints also prohibited me from observing Tim's history classes and interviewing his teachers. Nonetheless, I was able to interview Tim extensively in his freshman, sophomore, and senior years as well as two years after he left college to discuss his work in history. In all, he brought twelve papers to me, written across his freshman, sophomore, and junior years. Interviews were discourse-based—that is, Tim was prompted to explain his thinking processes, his decisions about each text, and the context of the courses in which the essays were written. In order to triangulate my analysis of his written work, I also interviewed several historians with expertise in the subject areas Tim was writing in to place his work within the larger context of the discourse community of historians and determine how closely he was approximating the work of historians.

As I indicated at the beginning of the chapter, in a retrospective interview at the end of his senior year, Tim reflected back on the writing he had done in history and was not able to articulate very clearly what genre expectations his professors had. Was it necessary to make an argument in a historical essay? What was the purpose of a close reading of primary or secondary texts? Looking at the different aspects of Tim's essays through the lens of genre reveals a number of problems in Tim's writing as a result of his having only vague awareness of genre expectations in history. Whether his professors made those expectations clear or not can only be surmised, but Tim could recall no explicit instructions about writing in genres in history. The problems that resulted from this genre confusion were numerous.

The first genre-related problem Tim faced was choosing an appropriate content or appropriate rhetorical purpose for an essay—if he was given the latitude to do so. Tim reported that he sometimes felt the only purpose of a writing assignment was to regurgitate a particular historical interpretation the professor advocated and to demonstrate that one had read the assigned materials. Of the writing task in one class his freshman year he said, "[The professor] would say you came to the wrong [conclusion]. . . . We talked about it afterwards. I walked him through my chain of thought and he followed it up to the very last link. . . . in order to get the grade on the paper . . . you had to say what you'd been told in class about the book. Maybe in a new way, maybe in more depth, but basically say the same thing."

In other writing assignments, Tim felt he had more latitude in terms of the type of topic he chose and the rhetorical purpose for the essay. But that latitude on writing assignments did not necessarily lead to writing that was appropriate to the discourse community. Perhaps his professors were thinking only in terms of getting students to read, not crafting their assignments to initiate students into genres of the discourse community of historians. But as this volume argues, the latter is a reasonable and attainable goal. One of Tim's essays in his first year was a comparison of Augustine's *Confessions* and Benedictine's *Rule*. He tried to argue their differences based on changing political conditions in the Roman Empire that transpired across the time period when each was written. A medievalist I asked to review Tim's essay for its fit within the discourse community of historians pointed out that the single major cause of the differences in the two texts was in fact that the texts were different genres. Augustine was writing a memoir, Benedictine, a guidebook for communal living. So Tim's essay took up a moot point. Tim had failed to consider the genres he was analyzing, which in turn led to an inadequate interpretation of the differences between the texts. If his professor had given some guidance about a framework for analysis of the two texts, Tim's analysis could have been more appropriate. This instance reiterates the importance of genre knowledge in history, not just for the sake of producing texts, but also for the sake of reading and interpreting a range of genres appropriately.

For an American history course his sophomore year, Tim's criticism of a historian's analysis of the causes of the Salem witchcraft trials again failed to take up a question that historians would consider relevant to the text under consideration: the author of the text Tim was analyzing was not concerned with the question Tim raised, so in essence, he was not evaluating the text on its own terms. In another essay for the same course, Tim attempted a rhetorical analysis of a letter from one Seventh-Day Baptist church in New Jersey to another in Rhode Island in the eighteenth century. Tim was able to enumerate many of the text's rhetorical features, this time considering carefully the genre of the text, the social context of the text, and the particular craft employed by the text's authors. But Tim's essay became a catalogue of rhetorical features without having an overall point. As an Americanist who read Tim's essay pointed out, it failed to answer the "So what?" question. Tim's understanding of the assignment was to "[focus] on one little document and squeezes as much blood as [I] can out of that." Based on what he produced and my interviews with him, Tim was not clear about the rhetorical purpose of the textual analysis, and as a result, his essay was less than successful in fulfilling expectations of the genre.

This crucial aspect of genre knowledge is often overlooked. To be effective rhetorically and fulfill readers' expectations of a genre, the subject matter of a particular text needs to link up with the "ongoing conversations" of the discipline (Bruffee 1984), and an appropriate framework of analysis must be used. Tim reported that a few times in his freshman year he ran an essay topic by the TA for the course. But Tim reported that assignments were generally open-ended, and in Tim's case, these open-ended assignments often resulted in choosing inappropriate content for his essays. Nor was Tim given guidance on appropriate analytical frameworks with which to generate the content of his essays.

Besides problems with content and rhetorical purpose in Tim's history essays, there were problems with executing a particular rhetorical purpose with ample development of ideas and with the aid of a structure that followed a clear line of argument. Of the twelve history essays Tim shared with me, all of which were five to seven pages long, an analysis of discourse-level structures revealed that only three of the twelve had a cohesive structure and only four had strong support for claims. And the strongest essays were not consistently the ones written in his junior year. A few of Tim's essays were a loose list of events or factors without any organizing thesis; in other essays the thesis was not substantiated in the body of the essay with concrete evidence. One of his professors commented on one unsuccessful essay, "Your hypothesis is interesting and sophisticated. The logic with which you apply it to the readings is sometimes faulty."

Tim attempted some complex structures in a few essays—a comparison of sources interwoven with a cause-effect argument, for example, or a chronology and a cause-effect argument woven together. He demonstrated a beginning understanding of the need, in history genres, not just to amass facts, but to incorporate textual evidence into a carefully constructed argument. But more often, he organized his essays as a list of points without clear interconnections among points. Even when he was doing the analytical work of comparing different historical documents, often there was no overarching central point to the essay. Although this is in part a critical thinking issue, it is crucial as well for fulfilling the persuasive aims of most history writing.

Patterns of citation usage, another indication of ability to work successfully analyzing historical documents (Greene 1993, 2001), were also irregular. In some instances, he gave citations for material that could be considered common knowledge. In three essays there were no citations. And in the two essays with the highest number of citations, there were citations for single facts but whole paragraphs of paraphrased material with no citations.

Matters of linguistic style were also a part of what Tim needed to learn as a novice writer in history. In retrospective interviews, he was able to articulate to me the difficulty of finding the appropriate authorial stance in writing his history essays: "[S]aying 'I' felt like, they are going to investigate my credentials [*laughs*]. I'd rather just hide behind the ideas and let them present themselves . . . saying 'I' would be like, well, who is this guy, anyway? Well, he's a student. I mean, come on, what does he know? So 'we' is little vague. You can hide behind it, I guess."

Tim experimented with authorial stances. In one essay he wrote, "Although only complete knowledge of Fletcher's character and values can explain his impressions conclusively, *we* can suggest a simple reason." In another essay, he wrote, "From both writers' perspectives *the reader sees that.*" He also felt that historians wrote in more formal prose than, say, his English professor might expect, although an analysis of the lexicon he used in his essays did not demonstrate a particularly "advanced" or sophisticated use of historical concepts and phraseology. Rather, he frequently employed colloquialisms and word puns (he enjoyed word play) that would not be appropriate to written discourse in history.

These problems—a combination of issues in critical thinking, subject matter knowledge, rhetorical skill, ability to structure material, and ability to assume an appropriate ethos in relation to his audience—all led to essays that were less than they could have been from the standpoint of appropriating not only the textual features of genres in history, but also the social roles enacted by those genres. Yet in spite of these indications of Tim's being still a novice in handling the genres of history writing even at the end of his junior year, Tim was successful in negotiating the expectations of his professors for his writing. Tim received As from his professors on the majority of his essays. Comments at the end of essays included "Good synthesis"; "Good analysis"; "Creative approach."

Tim's comments to me in interviews about his reasons for choosing the particular topics he did for his essays revealed that he was an independent thinker who cared about finding his own particular angle on historical situations. His professors, from the few comments written on his papers, appeared to value this independence of thinking and, as was the case in John's analysis of his own grading practices, did not assign grades based on a clear set of genre expectations other than these: that essays should analyze historical texts and incorporate textual evidence as support for arguments.

In addition, in analyzing the papers, it is evident that there was no clear "progression" from his freshman through junior years in incorporating more and more of the features of historical writing. It is also interesting that the writing assignments were not progressively more difficult, except for a requirement in one of his junior-level courses for a longer essay (fifteen to twenty pages). And outside readers in history whom I consulted judged many of his essays outside the realm of what historians would write. It is worth pondering whether, had genre knowledge been a clear learning objective in these courses, Tim's history writing skills would have developed further and enabled him to participate more authentically in the discourse community of historians. We turn now to a case of a professor consciously trying to help his students acquire the genre knowledge they will need to write effectively in his course.

JOHN'S GENRE EXPERIMENT

When I come to make a paper assignment for a lecture course, I have keenly felt many of the problems discussed in the literature on students learning to read and write history. I typically have a class of sixty to ninety students, in a junior-level course on South African or British Indian history. The historical material is unfamiliar to most students, and I need to spend most of the time establishing a framework of information.

But I want the students to write a historical essay, and I want to work out an assignment that will be difficult to plagiarize, where even the paraphrasing of secondary sources will not work. I believe that the classic research paper is not a practical option here; for that kind of paper I would want a seminar format so that I could lead students step-by-step through the research process. Here, I have not been worried about whether the students will be writing *history* but only that they will be thinking, casting their own sentences, doing the task themselves. Therefore, I tell them the assignment is not a term paper but an essay. This makes students stop to ask questions. They know what a "term paper" is, but what is an "essay"?

In effect, this assignment, which I have used for a number of years, invokes the issue of genre. My purposes in calling for an essay were two: first, to de-familiarize the assignment so that students might listen more closely to instructions; second, beyond this, to move students away from the term paper model in which they so often simply paraphrased sources. I wanted to say to them, "No one since creation has done this assignment; you are on your own." But my use of genre was akin to Molière's *bourgeois gentilhomme*, who realized suddenly that he was speaking prose.

Working with Anne in spring 2003 and learning about the newer, more flexible concepts of genre, I set out to make the question of genre more explicit and purposeful, to see whether we could improve student writing by giving detailed instructions. One of the things Anne noticed in looking at an earlier set of papers based on a similar assignment was that there seemed to be no consistency to the grades from her point of view. Good grades were given sometimes for the quality of expression, sometimes for the body of information, sometimes for the way the information was analyzed. In some cases it seemed altogether subjective. I realized that in some cases I rewarded engagement, effort, commitment to the assignment. I wanted to encourage students to take risks rather than settling for the easiest, safest approach to the assignment. Poorly written papers reflecting this commitment might not be graded as low as their quality seemed to merit. My expectations had not been clear enough, even to myself, and therefore the grading criteria were difficult to define. Introducing issues of genre would make expectations clear and grading easier.

In our spring semester 2003 experiment in the use of genre, the assignment for the paper was an outgrowth of ones used before. In previous assignments I had been most concerned about forestalling plagiarism. My method was to have students confront two books that were dis-coordinated, with no easy connection between them. It was a gimmick, designed to prevent cheating. Now I had a more positive goal—to make an effective writing assignment. Now I asked students to frame a hypothesis and an argument—this was new. It raised questions of critical reading that I have still to explore further. The assignment is not just about writing, but also about how to read: not passively for information but actively for responses and with a critical sense informed by some disciplinary knowledge.

The paper would cover material from the end of the course in South African history, the period from 1962 to 1994—the years of apartheid, the armed struggle, the transition, and the emergence of the new South Africa. The readings drew the students away from the political struggle itself to the lives of South Africans living through it, some of them important historical actors, others ordinary people, of all races, living through these dramatic times. All students were to read two books in common: Antjie Krog's *Country of My Skull* (1999) and David Goodman's *Fault Lines* (1999). In addition, each student was to read one more book, selected from a list of three dozen works—novels, memoirs, or journalism covering the same general topics. Krog's book is a multilayered work of journalism. It gives an account of her personal experience in covering the hearings of the Truth and Reconciliation Commission, and it provides a rich commentary on and analysis of the commission itself. In addition, it reflects on the author's own identity as an Afrikaner in the new circumstances of South African society. David Goodman's book provides a series of short biographical sketches in pairs—for example, of the activist Frank Chikane and the policeman, Paul Erasmus, who hounded him. David Goodman, an American journalist, had visited South Africa during the years of apartheid. This book is the result of a second visit. It is in effect a work of contemporary history, describing and assessing the realities of the "new South Africa." Whatever third book the student might choose, whether by Desmond Tutu, Nelson Mandela, or someone else, would offer an additional source of information and a further point of view.

Anne suggested that laying out specific criteria for grading was a good way to define the nature of the paper. I handed out the following to the class after the midterm examination, when they were starting work on the papers:

- Bases for grading the paper:
- Clear statement of argument, hypothesis, or purpose of the paper. What will your paper accomplish?
- Effective use of evidence drawn from the reading to support your points. This involves selecting key bits of evidence, not summarizing entire sections of the reading.
- Logical sequence of unified paragraphs to make your points and develop your argument. Is your argument accessible and easy to follow?
- Standard written English spelling and grammar.
- Historical concepts defined and used appropriately.
- Success of the body of the paper in supporting the argument or establishing the hypothesis.

With these guidelines, the students' task was to read three books, working out a way to respond to them. As noted above, they needed a statement of their hypothesis. I wanted them to decide what to say, construct an argument, cast their own sentences and paragraphs—in short, to write an original paper.

They were anxious. Many of them begged for a "topic." This would clearly carry them back to the "term paper" model. I pointed out in class that the hypothesis they developed would give them a principle of selection. They were going to have to omit at least 98 percent of the material they read in the books, and they would need good reasons for their decisions to include or omit material. What they included could not be arbitrary or random but had to be directly germane to their stated purpose.

I judge the results of this experiment in using a genre approach to teaching writing in history to be mixed. It turned out to be disappointing in some ways but with some significant successes. As the history department guidelines on the writing requirement have noted, large classes are not the best forum for giving instruction in writing. Yet we are probably stuck with them. Over the years, enrollment has edged up in our junior-level classes. The South African history course fulfils a diversified education requirement and is taken by many nonhistory majors. Also, attendance was a problem. Students cutting class on given days did not receive the handout or hear the class discussions of the assignment.

Some students simply evaded the assignment and found easier, more familiar paths. Some, for example, wrote a summary history of South Africa since 1652, reaching the time period covered in the assigned reading only in the last two pages of the paper. These papers mentioned the reading perfunctorily or, in a few cases, not at all. Other papers reverted to a "term paper" model, giving an expository account of the transition from apartheid to the new South Africa, drawn more from the classes and textbook than from the assigned reading for the paper. More papers recounted selected stories from the books, uncritically, with no evaluation of their own; these were close to the assignment but for their lack of any hypothesis or argument. One or two papers were statements of personal outrage—an element that could be used very effectively if the paper also addressed the material assigned.

The best single paper failed to follow the assignment in another way. It was thirty pages long, triple the suggested length. This paper selected long quotations from Antjie Krog's, David Goodman's, and Desmond Tutu's books, juxtaposing them and subjecting them to perceptive analysis and evaluation. The success of this paper at first made me wonder whether the ten-page length was fully adequate to fulfil the assignment effectively.

In the end, though, a number of the nine- to twelve-page papers met the assignment very effectively. It was a relief—I did not want to read ninety article-length papers. I can conclude from the fair number of successful papers that the assignment, with its emphasis on genre, did help some students write better and more convincing papers. The key elements for the most successful papers were an explicit hypothesis and an argument in support of it. As noted above, the hypothesis provides a principle of selection by which quotations and factual details can be included or left out.

Several papers addressed the question of the Truth and Reconciliation Commission and the controversial decision to offer amnesty in exchange for truth rather than seeking retributive justice through criminal trials. Here was fertile ground for speculation and argument. Whether the TRC should have attempted prosecutions for gross human rights violations was a matter the students would have opinions about. The authors they were reading also debated this question, and so did the people of South Africa whose lives these authors were writing about. This argument was the most obvious opportunity for hypothesizing; I wanted to see how many students would frame a hypothesis around this issue. In the end, only a few did. Students needed more training in thinking critically about the texts—a lesson I will note for future classes. On one level, these works of journalism are secondary authorities for the contemporary history of South Africa; on another, they are primary sources depicting the struggle individuals have with identities and moral commitments in a society undergoing deep and sudden changes. For students to get past the simplest level of engagement with the text—the summary—they need to engage more deeply than most did. They also need more training in how historians deal with such complex texts.

A series of topic sentences from one of the papers shows how a hypothesis could be used to sustain a paper. The paper asserts that all South Africans were victims of apartheid in one way or another and that the TRC offered a way to heal the society:

- "The system of apartheid has damaged not only black Africans, who felt it the most, but also Afrikaners, the very same ethnic group that institutionalized it."
- "Perhaps the deepest wound to black people under apartheid was psychological."
- "Mandela speaks in his autobiography about the inferiority complex among blacks as the greatest barrier to liberation."
- "The domination of the police force by Afrikaners further ensured them a psychological hold over blacks through the use of fear and violence."
- "In post-apartheid South Africa, many victims of apartheid crimes and their families still have not found psychological peace."
- "A key part of reconstructing black African culture was correcting history."
- "Apartheid made whites into drones, denying them the opportunity to think for themselves."
- "Separation, the very meaning of apartheid, bred racist theories because it denied whites interaction with blacks and other ethnic groups."

This unified structure enables the paper to carry well-selected and clear examples from the reading. The first topic sentence conveys the hypothesis. The second through sixth sentences introduce sections on the impact of apartheid on the African population; the seventh and eighth deal with the whites. In this paper, each of the generalizations introduces expository sections providing supporting evidence. The vast amount of evidence available, which overwhelmed some students, provided here a storehouse to enrich this paper. This was possible, I believe, because of its strong and explicit hypothesis.

Two other successful papers focused on women in the struggle against apartheid. This theme allowed students to draw widely from the reading, though these papers missed the opportunity to talk about Antjie Krog, the author of one of the books they were reading. They tended to use the books as windows on reality, failing to consider that Antjie Krog was part of that reality and the publication of her book a historical event itself. Although the papers missed many such good opportunities to make deeper connections, they did accomplish some good analysis. One paper in particular documented the pressures apartheid placed on African families and recounted examples of women who were destroyed and women who were made stronger by the struggle. The theme of women got these papers beyond the simple recounting of a few anecdotes. Neither of these papers developed a strong hypothesis, but they were halfway there.

In the end, a few papers, eight or ten out of ninety, give me some satisfaction that the assignment did have its element of success. I do not have any evidence of before and after to measure how these particular students might have improved. It is not unusual to get about this many "good papers" in a class. But what made them "good" was less specific. In this class, the "good papers" stood out precisely because they were engaged in the genre specifications set out in the assignment.

The task here is to define the historical essay in contrast to the term paper students are familiar with and to get students to take control of the paper, rather than following the authorities by paraphrasing. Papers that are extended paraphrases of secondary sources in narrative or expository form are evading this goal. This semester's experiment has pushed me to think further about the characteristics of the historical essay:

- It is a response to reading.
- As a response, it may have a personal element.
- It is critical, which does not mean attacking the work ("poorly written," etc.) but rather assessing its characteristics.
- It has a hypothesis and makes an argument.

- Its use of historical evidence and information is subordinate and supports the argument.
- It is multilayered, concerned alike with the content of the books students are reading, the points of view of the authors, the impact of the books on an audience, and the books' literary qualities.

The emphasis on genre in this semester's experiment also provided a basis for more consistent grading. The clearer expectations set down made the papers easier to grade, as the students and the grader shared a list of criteria for grading. The result was slightly lower grades for students who evaded the assignment, more consistent grades, and easier coordination with the teaching assistant who graded some of the papers.

I have said that some students evaded the assignment. That is true, but taken too far such an accusation is like blaming the victim. Many students simply needed more direction, closer supervision. The ideal would be the essay on assigned readings that Oxford students read to their tutors each week, as Eric Foner (2002) describes it in *Who Owns History?* But here we have one essay in a semester, in a class with perhaps ninety students.

Why did some students, despite the handouts and several reinforcing class discussion, evade the assignments? Students did cut classes, and some undoubtedly missed the class discussions of the assignments. A colleague who teaches writing at another institution offered another reason: he said that once students are by themselves, late at night with the paper due the next day, they are simply looking for a way forward—like a tennis player who has just taken a lesson but cannot apply what he has learned in his next match.

I plan to continue working to improve the writing components of my courses along these lines: closer definition of the assignment in terms of genre will certainly help. I will assign some short drafts early in the semester. In these, students can learn to develop a hypothesis, practice critical assessments of readings, and frame some arguments—all aspects of the historical essays I want them to write. To provide a model for these short assignments, I want to point out some of these features in the historical works they are reading, to discuss historical writing rather than content only. Finally, these written exercises will make it clearer that working on writing will help their grades. It will help the class get away from the "make-or-break" nature of the one paper handed in on the last day of the class.

For many reasons, the experiment in genre was worth doing, and worth repeating and developing in the future.

IN CONCLUSION

What have we learned? First, that the concept of genre and genre theory have been useful frameworks for our dialogue, deepening our understanding of what was going on in the two writing situations we encountered. History departments have always taught writing, but now they are discussing it more and are more concerned with how it is done. Still, we suspect that few history professors are familiar with the body of scholarship on genre theory and its application to writing pedagogy cited in this chapter and throughout this book. Perhaps they should be, for it addresses the very problems they have been discussing. We were impressed with the convergence between the historians talking about writing and the writing researchers looking at the problems of student history writing. Both looked at the diversity of historical writing, the way complex problems of interpretation intrude so quickly, even on the undergraduate level. Genre as a theoretical framework is neither too amorphous nor too ideological. It can be applied, practically, to designing writing assignments, conceptualizing instruction for novice writers, and evaluating writing.

Second, though genre theory is readily grasped by any academic, knowledge of genre theory as manifest in one's own discipline may well be tacit knowledge, a type of knowing hard to articulate when working with student writers. Anne, an outsider to the discipline, took the role of eliciting from John what the issues are in writing in genres appropriate to the discipline of history. And John, through the process of that articulation, made "real" the genre knowledge he had. The need to make expectations for student writing more clear and explicit came up in both Tim's case and John's class. The tacitly held conventions of historical discourse, and the difficulty of articulating them for students, lies at the center of this problem of expectations. John noticed a similarity, too, between the experiences Tim had (in Anne's case study), including the inconsistent pedagogy of some of Tim's professors, and his own experience with grading papers. While genre theory is not a panacea, these problems of pedagogy and evaluation can also be ameliorated by clearer articulation of the genres students should learn and a well thought-out pedagogy to teach those genres.

Third, genre theory forces us to ask ourselves if we aren't creating artificial barriers in our minds when we say, in subject areas outside writing and rhetoric, that we don't or can't teach writing. Certainly, in history, the real work of the discipline is reading and interpreting texts in writing.

And genre expectations in history—comparing textual sources, interpreting the contexts for those documents, creating reasonable interpretive arguments based on textual evidence—in fact describe the very work at the heart of the discipline. Genres really are the vehicles of social action for those in the discourse community with which the genres are associated. Tim was "doing" history in his more successful essays, as were the students in John's class who wrote the most successful essays. Less successful writing attempts missed the mark not just in some communicative sense, but in the sense of doing the analytical work of the discipline. So teaching history writing is in fact teaching history. Genre theory helps to make this evident. It would be interesting to hear from other disciplines: to what extent are the genres of the discipline at least in part "doing" the work of the discipline? And how are we teaching the mental habits, the philosophical assumptions, the practical activities of our fields as we instruct students in their writing? This is the real stuff of genre theory—and genres—in action.

4

MAPPING GENRES IN A SCIENCE IN SOCIETY COURSE

Mary Soliday

The writing allows us to gain "ownership" of the material being covered, as it enables us to explain, in our own words, the material rather than answer with textbook answers.

For me, writing for this course has been very different from my English courses. Ironically, my English teachers require very strict analysis, while this course encourages me to share my views and opinions.

These responses come from honors students who took Plagues: Past, Present, Future? a science course taught at the City College of New York in fall 2002. I begin with them because they confirm a theme central to genre theory: that individuals acquire genres by accenting alien forms with their own "views," "opinions," or purposes. To borrow from M. M. Bakhtin (1986), writers may most fully acquire "ownership" of communal forms when they assimilate them to their own social language.

From Bakhtin's perspective, acquiring genres sparks a struggle between collective forms *and* personal understandings. To study genres, we can describe their recurring textual features (see Swales and Luebs 2002), but if we're interested in how individuals acquire shared forms, we would focus on the interplay between "purposes, participants, and themes" that also shape form (Devitt, 1993, 575–76; Freedman and Medway 1994d). We would ask how individuals use typical forms to organize material in socially recurrent situations (Freedman 1995, 123).

In the fall of 2002, Professor David Eastzer offered the Plagues course at City College, and he agreed to participate in a study of genre with the WAC program. We began by wondering what genres David required, and how his students responded to his official requests for particular forms. We assumed that genre would be established through course documents, course texts, and David's goals, but, as we considered the social situation, also through classroom discourse, the students' responses, and David's judgment of what the students had learned. Four questions organize the study of genre in David's course that I describe in this essay:

- What genres did David ask students to produce in his course?
- How did David convey genre knowledge to the students?
- How did students approach those requirements to produce written genres?
- How did David judge whether a student's writing fulfilled his expectations for genre?

Two writers David chose as exemplary, Jonathan and Carson, spoke explicitly about genre when they described how they composed their assignments. Both seemed to use the genre knowledge they already had and were also acquiring, to some extent tacitly, in David's course. Notably, these writers used this knowledge to conform to, yet also depart from, David's instructions when they organized their work. A third student, Dawn, did not articulate her knowledge of genre explicitly, and while she was also successful in the course, her work did not stand out for David. Dawn seemed to absorb genre knowledge from David's modeling in class but did not consciously draw on her knowledge of forms from other contexts. Moreover, Dawn tended to adhere more closely to David's instructions—unlike the other two writers, she did not inflect the assignments with her own sense of what constitutes a genre. While quite satisfactory, her work in David's eyes was also more conventional and less analytical than Jonathan's or Carson's.

In the context of Bakhtin's theory and composition research, this qualitative research provides some evidence that writers acquire genre knowledge both consciously and unconsciously. This would suggest that teachers can teach genre explicitly and implicitly. Explicit instruction, such as the use of models, is crucial to learning, but it is also limited because no one can fully map out genres that must be learned implicitly. Implicit learning occurs through immersion in a social situation—for instance, through classroom discussions or assignment sequencing. The focal students in this study appeared to benefit from both kinds of learning. As important, this study also supports the conclusion that successful writers assimilate a genre by actively interpreting, not by just copying, a reader's requirements for particular forms.

THE COURSE AND ITS GOALS

Plagues: Past, Present, Future? is a 100-level general-education course for honors students who aren't majoring in the sciences. In his course introduction, David promises to explore the relationship between historical plagues, their current "upsurge," and future scenarios. Using the lenses of evolution and ecology, he will focus on the immune system, the organisms responsible for disease transmission, and the dynamics of the appearance and spread of infectious diseases. Though he will ground the course in biology, David hopes to discuss epidemics within their sociopolitical and moral contexts.

Because David knew the students would not become scientists, his overarching goal was to enhance their science literacy. In course documents, manuscripts, and interviews, he specified two other broad goals: that students would understand the process of how scientists reach conclusions; and, by distinguishing fact from interpretation, that they would think critically about scientific information, especially as it is reported in the mainstream media. Ideally, David hoped that, long after students had forgotten the specifics of the biology, they could make personal decisions about the scientific controversies that unfold regularly in our society.

THE WAC PROGRAM AND DAVID'S COURSE

In the WAC initiative at the City University of New York (CUNY), advanced Ph.D students from the CUNY Graduate Center come to individual colleges to help implement writing programs in the disciplines. In the program I direct at City College, these Ph.D students, called writing fellows, collaborate with faculty during one semester to conceptualize new approaches or develop materials that the professor will implement during the next semester. David Eastzer, a faculty member at City's downtown Center for Worker Education, developed materials for the Plagues course with two writing fellows, Holly Hutton from English and Robert Wallace from biology, in the spring of 2002. The following semester, Holly joined with writing fellow Rachel Nuger, from biological anthropology, to study genre in the Plagues course, offered at the uptown campus.

RESEARCH METHODS

The research method was naturalistic and followed the procedures of CUNY's Institutional Review Board (IRB) for gaining students' permission to conduct the study. Using the IRB protocol, I solicited volunteers for interviews from the whole class, so the six focal students who participated were self-selected. Holly and Rachel attended three hours of David's six-hour class every week for the semester. They both took observational notes, gathered course documents, and, beginning in late September, audiotaped the class sessions. In November they gave a midterm survey about the course assignments to eighteen students; in December, they interviewed six focal students and I copied their assignments. I met with David and the fellows informally throughout the semester, and the fellows and I took notes. In April and May 2003, I met with David for two taped interviews that focused on selected pieces of writing from the focal students.

HOW DAVID IMPLICITLY CONVEYED GENRE: SEQUENCING OF READING AND WRITING

David mapped out genre both implicitly and explicitly. In the former instance, David tried to immerse students in the genre they would have to produce by sequencing assignments so that they moved from annotation to summary and interpretation of articles they read throughout the course. The reading included three course texts (Jason Eberhart-Phillips, *Outbreak Alert* [2000]; Arno Karlen, *Man and Microbes* [1995]; and Paul W. Ewald, *Plague Time* [2000]), and articles from newspapers like the Tuesday science section in the *New York Times* or from periodicals like the *New Yorker*. Students watched films about the history of infectious diseases and gathered information from Web sites.

The articles from periodicals and newspapers reflected the kind of writing David hoped students could eventually produce in the course. For instance, for one of the first low-stakes assignments, David asked Holly to annotate one article to show students how the writer presented his information rhetorically; students then had to annotate their own articles and reflect in a page on the process of doing this exercise. When David presented this exercise to students in September, he was explicitly trying to convey to students that there is a difference between reporting facts and interpreting scientific debates.

The writing assignments thus began with introductory assignments, low-stakes writing or classroom genres, which included annotating articles, writing summaries, answering questions centered on the course texts, and writing in class. In class, David asked students to define terms like *evolution* or, while watching a film, to fill in an outline showing the typical pattern of how plagues spread. The more difficult high-stakes genres required students to analyze their summaries and to interpret data in a research study of a plague. Together, the high-stakes genres constituted about two-thirds of the course grade.

HOW DAVID CONVEYED HIGH-STAKES GENRES: EXPLICIT MAPS

David explicitly mapped out his expectations for written genres in official course documents including the syllabus, course introduction, and assignment sheets. The academic genres included "reading responses," one- to two-page critical summaries of the course texts, and the science in the media journal, one- to two-page critical summaries of five articles the students chose about scientific studies reported in the mainstream media.

On the assignment sheet, David stressed that students should "not simply copy sections of the readings. Rather, you must respond to the information by reworking the ideas in your own way and in your own words." David urged students to go beyond summary: "Note that your entry should go beyond simply notes on the reading or a rewriting of the author's words, although that is a good starting point. Rather, you should reflect on the reading and insert yourself, your experiences and knowledge and even your feelings, into an active engagement with the author's writing."

The final assignment, the West Nile virus research project, contained two parts. For the first part, David asked students to examine Web sites, to construct a flyer for the public about the West Nile virus, and to reflect on what they had learned. In the second part, a case study, students constructed a timeline, with a written commentary, of the events surrounding the evolution of the West Nile virus in New York. I will focus only on the second part of the project, the case study, which contained the timeline and the write-up.

Because David and the students used various terms to refer to the West Nile virus research, for clarity's sake, I will refer to it as the case study. The case study asked students to "create a timetable of the events of August–September 1999, when the epidemic was first recognized, initially thought to be St. Louis encephalitis, and then correctly identified as West Nile virus." David then listed what should be included in the timetable and told students that they could organize their data as either a list or a flowchart. In the middle of the page, he specified a purpose, or a *focus*:

This case study reveals how scientists (and their societal counterparts, such as politicians, administrators, etc.) work in complex social networks: competing and cooperating across research groups; crossing institutional and disciplinary boundaries; following their traditional protocols, methodologies, and "chains of command," as well as their hunches and intuitions; and using formal institutional arrangements as well as informal channels of communication for access to the facilities, resources, and expertise necessary to solve the problem.

In the instructions for "the write-up," David reminded students to relate this case study to others and to comment on how the assignment influenced their personal understanding of science.

MAPPING GENRE IMPLICITLY: USING CLASSROOM GENRES AND SOCIAL REGISTERS

David offered explicit maps for genres through his official instructions and annotated models; in so doing, he was also expressing a distinct way of thinking about evidence in his class. But teachers also map out genre and the way of thinking form can embody more implicitly through the social situations they establish in classrooms: for instance, in lectures, discussions, assigned readings, feedback, or even private talks with students. Patrick Dias and his colleagues (1999) argue that students in the law and finance classes they studied acquired genre knowledge by absorbing a disciplinary register—when the students in these classes learned the lexicon of the discipline, they also implicitly learned how to produce genre without explicit instruction. Similarly, while David implicitly mapped out genre through assignment sequencing, he also modeled ways of knowing through the repeated social situations he created in his classroom—for example, through class discussions, lectures, and impromptu writing.

For instance, in a class that David recalled as pivotal, Rachel recorded a discussion of Atul Gawande's article "Cold Comfort" (2002), which details scientists' attempts to unravel the mysteries of the common cold. One of our focal students, an English major named LaShae, raised her hand to ask, "How can we write our conclusions about the article when the article itself is inconclusive?" Rachel wrote, "David used this question as a platform to discuss what he wants the students to understand about science. He is trying to reiterate that science is an open-ended process, and the answer depends on the question that one is asking. David discussed the distinction between science 'in the making,' where the answer is not yet known, and the science that is 'made,' where an answer is generally accepted in the scientific community" In Rachel's view, "This was a really important moment in the evolution of the relationship between

David and the students, because it was the first time the students seemed to grasp that the answers to scientific problems or questions might not always be in front of them."

David then lectured on DNA, RNA, genes, and mutation, after which the students watched a film about natural selection and pesticide resistance. Rachel observed: "At one point, David stopped the film and asked the students if the enzyme that caused the mosquitoes to break down the chemical in the pesticide and become resistant was present before or after the pesticides came about. He forced the students to vote one way or another when they didn't all raise their hands at first. It turned out that about half the class was wrong, but by forcing them to vote either way David forced them to think about a concept and involved students in the classroom process when they might not normally participate."

In this and similar instances, David created a recurrent social situation that implicitly fostered a particular way of reasoning about evidence. His request for students to vote modeled the committed stance he wanted students to assume in the high-stakes genres. As he tried to show when answering LaShae's question, that stance required learning to distinguish between science that is made and science in the making. By encouraging participation and using in-class writing, David implicitly modeled the distinction between facts and interpretation. In turn, the genres he assigned—summaries and critical summaries—formally required writers to make this basic distinction.

HOW DAVID AND JONATHAN INTERPRETED CRITICAL SUMMARIES

Like the students I quoted at the beginning of this essay, Jonathan responded actively to David's invitation for students "to use their own words" and develop a point of view on the material. A music major and one of the focal students, Jonathan especially enjoyed the science in the media journal because "he asked us, sort of, for our opinion, and to make connections" between their thoughts and the reading.

Jonathan explained that the sequencing helped him to write because the assignment sheet was inadequate—it "was just a little paragraph." The reading responses pushed him to "jump right into the reading instead of sort of figuring out what was going on halfway into the semester." The regular short writings helped him to analyze information: "[W]hen you have to write something you [just] make connections to other readings in the course." In English classes, he found the assignments difficult because "they're so abstract, where am I going to come up with all this content?

But with this sort of thing, I had like a whole—in a lot of the questions I needed to do sometimes a whole synopsis of the subject material before I could go on and so I always had a starting point."

Jonathan imagined the kind of genre he thought David expected: "I would call a lot of this stuff that he had us do—I felt that the responding to news sources and the science in the media journal and that kind of thing was sort of like analytical op-ed, and that technique really developed [my thinking throughout the course]."

Jonathan said he began in September by plunging into the reading and just "guessing" what David wanted; by December, he explicitly mapped the features of the genre in his own words —a "synopsis" followed by "analytical" opinions. Possibly Jonathan's choice of naming the genre as an "analytical op-ed" was further influenced by his reading of newspapers and periodicals, which David thought was more extensive than that of the other focal students. From a Bakhtinian perspective, writers assimilate the official or authoritative genre by accenting it with their own purposes and experiences. Similarly, the genre of analytical op-ed suited Jonathan's critical perspective toward the media, since in his papers he tended to editorialize on the media's role in, for example, sensationalizing scientific information. Jonathan's skepticism suited David, as we shall see, because analytical op-ed accommodates a strong point of view.

For one journal entry that David chose to read aloud and comment upon, Jonathan compared two articles, one by Boseley in the *Guardian* on December 7, 2002, and another by Askari in the *Detroit Free Press* on November 12, 2002. David noted that Jonathan began well because he swiftly summarized the key points of the articles (what Jonathan called "the synopsis"), therefore establishing the scientific facts of the cases as they unfolded in Europe and Detroit. For instance, Jonathan wrote: "Both articles concern new threatening strains of the bacterium staphylococcus aureus. The *Guardian* article describes a case of linezolid resistance in Europe and the *Detroit Free Press* describes a case of vancomycin resistance in Detroit."

David commented that Jonathan chose good articles because he could relate them to debates over antibiotic resistance. But also, as David commented, Jonathan's choice to use two articles instead of one enabled him to develop an argument: "I don't play this up, but sometimes I say, you might use more than one article if they make a good contrast. In this case, they're sort of saying the same thing in different contexts."

In his long opening paragraph, Jonathan completes a "synopsis" and then gradually draws evaluative comparisons and contrasts between the two reporting styles. By the paragraph's middle, a distinct point of view, or an argument, emerges. For example, Jonathan argues that the *Guardian* relies on more neutral language to describe the event than does the *Free Press*: "The *Guardian* recognizes the significant resistance [toward antibiotics] but is much less shocking" in its choice of words. Jonathan argues this is "a very subtle difference in communicating the situation [since] both articles basically warn that through evolution all antibiotics will eventually lose their effectiveness."

Jonathan develops the difference by examining the *Free Press's* rhetoric, which includes "words and phrases like 'dread,' 'the most remarkable and significant events in my lifetime,' 'serious threat,' and 'getting worse fast.'" He contends that the *Guardian* also exaggerates fears, but in a different way. The British newspaper reports "on the possibility of the number of deaths by infections rising above 100,000 per year in the United States. [This is a useless comment] because it is broad, general, and out of context. They should also include how many people died from infections last year, the year before, and in 1920 to make this all relevant. It is not that these things are necessarily untrue or insignificant, but seem more like shocking entertainment than news. [So] the *Guardian* has its own hair-raising statistics; they just leave off the 'we're all doomed' comments, which I found in the *Free Press* and the ABCNews.com article."

David evaluated Jonathan's opening paragraph positively: "So what he's doing here that's good is that he's saying both articles describe the bacteria as benign only the *Guardian* recognizes the significant resistance [without using melodramatic language]." Jonathan's journal entry fulfilled David's expectations of the genre because "what he's doing here is taking an article that is important scientifically but basically factual and he's going the extra step of comparing two articles and talking about the rhetoric that's being used in the two different contexts."

Jonathan next compares how the doctors in the two cases reacted differently. When describing the *Guardian*'s reporting of how doctors reacted to a possible plague, Jonathan remarks, "according to the *Guardian*, it would seem like nothing was done about the case. The public health laboratory revealed its findings and then, nothing." By contrast, the American paper stressed "the imminent threat to our lives and the swift expansive actions to secure" our public health, which he attributed to the paper's desire "to want us to feel scared and taken care of at the same time."

David appreciated this analysis of the papers' different rhetorical aims—he thought that Jonathan was reading critically: "[He is thinking] that maybe they just didn't tell me in the article, recognizing the limitations of information and the way the choices that the writer of an article makes can affect the information that [the reader] has to go on."

Using the basic scientific facts as his "starting point," Jonathan developed a case about how the two articles expressed the same story using different styles. In the process of showing how the media interpret scientific facts rather than report them neutrally, he also judged those styles, commenting for instance on the "reactionary" character of the Detroit paper.

Jonathan fulfilled David's genre expectations, but to a certain extent, he did so on his own terms. Jonathan did not fully grasp what David wanted through the official description of the assignment, but, as he indicated, he understood the genre by completing the low-stakes assignments. Jonathan thought that the more he read, the more he was able to draw connections between articles and course themes. When he decided he was writing an analytical op-ed piece, he accented his writing with the stance appropriate to this form—hence his tendency, as David noted, to view the media more judgmentally than the other students. Jonathan used the form to express his skepticism about the mass media and the extent of journalists' scientific knowledge. Jonathan liked writing in David's class because he had a content, an article, with which to begin, but he could also bring his own opinions to bear on what he read. The genre he selected conformed to but also reworked David's expectations because it suited Jonathan's personal stance while meeting David's goals.

HOW DAVID, CARSON, AND DAWN INTERPRETED THE CASE STUDY REPORT

Unlike Jonathan, Carson, an English major and another of our focal students, found writing the science in the media journal one of the less enjoyable assignments because "what [David] always said, don't just summarize, analyze it . . . you have to relate it to something bigger and that's difficult." Though David never used the word *argument* on the assignment sheets, Carson assumed that what he had to write would "be an argument and you're supposed to . . . know which side you came out on. Like for instance, we just have this one on smallpox vaccinations and if you would do that or not [a classroom genre]. So basically what I would do, and what's done in most other writing assignments, is you just lay out the argument first. I'm taking a law class too and they kinda go together, you just lay out, not the facts but each side, and then, put whatever you think at the end."

Carson consciously related the writing he was doing in David's class to his prior experiences with other academic situations like the law class. In drawing this comparison, Carson also distinguished writing for David's course from writing for other courses: "[A] lot of the assignments were actually a lot more personal, not personal, but he'd ask, like, what's your opinion on this? The writing was very different from other courses because in other courses they're, like, don't say anything about yourself."

When he read the assignments, Carson, like Jonathan, interpreted requirements—he assimilated David's instructions to his past experience as a writer in other situations, and he used his own language to describe David's expectations. What Carson "got from the assignments" was that David "wanted opinions, wanted first person." In some ways, this expectation conflicted directly with writing for other classes, which he thought required students "to write in the passive voice a lot," and where "'I' is a dirty word."

David selected Carson's West Nile virus research project as exemplary of the kind of reasoning he hoped to see in the course. Here is an excerpt from Carson's timeline, which, along with a write-up, comprised the second part of the West Nile research project, the case study.

West Nile Timeline

- 7/99 Dr. Tracey McNamara learns that "a large number of crows had been dying around the zoo," which she later reports to the *New York Times* (9/25/99). Bronx Zoo receives numerous calls concerning dead birds.
- 8/9 Dr. John Andresen receives a dead crow from Nassau County—test results are inconclusive; the bird has decomposed too much.
- 8/23 First call to New York City Health Department—unknown "neurological disease" is affecting patients at Flushing Hospital—meningitis, encephalitis, and botulism are suspected.
- 8/25 Birds in outdoor cages at Bronx Zoo begin to fall ill.
- 8/26 Dr. Andresen attends dying horse on Long Island.
- 8/30 Elderly patient at Flushing Hospital dies; encephalitis is suspected cause of death.
- 9/3 CDC announces that tests confirm St Louis Encephalitis, Mayor holds press conference; Malathion spraying begins soon after. Animal pathologists and human pathologists begin considering connection between animal and human incidence of disease.
- 9/7 Bronx Zoo workers come to work to find sick and dying birds.
- 9/21 Fort Detrick, Maryland—Dr. McNamara calls in a favor with an Army pathologist and sends in samples for test.

This timeline fills another page, and a three-page commentary follows it. Carson begins the write-up with what I read as a strong topic sentence: "The most unnerving element of the West Nile outbreak was its difficulty to diagnose," and then follows with a long paragraph detailing the twists and turns of this biological mystery. Carson highlights the fact that Dr. McNamara got a break because she knew a pathologist at the army laboratory and called in a favor, an example of informal channels of communication that David emphasized on the assignment sheet.

Carson opens his next full paragraph with, again in my view, a definite topic sentence: the timeline cannot show the first "actual incidence of West Nile in the U.S." He then develops that idea by detailing the biology of plagues. In the third paragraph, Carson analyzes the media's relationship to scientists and their role in spreading "public fear and panic." In my view he deftly ends with two short paragraphs reflecting on the difference between scientific fact and interpretation, a central goal of the course. While Carson does not judge the media's intentions in the way Jonathan did, I find that his focused topic sentences provide a sharp point of view on the material. He also seemed able to infer the basic shape of a case study from David's assignment sheet: that the timeline's events provide the data for an argument, so that the two parts are closely related. When Carson ordered his essay, he inferred what David's instructions only imply—to begin with data and then move toward analysis and reflection.

David thought that what made Jonathan's and Carson's work exemplary was their ability to "bring in their own stuff." Carson, for instance, "goes beyond what he reads to say something he might have been interested in knowing more about. So the timeline doesn't tell when the first incident was and he talks about the science of the incubation period. . . . He's asking questions that are actually quite important but not explicitly raised [in the articles] and so he's saying this is what I'd like to know."

By bringing in their own stuff, David meant picking extra articles but also choosing appropriate articles, drawing inferences, taking an argumentative stance, and thinking comparatively.

These qualities seemed to stem from the active rhetorical stance that David required in the class. But these writers also assumed a stance that suited their personal preferences—Jonathan the editorialist and media critic, Carson the English major and future lawyer who reasons a case based on the facts. While Jonathan organized synopsis, argument, and judgment together, and Carson employed a more traditional paragraph structure, both satisfied David because they projected a clear point of view on the evidence. In this way, they were successful because they understood when to depart from, yet also stay close to, the assignment sheet.

In contrast, Dawn aligned herself more closely both with the articles and with what David said in class about the assignments. An art major, Dawn was successful in the course, but David did not find her work to be as keenly analytical as Jonathan's or Carson's. In her interview, Dawn found it more difficult to articulate her approach to the assignments; she never used words like "argument," "opinion," or "analysis," as did Jonathan and Carson. She said she enjoyed the science in the media journal the most because she read a newspaper regularly for the first time. Dawn said she liked to write and that she had done writing like this "before," though when Holly and Rachel asked her where, she didn't specify any particular situation. But Dawn specifically referenced David's modeling in class as the basis for her understanding of his requirements: "Well, we did a few examples—like in class, . . . we would come to class [and] he'd give us an article [to] read and put up some sample questions on the board and then we would take like fifteen minutes to write out what we thought and then we would go over it. And he would say, "You know, this is the kind of writing you need to do for the question.'"

When comparing her science in the media journal to Jonathan's, David noted that Dawn tended to select articles that covered the same topics discussed in class, unlike the other two writers, who selected articles that could be related to topics discussed in class. Dawn's close alignment with David's expectations did not mean she was less successful in terms of the course grade—David felt that her work was closer to what he would normally expect from good students in other general-education courses. But her work didn't stand out for him in comparison to students like Jonathan or Carson because she didn't bring "her own stuff" to the writing.

For the West Nile virus case study, Dawn chose to organize events in a flowchart rather than in a timeline. Here is Dawn's first event, compared to Carson's:

Dawn: Dr. Tracey S. McNamara (head of pathology at Bronx Zoo) Ward Stone (chief wildlife pathologist for the State Dept. of Environmental Conservation): notice large numbers of dead birds.

Carson: 7/99 Dr. Tracey McNamara learns that "a large number of crows had been dying around the zoo," which she later tells the

New York Times (9/25/99). Bronx Zoo receives number calls concerning dead birds.

When he read both papers aloud, David thought that Carson's stood out because he provided so much more detail—a quality he also had seen in Carson's science in the media journal. Referring to Dawn's paper, David commented: "Hers is basically quite good but it's much, much sketchier than Carson's. [He] writes it out, and just gives a lot more detail. I would say that hers is very good [compared to other students he has had in the past], and touches on most of the main points. But it's not as much detail; if you're thinking in terms of a concept map, it's sort of missing the connecting pieces that Carson fills in."

When David says Carson is more specific than Dawn, we might say that he is more appropriately specific—he understands what is new and what is given or presupposed information, a crucial component of genre knowledge (Giltrow and Valiquette 1994). In my view, while Dawn provides the institutional affiliations of McNamara and Stone, which is given information, Carson focuses on what McNamara did and when, which is new information. As an outside reader, I find that Dawn clutters up her timeline with scientists' titles to display affiliation (also a tendency, David remarked, in her science in the media journal), but, as David noted, Carson focuses on the details that will eventually display connections—that when McNamara learns birds died at the zoo, she communicated that to the *Times* two months later. While Dawn may just not have spent as much time on this assignment, the obvious care with which she completed her work suggests to me that the weaker connections in her paper reflected her weaker grasp of the genre of the case study.

David commented when he read Dawn's write-up, "She makes [good points] but she's not really backing it up; what she does nicely is relate [her points] to other issues we talked about in the class." David reiterated that Dawn was a very good student but her understanding of genre was less sophisticated. "In a way," David concluded, Dawn's work was consistently "more literal" than Carson's or Jonathan's. Her approach to genre was more closely tied to the texts, the assignment sheets, and to what she heard in class—she did not accent the genres with her own preferences as freely as did Jonathan or Carson.

For David, Dawn's work stood out in the context of classes he usually taught at the Center for Worker Education—she was a diligent student who had learned the basic concepts of his course. However, within the context of the honors course at City College, her work was not as memorable as Jonathan's or Carson's. In her interview Dawn did not reference specific past experiences that she could bring to bear on what she was composing in David's class, nor did she speak explicitly about generic forms and textual features. Reading a newspaper regularly was also a new literacy activity for her, as it may not have been for the other two focal students. Using Bakhtin's terms, we could speculate that Dawn did not bring what she already knew about genre into direct engagement with David's expectations for genre.

ASSIMILATING GENRES AND DIALOGIC LEARNING

In "The Problem of Speech Genres," Bakhtin famously describes the dialogic process of acquiring genre, and it is worth quoting in full:

> [T]he unique speech experience of each individual is shaped and developed in continuous and constant interaction with others' individual utterances. This experience can be characterized to some degree as the process of assimilation—more or less creative—of others' words (and not the words of a language). Our speech, that is, all our utterances (including creative works), is filled with others' words, varying degrees of otherness or varying degrees of "our-own-ness," varying degrees of awareness and detachment. These words of others carry with them their own expression, their own evaluative tone, which we assimilate, rework, and re-accentuate. (1986, 89)

Even established scholars struggle to fit what they know about genre to their readers' conceptions of a finished form. For instance, Carol Berkenkotter and Thomas Huckin's (1995) case study of a biologist shows how this researcher's initial sense of the meaning of her experiment conflicted with her readers' desire for her to relate that meaning to a broader scientific narrative. Consequently, the biologist, as the individual writer, and her editors, as the collective voice of the discipline's premier genre, the research report, spent months negotiating over their competing expectations as the final article took shape.

Similarly, Bakhtin's theory suggests that if we want to help writers to assimilate genre, we must remain aware of the dynamic between the individual writer's intentions and the constraints of form. In composition, two approaches to genre reflect this dynamic: explicit knowing, which reflects a community's traditions or expectations, and implicit knowing, which reflects how individuals meet those expectations. In my view the first approach includes making tacit knowledge explicit by designing rubrics, describing the purposes of form, and providing maps of textual features such as annotated models. Though of course these approaches will overlap, in general implicit learning includes modeling genre through class talk, offering regular feedback, and sequencing assignments. In David's class, students appeared to benefit from both approaches.

Explicit knowledge of form did appear to be generative for students like Carson. Though some theorists dispute the value of teaching genre explicitly, in their reply to Aviva Freedman, Joseph Williams and Gregory Colomb (1993) cite research that supports the direct teaching of textual features (256–57). Williams and Colomb speculate that form can help writers to generate content as much as the other way around (262). When we asked the students how they knew how to organize specific assignments or select articles, Jonathan and Carson referred to genres, rhetorical stance, and to David's verbal or written instructions. Carson said he composed by drawing on what he knew about argument, and he distinguished between "argument" as it was defined in David's and other classes. Jonathan and Carson also used words to describe the textual features of college writing: summary, synopsis, argument, opinion, analysis, first person, passive voice. In contrast, Dawn did not refer specifically to prior experiences with genres or to textual features and rhetorical stance.

There was a gap between David's tacit knowledge of genre and his explicit instructions. David stressed the strong stance he preferred in the writing, but he didn't dwell on the importance of choosing appropriate articles, a key feature of his evaluation of the students' texts. He didn't use "argument" on official documents, though argumentative stance was central to his course and to interpretations of students like Carson. While the second (and most heavily weighted) part of the West Nile virus project was a case study, the official term was buried in the middle of the assignment page and was never used by the students. Indeed, David seemed also to view some of the articles that had been assigned as case studies. Describing the case study could have helped industrious students like Dawn better understand the link between data and analysis, while David's lengthy instructions for the research project, which some students found daunting, may have been easier to organize around the concept of case study.

However, while I advocate teaching genre explicitly, some genre knowledge will always remain tacit, possibly because, as Paul Prior (1998) has argued, genre is also realized locally by individual writers and readers. It would also be difficult for anyone to teach the specificity that David found in Carson's work, for instance, because that feature may be contingent upon presupposed knowledge. For these reasons, while WAC programs should help teachers to articulate what they know about genre and to speak consistently about their expectations, explicit maps will provide just one window on genre. We must also provide occasions for writers to assimilate genre, or to accent explicit instructions "in their own words."

Assignment sequencing played this role for students in David's class; while divided on whether the reflective writing helped, they consistently mentioned the positive influence the short reading-based writing assignments had upon their mastery of content. Students seemed to appreciate the requirement to read actively, "pen in hand," as Andres, another focal student, explained; "Actually, I wish I had had some of the initial [low-stakes] writing in my English 110 [composition] course, freshman year," wrote another on the midterm survey. Additionally, a student like Jonathan thought these assignments immersed him in a genre—the more he read, the more he understood the interpretive stance David expected writers to take. Beginning with summary and moving toward interpretation, the sequencing scaffolded the interpretive stance central to learning genre in this class.

Finally, this study suggests that writers learn genre interactively. While congruent with David's expectations, Jonathan's and Carson's genre maps were based partly on inferences they made about what David wanted. To some extent, both writers reworked David's explicit expectations into their own language. Perhaps the most successful students have learned how to assimilate, not copy, official instructions. Unlike some struggling writers in courses Barbara Walvoord and Lucille McCarthy (1990) studied, Jonathan and Carson did not cling to David's assignment sheets— they stayed close but also departed from them when they needed to. Even though Dawn stayed close to the assignment sheet, she did interpret the requirements through what she remembered David had said during class. A successful honors student, Dawn contextualized David's instructions and produced competent writing. Future research could focus on those writers who, unlike our focal students, did not develop successful strategies for producing genre. Possibly writers who struggled in David's class—those who didn't volunteer to participate in our study—were also those who haven't learned to translate a teacher's requirements for genre into their own words.

Genre expresses a complex mix of individual and communally sanctioned ways of knowing, and for this reason, there is no easy formula for teaching writers to assimilate new forms. As this study of David Eastzer's Science in Society class strongly suggests, writers do not learn to assimilate forms in just one way. The students in this study benefited from both implicit and explicit approaches to teaching genre. Equally important, successful writers do not merely copy a new form: they translate the words of the other into their own language. Perhaps, then, we can say that genuine learning occurs when writers rework the voice of the other, the communal form, into their own individual words, intentions, and worldviews.

5

"WHAT'S COOL HERE?"
Collaboratively Learning Genre in Biology

Anne Ellen Geller

I ran into David Hibbett at a convocation reception a year after we had collaborated on writing workshops for his Biology of Symbiosis class. Over cheese and crackers, surrounded by a throng of noisy faculty catching up on one another's summers, David, a mycologist in the Clark University biology department, revealed that he was in the throes of writing a *News and Views* column for *Nature*, a commentary based on a primary research article in the same journal. The column is smaller in scope than the "mini-reviews" David had asked his symbiosis students to write, pieces that survey and comment on the research in a subdiscipline. But writing and revising his own work left David remembering the questions his students had faced a year earlier as they had written their mini-reviews. That is, he needed, and wanted, his writing to be accessible to a general audience who might not know the fungi he knew well, and he needed to stress what made the fungal/plant associations he was writing about distinctive—what made them "cool." David was striving to engage his readers, even those who might not expect to be interested in, or able to understand, his subject.

David's *News and Views* column was published just a few weeks after we spoke. It has a clever title: "Plant-Fungal Interactions: When Good Relationships Go Bad" (Hibbett 2002). He practices what his students told me he preaches—that articles should have titles that will intrigue readers. In the first lines I find out that I will learn how "some non-photosynthetic plants cheat their fungal partners" (345). I am enticed. I have to read on, even though I know nothing about mycorrhizae, the "ancient, widespread associations between fungi and the roots of many species of plants" (345). I am one of the literate laypeople David envisions as his audience, and I become interested in fungi because his language invites me into a world I know nothing about.

As a scientist David thinks about the power of mutually beneficial symbiotic relationships. He also cares deeply about how scientists can form better relationships with those outside their area of expertise. He has made me realize how much scientists depend on those outside their laboratories for support, financial and otherwise, and support comes only when those outside the work of a laboratory—other scientists and nonscientists alike—can understand the work inside the laboratory. David wants his students to realize this, too. Like other research scientists, he writes and encourages students to write and coauthor primary research articles about the work of his lab. But he also always seems to ask: what other genres can scientists use to communicate scientific work on complex topics to the lay reader? And how can science students learn to write in these genres so they can learn how to show a nonscientist what is "cool" about their work, no matter how specialized it is?

In the fall of 2001, Biology of Symbiosis was not a writing course; it was an upper-level seminar for sophomores, juniors, seniors, and a few graduate students. David was under no university mandate to "teach" writing. However, in a course where developing deep understandings of symbiotic relationships and synthesizing bodies of research about those symbiotic relationships were integral to his goals for the course, David saw writing, the writing of mini-reviews in particular, as integral to his students' learning.

Mini-reviews, most familiar to scientists but published in a variety of disciplines, are short articles that summarize and comment on the most recent scholarship within a narrow subdiscipline. Writers of mini-reviews must know their subject incredibly well, well enough to make judgments about current research in that field. So mini-reviews also teach science students how deeply and thoroughly one must understand a subject to write about it clearly and elegantly. The assignment was particularly well suited to this upper-level seminar, in which students could be expected, after their library orientation, to independently gather research from sophisticated and respected scientific journals.

David and I held only two workshops together, yet what we—David and his students and I—learned from those sessions was significant. His students—majoring in biology, biochemistry, molecular biology, and environmental science—seemed to have had very little experience in thinking about how to communicate their science to nonspecialists. Most knew how to write science only in the genres they had been taught: lab reports, essay questions, and case studies. Some had completed creative science projects meant to encourage writing to learn. Almost all, it seemed, had completed some form of research paper in the social sciences or humanities.

What I now understand is that for David's students to be able to success-fully produce a mini-review, a new genre for them, they had to be able to tell themselves what distinguished it from other genres in which they had written.

From their previous writing experiences, David's students had:

- an understanding that writers must gather evidence
- some knowledge of how to employ a thesis, controlling idea, or question
- a basic understanding that the parts of a text must relate to the whole of a text
- a superficial understanding of audience

But to write a mini-review, David's students had to:

- know their subject *and* know how to convey their knowledge with author-ity
- find a central, organizing idea or question sophisticated enough to be of scientific interest, but uncomplicated enough to engage nonspecialist readers
- feel comfortable synthesizing, organizing, and analyzing a great deal of evidence
- be aware of audience and translate specialized information to a nonspe-cialist audience

David himself certainly had experience moving among genres, publish-ing the *News and Views* piece in the same year he published three primary research articles. Yet what he didn't realize was that he had internal-ized the writing strategies he used to negotiate the differences among genres. He knew, for example, how writing to nonspecialists was different from writing to specialists. He knew how to reduce jargon and simplify concepts, even when the science was complicated, and he knew how to structure a short, complex text by what makes it "cool." But it wasn't until the writing workshops that David could articulate the central motive for writing a mini-review. In a mini-review, a professional scientist has a sense of "what's cool" and can advance his or her own scientific agenda. David's goal was not just that students learn to write a new genre. He also hoped his students, less experienced scientists, would learn to take on the inter-ested stance of the professional scientist. He hoped that the mini-review itself would be "cool," a complex, hybrid genre that would push students to think through their roles as scientists, readers, and writers. In the end, the craft of learning to teach the genre of the mini-review was almost as complicated for David as the craft of writing the genre was for his students. Yet it was as satisfying for David (and for me) to learn to teach the genre as it was for his students to learn to write it.

In this chapter, I want to consider the relationship between the structure and goals of Biology of Symbiosis and the mini-review assignment, for I believe it was the collaborative environment of David's classroom that made negotiation of genre a possibility. Then, I'll consider the mini-review assignment and its relationship to students' previous writing experiences. Finally, I'll describe the writing workshops David and I held with his students and explain what they revealed about David' teaching goals, his students' struggles, the genre of the mini-review, and David's deep understanding of the mini-review. Throughout, I will include excerpts from David's class materials, as well as excerpts from conversations with him and two of the students in his class, Caitlin Dwyer-Huppert and Ewa Zadykowicz. I will include writing from these same two students.

BIOLOGY 256: BIOLOGY OF SYMBIOSIS

I am offering this course because I want to learn more about symbiosis and share what I have learned with you. This is the same attitude that I expect you to bring to the course.

—Biology of Symbiosis Syllabus, 2001

Over the first weeks of the semester, David lectured and led discussions on selected symbiotic relationships—relationships in which two or more species live in intimate association—and on the general evolutionary theory of symbioses. Students took a short-answer quiz on that course material. But then the course format changed. David's expectations were clear. From that point on, each class would be planned by a student. Each student would be responsible for choosing a symbiotic relationship and presenting it to the class. No matter what symbiosis the presenter chose, and no matter what aspect of the symbiosis the presenter emphasized, he or she would be responsible for assigning readings from the text to introduce the symbiosis and he or she would also select one or two peer-reviewed primary research papers and assign these. Thinking back on the semester after it ended, David said he had intended to give himself a bit of a break by turning much of the course over to his students. His students, however, saw the change in course structure as an opportunity to take greater responsibility for their own learning, and once they took that responsibility, they began to practice the expert stance they would need to have in their mini-reviews.

From the first day of class, when the syllabus was distributed, students also knew a discussion leader would be chosen at the beginning of each class. The gravity of that assignment of responsibility did not strike me until Caitlin Dwyer-Huppert explained: "We would all read the papers for class, and we were *all* accountable for understanding them as best we could and being prepared to talk about them because David chose a name out of a hat and whoever he chose had to lead discussion of that day's paper." This led to what Caitlin termed "accountability." Students could not, and did not, slack off; they had committed to being prepared for every class, and as Ewa said, they never knew until the moment the name was drawn who would be held most responsible.

This was not unlike the accountability David had created for himself. As he said in his syllabus, David was not knowledgeable about every symbiotic relationship they would study. While he did approve the papers students chose to present before they prepared presentations, and he clearly had more knowledge of symbiosis than the students, he was sometimes just as likely as his students to encounter the week's symbiosis for the first time when reading and preparing for class. Caitlin told me she remembered days when "David seemed to have as many questions about a paper as we did as we all tried to understand it." To her, this meant that he was as engaged as his students were in learning. He was exploring new material with them. This, too, kept them committed.

To Caitlin it was even significant that David asked students to sit in a circle in class. David laughed when I told him this. "It was just so we could see one another as we talked," he said. But the spatial organization of the room set the intellectual tone of the class. Ewa remembered in-class discussions fondly, saying, "When you have a lot of people working together, the group becomes much more intelligent than any individual would ever be and together there is a feedback loop. You end up thinking about things you wouldn't have thought of yourself and you start making yourself think in different ways than you used to." It was the workshops, I think, that helped David realize what a powerfully collaborative scientific community he had created in class. Originally, he hadn't been sure he'd be comfortable in writing workshops. He'd never held a writing workshop for his students. But reflecting on them once they were over, he said the workshops had surprised him; they reminded him of "lab meetings," times when all who work in a lab get together with the PI (principal investigator) to talk about and negotiate projects, experiments, successes, challenges, and pending publications. Interestingly, it was attending lab meetings just like those David describes that Christina Haas, who followed one biology student over four years, termed "mentoring in a socio-cultural setting," a type of discipline-specific mentoring she found very important (1994, 77) to that student's rhetorical development. I'm not sure that David knew his students appreciated the collaborative, inquiry-based atmosphere of his class long before and long after the writing workshops ended. I didn't know it until I began to talk with Caitlin and Ewa.

Most significantly, David Hibbett asked his students to invest in new ways of learning over the entire semester. Students' in-class experience scaffolded their writing, and thus, their writing made sense to them in the context of their in-class experience. We too often forget how necessary it is to relate in-class learning to the writing done outside class. We may assign new genres to be completed outside of class, but those assignments may necessitate changing in-class instruction, for in-class instruction can lead students to rely on familiar writing strategies even when facing new genres, or can encourage students to take on the challenge of new genres with all their inherent tensions. In "The Life of Genre, the Life in the Classroom," Charles Bazerman notes that "our strategic choice of genres to bring into the classroom can help introduce students into new realms of discourse just beyond the edge of their current linguistic habit," but it may also be up to "us as teachers to activate the dynamics of the classroom so as to make the genres we assign come alive in the meaningful communications of the classroom" (1997, 24). With that in mind I turn to how the mini-reviews David asked his students to write kept them working just beyond the edge of the linguistic habits they relied on as science students, just as the in-class work they practiced together did.

BIOLOGY OF SYMBIOSIS MINI-REVIEWS

> I remember thinking how can I write this in a way that it is really understandable. I remember other people struggling with that too. Being forced to do that is what really allows you to internalize and understand something.
>
> —Caitlin Dwyer-Huppert

A few weeks before the class format changed, David invited Clark's Goddard Library reference staff to talk about strategies for researching scientific papers. David wanted his symbiosis students to become sophisticated researchers of published scientific texts, researchers who could identify quality research and would know a peer-reviewed article when they saw one. But David also told me he used the librarians' visit as an opportunity to discuss how to "find, read, evaluate, and explain" a scientific research paper. In fact, his syllabus committed him to taking "time to discuss the anatomy of a scientific research paper, the process of publishing in science, and the difference between reviewed and nonreviewed publications." Students would need to know all of this for the research they would eventually do for their mini-reviews.

In a sense, students' mini-reviews served as a test of what they had learned about choosing quality primary research articles and reading them well. In addition, David wanted to emphasize how readers, how scientists reading their peers' work, respond to scientific writing. As they researched, David's students knew to think of themselves as critics, hungry for information but also slightly resistant, full of questions. I would now suggest to David that he make this more explicit to his students, though I think most students understood that he expected them to think about how successful the primary research articles were as they were reading and presenting them. Teaching his symbiosis students how to research and read primary research articles, David prepared them to write mini-reviews. Teaching them how to write mini-reviews—a genre new to most of them—he strengthened their researching and reading as well as their understanding of course content.

There were two times during the semester when Biology of Symbiosis students were required to write mini-reviews. One mini-review focused on the subject a student covered in an in-class presentation; the other mini-review could be on a second symbiosis of a student's choosing. Depending on the content of a mini-review and on who is writing it and on where it will appear, it may take on very different forms and styles. David has explained to me that published mini-reviews in journals such as *Science, Nature,* and *Cell,* and in more specialized journals such as *Trends in Ecology* and *Evolution* can be "very influential," for they are "authoritative and critical," yet they are highly "accessible." Greg Myers (1990) argues that "such articles may not directly advance the career of the individual writer" but "are essential to the survival of the discipline, dependent as it is on public support for research" (145). David disagrees, noting that because reviews are often well cited, they bring a scientist's opinions to a broad audience.

In his mini-review assignment, David suggested a fairly rigid textual structure. "In your introduction, describe the system and explain its relevance to general issues in the study of symbiosis. Later, briefly recap the major research initiatives in the area, and review their successes and failures. Conclude with a perspective regarding the state of the field, perhaps suggesting new experimental approaches that could resolve remaining questions." The assignment made a mini-review seem quite straightforward. To me, David seemed to be offering a template, but later he would say that all he thought he was offering were "the basic elements of any scientific paper." While David knew the ways in which all scientific papers are alike and different from one another, he did not, or could not, articulate these until the writing workshops.

David's assignment did strongly encourage student writers to pay careful attention to their audience, an audience of nonspecialists. In class he reiterated that a literate layperson needed to be able to understand the complicated symbiotic relationships explored in the mini-reviews. In his assignment, he suggested students "avoid jargon, define essential scientific terms, and clearly describe experimental methods" of any studies reviewed.

As David has taught me, mini-reviews are not meant to collect all that is known about a subject. A mini-review's bibliography need not cover every publication related to the subject. David told me a mini-review should "highlight the critical issues in an area of research, expose the assumptions and limitations of current approaches, and suggest promising avenues for further inquiry." Because most readers of a mini-review will not be familiar with the particular subject—whether or not they are scientists—a mini-review writer should explain "the general motivation and broad relevance of research in whatever area is being discussed." Just to add to the challenges of writing such a text, the best mini-reviews, according to David, "include a novel synthesis and new ideas." This seems to be what challenged Biology of Symbiosis writers most. New to the symbiotic relationships they were writing about, and new to the role of scientific expert, student writers struggled to find their authority in relation to the scientific research they incorporated into their mini-reviews.

David's written assignment did note that a mini-review should be a "critical summary" of the major issues of "an active area of research," and the phrase "critical summary" proved to be an interesting one for students to unpack. As Judith Langer notes, when faculty "talk about thinking," we sometimes fall "short of the kinds of explication that would convey disciplinary argumentation" and "structures" (1992, 78, 80) to students. Langer argues, "While the forms of comparisons, critiques, or summaries can be discussed in general ways, if only the general character-istics are discussed, then the use of those forms in particular disciplinary contexts will be lost" (85). Langer also says that we "need to look beyond generic terminology about thinking and reasoning" and find more "spe-cific vocabulary to use in discussion with students" (85). As the descrip-tion of the workshops will reveal, David did come to a much more specific articulation of what it meant to him for a scientist writing a mini-review to summarize critically.

Students knew they would need to account for a body of scientific research; they knew to summarize and present current research, but they didn't know how to set primary research studies in conversation with one another. They knew they were expected to make judgments about current scientific approaches to the symbioses they studied, but as novices they felt unprepared to do so. This is the writing work they learned to do as they wrote their mini-reviews and as they revisited them in the workshops.

Most of the students in Biology of Symbiosis had never written any-thing like a mini-review, especially for a science class. Joy Marsella (1992) suggests that students "consider what they know about their professor's expectations in such areas as format, structure, and appropriate sources of information" when they write to an assignment, yet "many, perhaps most, of their decisions are driven less by their reading of the teacher's expectations than by their own prior experience as writers and by the present contexts of their lives" (178). I was left wondering what prior aca-demic writing experiences inside and outside of science David's students drew upon when faced with this new genre.

Students' answers are revealing; both Caitlin and Ewa did draw on prior experiences of academic writing and both tried to adapt what they knew to this new genre. In doing so, both had to face questions raised for them by David's mini-review assignment. Was the mini-review creative writing because it was writing for a nonspecialist audience? Should the mini-review focus on some controversial aspect of science to appeal to a more general readership? Should the most complicated aspects of the symbioses simply be left out because readers might not understand them? How expansively should one attempt to cover the symbiosis? How many specifics of the research should be included? Caitlin and Ewa's negotia-tions with their prior academic writing experiences preview much of what all the symbiosis students raised in the workshops.

When I asked Caitlin what she had written in other science classes, she had few writing experiences to describe. She was more interested in telling me about in-depth projects she had taken on in history and sociology. In fact, no matter how scientific the topic of a mini-review may be, mini-reviews may at first appear to students to be more like the research papers they write in humanities and social science courses, simply because they seem less like what most have written in science.

The introductory chemistry and biology classes Caitlin had taken required only short answers on exams, and though she felt those short answers had led her to practice writing out her understanding of processes as she studied them, they never required extended analysis. Lab reports, written in almost all of her science classes, felt "canned." As she said, she "pretty much knew the whole abstract, introduction, blah, blah, blah." Caitlin felt she had one previous science writing experience that came close to the type of writing David was requiring. In an evolutionary biology class she had written a story in a "Dr. Seuss style" to explain how a fantastic population had evolved. She saw both that story and the mini-review as the types of assignments developed by faculty who are interested in writing and the creativity possible within the teaching and learning of science. Yet she felt the story assignment was still very different from the mini-review. The story was "fun" and "creative," and she felt it was meant to be. She remembered it was due just before the December break, when she and the other students welcomed the opportunity to play.

For Caitlin, the mini-reviews were about "research, bringing together different sources, and going with some kind of idea." In addition she felt students in Biology of Symbiosis were "learning to be familiar with how scientific papers are written," synthesis, and something she named *craft*. For Caitlin, craft was "about using language." Through "grappling with what was appropriate" in the language she used in her mini-reviews, she was left feeling as if she were *crafting* them.

In his comments on Caitlin's first mini-review, David noted that some of her language was "florid." Without looking back at her writing, that was a word Caitlin remembered him using. She "had a really hard time with that" comment, because while she worked to "tone down" her language, she told me she "couldn't divorce myself from what I found fascinating" and she wanted to write in a way that would reveal "how magical things were" to her. Here is the first paragraph of her first mini-review.

In the cold, montane environments of the western U.S. wingless seeds of the Whitebark pine (Pinus albicaulus) lie locked in their cones, waiting for the beak of the Clark's nutcracker (Nucifraga columbiana) to shred the fibers and peck them from the dark. Unlike most pines, the cones of this species do not open at maturity to liberate the seeds. This pine cannot reproduce without the help of Clark's nutcracker. The nutcracker, in turn, depends on the pine's nutritious seeds as its main food source (Tomback 1982). This paper will examine the mechanisms that perpetuate this mutualism, its evolutionary origins, and profound effects on the surrounding ecosystem.

In those first lines of her mini-review, Caitlin confidently sets a scene and beautifully describes the symbiotic relationship's players—pine and bird. But when she reaches the final line of the paragraph, she does not express a novel synthesis; she offers only a description of what the mini-review will "examine." She was unable to transfer her fascination to her readers through anything but description. Her language play alone does not convey an argument or a reason to care about the symbiosis.

Caitlin struggled with this in her second mini-review as well, but after the writing workshop, she did move closer to articulating a central idea. What Caitlin may have begun to learn in the writing workshop and through David's comments on her mini-reviews is that language choice is not the only way for a scientist to express fascination with a subject. "Honeybees themselves are proposed to negatively affect the populations of native pollinator species. This paper will address the impact of fragmentation on honeybee and native bee populations. It will then explore the extent to which honeybees disrupt native pollination systems."

When she wrote that second mini-review, late in the semester, Caitlin was still uncomfortable with her expert knowledge. "What could those impacts be?" David wrote in the margin, prompting her to say what he believed she knew. "Some complex ideas here," he wrote in his final comment. "It would have been helpful to synthesize the hypotheses addressed in the different studies. Perhaps in the introduction?" Even as a senior, Caitlin needed to learn to find a central, organizing idea sophisticated enough to be of scientific interest to her readers. She also needed to learn to articulate that idea in the beginning of her text and use it to organize the whole of the text.

Ewa Zadykowicz, who was a sophomore the fall she took Biology of Symbiosis, had taken few other upper-level courses, and she felt that she had had only one writing experience that was at all comparable to the mini-review. In a class on environmental hazards, she had written a case study on the Woburn, Massachusetts, leukemia cluster described in Jonathan Harr's book, *A Civil Action.* To complete her case study she had been required to read beyond the required text, *A Civil Action*, gather research, and make sense of many conflicting scientific opinions. Yet it seemed different from the mini-reviews because to her it was "more controversial and socially pertinent" than the symbioses of the mini-reviews.

What Ewa thought was similar about the two projects was that she was reminded that "there are always a lot of arguments going on in science, and it's difficult to pick out the important points. To do that you have to be able to take a lot of notes and organize them and then figure out what's important." She didn't enjoy dealing with the politics of her case study, but she did enjoy the mini-reviews, which were not "socially controversial per se" and through which she could focus on the ecology of systems, her interest. Because Ewa was a sophomore, the mini-reviews were Ewa's first experience of scientific research—"going through a huge body of other peoples' research, analyzing it," and coming up with her own conclusions about it. This was something she had practiced in her case study, but the materials she researched for that project were less scientific and the actual text she produced was longer. It was a challenge for Ewa to determine how to synthesize all the information she gathered for her mini-reviews and present it to her imagined audience. "I have problems clearly presenting scientific information to an educated layperson because there is a lot of information, background information, and I'm not sure if the readers need it or not so I either make my sentences clear but complex, scientifically dense, or I try to make them more understandable to a regular reader, but that makes them longer and more complex and, in a way, less understandable."

David made comments on both of Ewa's mini-reviews related to this issue: "avoid excessive use of parenthetical comments" and "too technical." Ewa willingly immersed herself in the science of the symbiotic relationships she wrote about, but because she had little experience writing for real readers she struggled to choose which details to convey. Yet Ewa's writing changed significantly in her second mini-review. As I'll explain in the next section on the writing workshops, this had as much to do with the process modeled in the workshops as it did with the writing skills modeled.

BIOLOGY OF SYMBIOSIS WRITING WORKSHOPS

[The workshops] helped me realize that I often approach topics in a broad way and want to include too much! I need to hone in on one area and really explore its issues. . . . I love seeing how others write, how their minds deal with the challenge of presenting material.

—Anonymous Workshop Evaluation from Biology of Symbiosis

The two workshops David and I held took place in a wonderful seminar room in the science building where all four walls are lined with half bookshelves. Six students signed up for each workshop so David, the students, and I were able to sit comfortably around a rectangular table and see one another as we talked.

David had already graded the mini-reviews and returned them to students, but he had copied them for himself, and he had gone back over them with red pen, noting what he might raise in the workshops. As he had responded to students, he had looked for what each mini-review would be about, but he had found few articulations of writers' overarching ideas or analyses. He wrote comments such as "Tantalizing, but what are we talking about?" and "Make the case up front" and "Is this the question?" on their mini-reviews. He had a sense that where and how students began their mini-reviews was crucial to the mini-review's success, but I don't think he knew quite how to articulate this to his students until the workshops.

What I don't see in David's notes in preparation for the workshops is what he eventually ended up articulating to his students, something central to his mini-review assignment but missing from the actual assignment, something that I see as central to his rationale for teaching students to write mini-reviews. What he told his students in the workshops was that writing decisions in something as complex and as compact as a mini-review are dictated by what a scientist-writer finds most "cool." When "what's cool" is identified, all writing decisions can be made through that lens. It's difficult enough as a disciplinary novice to make a solid intellectual claim when submerged in a vast sea of research, but mini-reviews also require writers to make the claim accessible to readers unfamiliar with the specialized research, a task much more difficult than David's assignment guidelines might have suggested.

For David, "what's cool" is the solid intellectual claim a writer makes in a mini-review. That solid intellectual claim, which is what Gordon Harvey names "motive," is what helps a writer sort through the vast amount of research he or she has collected and articulate "why it should interest a real person . . . : why it isn't simply obvious, why there's a mystery to unfold, how the matter is different from what one might expect or some have said" (1994, 650). For Harvey, that "sense of motive needs to be sustained through the essay, but establishing it is the essential work of the sentences we usually call the introduction" (650). However, the establishment of motive may itself be a process of discovery for a science writer.

In "Scientific Composing Processes: How Eminent Scientists Write Journal Articles," Jone Rymer reports that seven of the nine scientists who participated in her study "readily acknowledged that they discover new aspects about the scientific information while writing their papers" (1988, 238) and, as one told her, "'I'm pretty interested in [publishing my data], pretty excited about it because there's no point in publishing it unless you find it interesting'" (220). This reveals, as Rymer notes in her conclusion, "that scientists are tellers of tales, creative writers who make meaning and who choose the ways they go about doing so" (244).

In fact, Greg Myers proposes that not only do those who write review articles in the sciences choose the "story" (1991, 52) they want to develop to "enlist readers in a particular view of the present and future of the field" (64), but that the story the review writer highlights and the style the writer chooses to use for the review both have something to do with how well cited the review becomes. As Myers notes, when a specialist writes for nonspecialist readers, he or "she sees it from outside, with these readers, and has to ask the always risky question, 'So what?'" (46). This creates a relationship between the writer and the topic, for "the discovery of this broad audience is also a rediscovery of the topic" (46).

Although the very beginning of Caitlin's "Beaks and Seeds: The Mutualism of Clark's Nutcracker and Whitebark Pine" does not set up the mini-review's story, and Caitlin's first paragraph suggested only this—"This pine cannot reproduce without the help of Clark's nutcracker. The nutcracker, in turn, depends on the pine's nutritious seeds as its main food source"—there was a tale that ran through the first few pages of the review. What fascinated Caitlin was how the nutcrackers remember the locations of their cached seeds and return to their caches by using "landmarks like compass bearings." Two years after writing the mini-review she still remembered this and wanted to tell me about it. And on the fourth page of her mini-review Caitlin refers to the nutcracker's memory capacity as "astounding." I don't believe her word choice was arbitrary. I don't think Caitlin knew her mini-review could so explicitly articulate just what it was she found astounding. In fact, I don't think the symbiosis writers realized that mini-reviews would allow them to tell tales to get at meaning, or would allow them to reveal what they thought was "cool," until David was able to explain to them why that is just what the genre requires.

As the director of the writing program, when I begin collaborating with faculty in the disciplines, I ask two questions: What do you think your students already know how to do in their writing? What do you wish your students were able to do in their writing that you don't think comes easily to them? The answers to those questions guide me as I decide what I can and should offer as we work together. David had already thought through how his written assignments for the course—two mini-reviews—might lead his students to consider the importance of being familiar enough with primary literature to synthesize it, but he told me he was also interested in teaching students to "have compassion" for readers as they wrote. David felt students, especially science students, seldom wrote "from the perspective of the reader" or "considered readers' expectations." For him, the best example of this was students whose paragraphs were long and unwieldy, allowing no break for the reader. I am now not so sure that long paragraphs were all he was referring to when he described writing from the perspective of the reader.

I know that we came to the idea of holding workshops between the first and second mini-reviews because we wanted to remind student writers that they, too, were readers who had to be satisfied. But David has reminded me he was also interested in having his students imagine one another as their audience, for he felt they would have an understanding of the "expectations and needs of their peers" and would thus write with greater clarity. Beyond that, he wanted students to realize "what will be 'cool' to one reader may not be 'cool' to another." He wanted his mini-review writers to identify with their readers in hopes they might then identify what would be "cool" to those readers. In this way, the workshops enacted one of the goals of the mini-reviews. Students were supposed to think of general readers as their audience, and while in-class peers may have had some sense of the science a mini-review writer was describing, they were, by no means, the same expert audience David was. By encouraging students to anticipate the workshops as they wrote their mini-reviews, David also reminded them to write for their readers.

There was also a practical reason we decided on workshops, rather than on prewriting assignments or group work around drafts—other possibilities I might have suggested for helping students negotiate the genre of the mini-review. David saw his syllabus as a "contract." We couldn't add on new required work, but we could offer an "experimental" (David's word) and optional experience with writing. David titled the workshops Writing from the Reader's Perspective, described them, and asked for volunteers when he distributed the detailed assignment for the mini-reviews. The workshops would take place after students wrote their first mini-reviews and before they wrote their second. David stressed how useful the workshop experience might be for students when they drafted their second mini-reviews later in the semester.

Preparing for the workshops, it turned out, was more of a test of my expertise than I had expected. In what one of my colleagues has taken to calling my "grassroots" WAC/WID work with faculty at Clark, I had already stepped into co-teaching in a number of disciplines that I had never taken a class in—sociology, psychology, and screen studies. But the truth is those were all classes in the humanities and social sciences, my own background. In my own education I've avoided the lab sciences. When I opened the envelope that contained the students' mini-reviews, I had a terrible feeling I was finally in way over my head.

These texts were about stickleback fish and cestode parasites, tubeworms and hydrothermal vents, and sea slugs and plastids. They described complicated symbioses in great detail. The writers used words I had never heard, and although they were words I knew I might find in the dictionary, especially the heavy, unabridged dictionary that sits on the shelf in the writing center, I couldn't imagine laboriously working my way through the mini-reviews. I felt guilty. So I convinced myself I could read them, if I read them slowly.

Once I allowed myself to take guesses about some words in context, and ignore other descriptions of scientific processes I didn't understand, I actually began to enjoy the mini-reviews. Many of them were quite detailed and used colorful language. Some described symbiotic relationships I might notice around me were I to become more aware. One mini-review, for example, which still fascinates me, was about cowbirds, birds that take over other birds' nests for their own young. In one of the workshops, David joked about how his daughter was both fascinated and horrified by the same symbiosis. As he said, she seemed to wonder if someone could come to her house and do the same to her. What a wonderful moment, I think to myself now, in which David modeled what was "cool" to his daughter about that symbiosis.

When I let myself relax, I could see I was indeed just the educated, nonspecialist reader David had imagined for his students. But that was not all I was. I was also supposed to be co-teacher as David and I co-led the workshops, and the morning of the first workshop I still felt nervous. I wrote to David and reminded him I had very little science experience. "This is challenging work for me," I admitted in the e-mail. "The genre of these texts is so new to me—I am truly the unknowledgeable reader, and thus I worry that the texts I find more satisfying (meeting my expectations) may not be the ones you would find satisfying." In his response, David reminded me the students were supposed to be writing for readers like me. He wrote, "One of my general criticisms is that the students too often used technical jargon without explanation, or failed to convey the general motivation for studying the system in the first place. So I think that our expectations about the form of the essays are probably similar."

In the same e-mail I listed how I would rate the mini-reviews I had read on a spectrum of "most satisfying to least satisfying," asking self-consciously, "does that jive at all with your reading?" "Your ranking matches mine almost exactly," David wrote back, listing the grades. What he and I agreed on was that the most satisfying mini-reviews were engagingly descriptive. They described the symbiosis with detail that helped the reader to picture it. They minimized jargon and did not rely on citations in every single sentence. When I look at those we were less satisfied by, I see overcomplicated descriptions of organisms and symbiotic relationships. I see citation after citation after citation. Some of the mini-reviews I found least satisfying had very, very long paragraphs.

The mini-review writers did not know what experts David was asking them to be. They did not realize they could turn their readers' focus anywhere they chose. They did not fully understand that they were working as translators and that they were meant to confidently lead their readers through specialized subjects with familiar language.

David and I began each workshop by asking students to brainstorm about these questions:

- What were the goals of this assignment?
- What does this assignment/this type of writing require you to do?
- What did you need to pay attention to in order to have your writing meet the goals of this assignment?

I too was a translator; I wrote the answers students offered on the board with my version of language I heard them use as they described their writing processes and struggles. In both workshops the writers reported that it was as they wrote their mini-reviews that they realized how much research they had done. "How to condense" came up again and again, but that question remained in conflict with students' accurate understanding that they were responsible for bringing a large body of research together for their readers. "How to evaluate the research," "how to review it with judgment," and "how much background" were questions they all had. They did not feel they knew how to explain the significance of the symbiotic relationship they were describing, or offer—as the assignment had required—"a novel synthesis." They said they found themselves mired in description, even when they knew they needed analysis as much as or more than description. They had considered how they could make their reviews "interesting" and "lively," and they wondered how much "creativity" they could use. Most of all they wondered "what to leave out," "what to exclude." As new experts, everything seemed necessary. They faced simple questions they simply did not understand. For example, why had David told them they could not use graphs and diagrams? Could they use direct quotations? Writing for the designated audience of literate laypeople left the writers asking how to simplify without oversimplifying and how to change scientific jargon to everyday English. They struggled with just what David might have hoped they would struggle with and their explicit articulation of their struggles in the workshops allowed David a way to join the conversation with them.

As we talked, David added to the lists and responded to their questions. It was when students described how difficult it had been for them to make complicated symbioses significant to readers that David described why it is important for writers of mini-reviews to keep in mind: "What's cool?" He raised this a second time when students described struggling with what to include in, or exclude from, their mini-reviews. For David, the best way to make decisions about *how* to structure a mini-review and *what* evidence to use is to decide *what* is "cool," and then determine *how* to make that "cool" for readers. David reminded the student writers of their role—they were disciplinary experts speaking to nonspecialized readers, and they had the authority to decide what to include and what to leave out. Transcribing what I thought were the most important comments he made, I wrote this on the board: "Writer is knowledgeable enough to make this decision. Clarity is more important than completeness. Can't always, and don't always, have to cover everything. New ideas take more time and space."

In each workshop, we considered each student's mini-review one by one. We took a few minutes to jot down thoughts about each mini-review before we talked about it and then spent ten minutes for each on these two questions: What strategies is the writer using that are working well? Which aren't or which are missing (if any)? There were productive exchanges as we talked about each writer's text and considered which aspects of the writing were succeeding and which were failing in terms of the genre requirements of the mini-review, but what I believe was most worthwhile about each of the workshop hours was the opening conversation David, the students, and I had together. In the give-and-take of workshop conversation, David and his students could develop their shared understanding of the mini-review.

David told his students that their answers to "what is cool" would help them make decisions about *how* to structure their mini-reviews and *what* evidence to use, but there were many other writing decisions to make that forced them to negotiate between how they may have previously written and how they now had to write. Perhaps what becomes important then is how the workshops provided a space where the students, who were not quite disciplinary insiders and not quite disciplinary outsiders, were able to negotiate the demands of the mini-review. As David Russell and Arturo Yañez point out, it is students and teachers alike who need to remember that "writing is never writing period," but "is always . . . part of some system of human activity" and people "act in multiple, interacting systems of activity where writing that seems the 'same' as what one has read or written before is in practice very different—and not only in the formal feature, the 'how' of writing." As Russell and Yañez go on to say, "Lying behind the how are the who, where, when, what and—most importantly—the why of writing, the motives of people engaged in some system of activity" (2003, 359). In the workshops, David and I could certainly offer the symbiosis writers the "how," as in "how to write" a mini-review, but we could also explicitly remind them of the where, when, what, and why of writing mini-reviews. We could remind them the text was more than a template: it was a conversation.

Thinking back on the workshops, David has said that what he appreciated most was the verbal exchange; he had the opportunity to give students feedback in the form of conversation. For David and the students the workshops seemed to offer space to have the same kinds of negotiated and collaborative conversations about writing that students felt they were having about disciplinary content in their in-class discussions. It was once again just as Ewa described, "a feedback loop," where "you start making yourself think in different ways than you used to." We often forget the power of this type of conversation, perhaps because it is so difficult to fit it into a semester's discipline-specific teaching and learning.

We also underestimate the power of allowing students to see one another's work. Many students noted in their workshop evaluations how powerful and educational it was to see that their classmates were struggling with the same aspects of writing the mini-reviews that they were and how useful it was to see the many different writing strategies their classmates had used in their mini-reviews. It might be more effective to incorporate these workshops into the plan for the semester and hold them before mini-reviews are due. But, as David had hoped, the writing we looked at in the workshops was already quite strong because students had written it to be graded and knew beforehand that their peers as well as David would be reading their mini-reviews.

Ewa's experiences writing her second mini-review reveal what she learned from the writing workshops. I am struck by the significant difference in the beginnings of her two mini-reviews. Ewa chose the topic for her first mini-review because the symbiosis "seemed cool," but in the beginning of that mini-review she could not express her fascination. Like Caitlin she ended up focusing primarily on description. "No clear question or thesis," David wrote back to her. But it is interesting to note that the beginning of her first mini-review follows David's assignment guidelines fairly closely.

> The sea slug Elysia chlorotica depends on the chloroplasts derived from the alga Vaucheria litorea for survival. This mollusk is a specific herbivore and has been shown in the lab to forage for V. litorea— its only food source—exclusively during its larval stage. From then on, the slug relies on photosynthetic material derived from the chloroplasts of V. litorea for a source of organic carbon.
>
> Some would argue that this relationship could not be considered symbiotic, in the traditional sense of the word, since it involves an association between an organism and only part of another organism. Nonetheless, whether one chooses to call it chloroplast symbiosis, chloroplast retention, or kleptoplasty (the stealing of plastids), this association is no less complex than any other more conventional symbiosis (Pierce et al., 1999).

Ewa said she wrote her second mini-review to feel more like "a walk in the woods" because she had been impressed by her classmates' play with language. This second beginning reveals a much greater understanding of the importance of "what's cool." She sets up an argument about the possible implications of the symbiosis she presents, and while the success of her second mini-review may be partly attributed to the fact that she had previously studied and researched this symbiosis and was therefore able to take on the necessary expert stance more easily, Ewa also said she thought deeply about what she had heard in the workshops. In fact, Ewa has, by her own admission, seldom been a draft writer, so she was proud to tell me that after the workshops she asked two of her classmates if they would read and respond to the draft of her second mini-review before she handed it in to be graded. They agreed. On her own, she carried the message of writing for the reader out of the context of the course and into her own process.

Here are the first two paragraphs of Ewa's second mini-review:

If you walk through a grove of healthy hemlocks, you will notice that their canopy creates much more shade than the canopies of most other trees that are common in the northeast. In fact, the density of hemlock canopies provides enough shelter to effect a different microclimate underneath the hemlocks. In the winter, the temperature in the immediate area is several degrees Celsius higher than the rest of the environment, while in the summer, hemlocks cool down their surroundings by several degrees. A hundred species of plants alone are known to rely on hemlocks for survival. One of the most well known and valued animals that require shelter of hemlocks for thermoregulation is the brook trout, which could die out if summer temperatures in streams increased (Quimby 1995).

Unfortunately, the fates of the eastern (Tsuga canadensis) and Carolina (T. caroliniana) species of hemlock in North America are uncertain. The hemlock wooly adelgid (HWA, Adelges tsugae), an aphid-like insect that was accidentally imported to North America from Japan in the 1950s, has been decimating hemlock trees and altering the forest ecosystem. Because the adelgid did not encounter any serious natural enemies on this continent, it has flourished here. It is now found in all states from Virginia to Massachusetts and is about to invade northern New England. After years of careful research the most feasible method of HWA control in sylvan setting has been importing a specific predator of A. tsugae, known as the Japanese predacious ladybird beetle (Pseudoscymnus tsugae). Obviously, introducing one nonnative species to combat another involves a great deal of risk, but so far (six years after the first release) Pseudocymnus tsugae seems to be gaining control over the adelgid population without causing visible ecological damage (McClure 2001). Nevertheless, most of the research and some potential surprises may still lie ahead.

Perhaps this second beginning feels satisfying to me as the literate lay reader because Ewa realized that rather than producing a "narrative of science," she should produce what Greg Myers terms "a narrative of nature," which succeeds by "foregrounding the activity of the object and obscuring the activity of the scientist" (1990, 189). In a narrative of nature, Myers argues, "the plant or animal, not the scientific activity, is the subject, the narrative is chronological, and the syntax and vocabulary emphasize the externality of nature to scientific practices" (142). To produce a mini-review Ewa had to turn to a symbiosis she knew well. She had to claim her expertise and authority. She had to assert motive. She had to acknowledge that as the writer of a second mini-review she found herself once again in a recurring social situation, a situation in which she was striving to satisfy nonspecialist readers as well as David, and so she not only changed her writing, she changed her process of writing. She sought out readers' responses to her draft. Maybe it is good experience for students writing in biology—or in any discipline—to be asked to write in the various genres of the discipline. For Ewa it was.

It was only after the convocation reception that I realized just how cool the work David and I had done together was. A year later, the experience still affected David as he wrote his own review article. A year later, I found myself wanting to think and write about symbiotic relationships and mini-reviews and my work with a mycologist. In working together to plan workshops for students writing about symbiotic relationships, we had formed our own symbiotic relationship. How often, really, do mycologists and compositionists collaborate?

I may have known little about the science of mini-reviews, but because of what I know about the teaching of writing, I was able to name, and help David name, the writerly moves mini-review writers must make. David had experience writing in a variety of scientific genres, and while the students and I had to determine how mini-reviews were different from other genres we had written and read, we also had to help David understand that he knew the differences tacitly, but needed to teach them consciously and actively.

It was, however, the awareness of audience that I believe was most important in facilitating all of our learning. Each of us—David, the student writers, and I—had to consider what a mini-review is, why mini-reviews exist, and why we would want to read them. What was cool about the workshops was that they created a space where David and I, symbiotic translators, could help the students explore a new genre. Though written for David's class, the mini-review required the students to own disciplinary knowledge and speak to others as working scientists. By working to articulate what was cool about pines and nutcrackers, or sea slugs and chloroplasts, students learned to stake a claim for themselves as scientists writing to other learned readers. The workshops remind me, even today, that the relationship between writer and reader, between one genre and another, or even one field and another, is itself a symbiosis.

ACKNOWLEDGMENTS

While David Hibbett, my collaborator, is not named here as coauthor, he actively read and responded to drafts of this chapter as I wrote and revised. His ideas are, I hope, as present here as mine.

Thanks to Caitlin Dwyer-Huppert and Ewa Zadykowicz, who spoke about their writing experiences and graciously offered their writing for this chapter. Appreciation also to Michele Eodice, Pat Hoy, Neal Lerner, and Jim Mancall, who all read drafts of this chapter.

PART TWO

Genres in First-year Writing Courses

6

"I WAS JUST NEVER EXPOSED TO THIS ARGUMENT THING"
Using a Genre Approach to Teach Academic Writing to ESL Students in the Humanities

Rochelle Kapp and Bongi Bangeni

"The school essays were just like retyping, and plagiarising was not the issue, so I didn't have to read" (Garth).

"[At school] we copied from the textbook . . . you were not expected to have your own point of view" (Andiswa).

"I prefer to say things out loud . . . it's hard when we have to write about them" (Dudu).

"I have the stuff in my head, but it's hard to put it down" (Andrew).

"I don't think I can manage the critical analysis thing. I prefer writing what I think and feel. The kind of writing here does not allow me to write freely" (David).

"I do not enjoy writing because I can't write what I want here, and sometimes I can't express myself properly" (Yandisa).

These quotations are typical of remarks made by a group of twenty first-year students whom we interviewed (as part of a case study) three months after their entry into the humanities at the University of Cape Town (UCT). In some ways, the students' experiences echo those reported in studies about the transition from school to university in many parts of the world. The students find the new discourse constraining and demanding in its many rules, its formality, its requirement to engage in close analysis and to consider the views of others in producing an argument. And yet the quotations also bear the quite specific imprint of the South African legacy of apartheid. Despite the many changes in the political system, the majority of "black"[1] working-class students are still educated in print-impoverished environments, often characterised by teacher-centred, predominantly oral classroom cultures. In a context where close to 90 percent of students study through the medium of English (their second language), literacy practices take on an instrumental character, functional to the externally set examinations that students have to pass in order to gain a school-leaving (matriculation) certificate (see Kapp 2000 for detailed description). These students are nearly all the first in their families, sometimes the first in their communities, to attend university. Yandisa and David's statements also allude to the fact that like many students who enter the academy from traditionally marginalized communities, these students feel constrained by the cultural and intellectual context of the university, where many of the norms and values are different or at odds with their own experiences.

When they enter into the humanities, students from such backgrounds thus have to negotiate a chasm that is not only cognitive and linguistic in character, but also social and affective: they "navigate not only among ways of using language but, indeed, among worlds" (DiPardo 1993, 7). In the words of new literacy studies theorist Gee they are entering into new discourses (he uses a capital D), a process entailing new ways of using language that are intricately connected to disciplinary processes of knowledge construction. Entering the discourse is a social and affective process because students have to negotiate a sense of self in relation to new ways of "behaving, interacting, valuing, thinking, believing, speaking and . . . reading and writing" (1990, xix).

In this chapter we will describe why and how we use a genre approach to help students "navigate" their entry into the disciplines in their first semester in Language in the Humanities, an academic literacy course that is situated alongside a range of disciplinary-focussed introductory courses and is designed to address the needs of students from disadvantaged school backgrounds.[2] We focus on our use of the social science essay as a tool to open up a conversation about the nature of the discourse. Our data are drawn from course material from our teaching in 2002. We also use data from our case study of twenty students who took our course in 2002. These comprise extracts from student essays and interviews (conducted during their first and second semesters), as well as informal discussion. Our chapter illustrates the ways in which we have used genre theory alongside process and academic literacy approaches to suit the specific needs of our context. Through an exploration of its strengths and weaknesses, we argue that while a genre approach is a key resource for providing metaknowledge of the discourse conventions, it does not provide the necessary exploratory talking and writing space to enable students from outside the dominant discourses to become critical participants.

GENRE IN OUR CONTEXT

Cope and Kalantzis have been among the leading proponents of an approach to literacy pedagogy that foregrounds genre. They define genres as "conventional structures which have evolved as pragmatic schemes for making certain types of meaning and to achieve distinctive social goals, in specific settings, by particular linguistic means. (1993b, 67)

They emphasize the need to facilitate access to dominant discourses by teaching explicitly the text types that characterise the discourse. In this approach, students are conceptualized as apprentices who are inducted into the discipline through careful scaffolding. They are taught a meta-language ("a language with which to make generalizations about language") that enables them to describe, produce, and critique a range of genres in the context of the discourse (Cope and Kalantzis 1993a, 6). The writers distinguish their approach from that of traditional (transmission) literacy pedagogy by emphasising the socially situated nature of language and literacy learning (see also Johns 1997).

They also argue that "students should be allowed to cross the generic line" (1993a, 10). This position is distinct from that of genre theorists like Martin (1993) who emphasize the need for modeling the genre first, and argue that students first have to know the genre thoroughly before they can attempt critique. It is also distinct from theorists who view genre acquisition purely as a process of acculturation (see, for example, Berkenkotter and Huckin 1995). Like Dias (1994), Luke (1996), Clark and Ivanič (1997), and Herrington and Curtis (2000), Cope and Kalantzis (1993a, 1993b) argue that genre teaching has to go beyond focusing on how texts function to teaching the ideological underpinnings of form (the "why"). This is especially relevant in a world where there is an increasing emphasis on instrumental educational outcomes (Luke 1996), as well as persistent calls for a return to teaching decontextualized grammatical form.

Besides constituting a reaction to traditional transmission approaches to literacy pedagogy, the genre approach, particularly in the form emanating from Australia, has reacted strongly to process pedagogy. Cope and Kalantzis argue that the emphasis on "natural" learning through free writing, on students' generating their own topics, and on affirming student "voice" "favours students whose voice is closest to the literate culture of power" and simply reproduces power inequalities by failing to teach explicitly the genres that characterize dominant institutions (1993a, 2, 5; see also Delpit 1995). They also critique the "analogy" of orality and literacy in process writing and whole language approaches (5).

While we have found the genre approach enormously valuable in its conceptualization of the student-teacher relationship as an apprenticeship that focuses on the explicit teaching of the manner in which texts are structured and on their social purposes, the outright dismissal of process pedagogies, and the denial of the possibility for students to be critical participants (by some genre theorists), seems problematic in our context (see also Coe 1994 for this observation). On the basis of our experience and research, we believe that for literacy teaching to be successful in contexts where students are entering into discourses substantially different from their earlier socialization, students' identities have to be taken into account because they are entering into new subjectivities (see Johns 1997; Herrington and Curtis 2000). In Gee's (1990, xviii) terms: "There is no such thing as 'reading' or 'writing,' only reading and writing something (a text of a certain type) in a certain way with certain values while at least appearing to think and feel in certain ways. We read and write only within a Discourse." If students are to become critical members of, and contributors to, the discourse, rather than instrumental reproducers, they have to be allowed the time and space to engage with the messy process of exploring (through talking, reading, and writing) who they are (and who they are becoming) in relation to the authoritative voices in the field. In our context, the authoritarian, examination-driven school environment has meant that students have had little opportunity for such exploration. They are accustomed to accepting the answer sanctioned by teacher and textbook.

Cope and Kalantzis (1993a, 18) advocate "a dialogue between the culture of schooling and the cultures of students," but it is not clear from their work how this dialogue will be facilitated. They seem to underestimate the extent to which individual mastery of genre entails negotiation and (re)construction of identity (as both Clark and Ivanič 1997 and Herrington and Curtis 2000 demonstrate). Cope and Kalantzis interpret a process approach narrowly, as a validation of student voices; whereas the approach can provide a space for students to enter the academic conversation through exploration and dialogue. For us, this is a key point of departure from the genre school. Our goal is to combine genre, process, and academic literacy approaches in such a way that conscious "learning" of genres through explicit mediation of form, and the development of a shared metalanguage, is placed alongside "acquisition"[3]—a more unconscious process of using writing to clarify one's own position in an argument. Learning the form of the academic conversation is combined with working out its semantics and one's own role as a critical participant. Our approach conceptualizes the genre of the academic essay as an instance of discourse. The task is not to romanticize students' home discourses, nor to reify the authority of academic discourse and the form of the academic essay. To become members of their disciplines, students have to learn how to situate themselves within the academic conversation with critical reflection.

Developing this critical awareness entails metaunderstanding of the culture of the disciplines and their social constructedness, and fluency in the register of the conversation. It entails knowing what subject positions are available to one. Whereas Cope and Kalantzis conceptualize "voice" as personal opinion, Clark and Ivanič (1997, 136) develop a more nuanced view of textual identity in academic writing. They use a poststructuralist understanding of identity as social, multiple, and fluid in order to identify three aspects of writer identity, which they categorize as the "discoursal," "authorial,"and "autobiographical" self. The discoursal self refers to the discourse choices that the writer draws on in the writing process, which reflect an awareness of the discipline. The authorial self has to do with the writer's "sense of authority and authorial presence" in the text, which reflects the degree of ownership; and the autobiographical self refers to the extent to which the writer's life history is represented in the text. These concepts overlap, but the distinctions provide a metalanguage about textual identity, a framework for understanding our students' writing and for giving feedback that may help them enter the discourse. Clark and Ivanič point out that we need to make writers aware "that their discoursal choices construct an image of themselves and that they need to take control over this as much as they can, *not* so that they can deceive their readers but so that they do not betray themselves" (231).

THE LANGUAGE IN THE HUMANITIES COURSE

The Language in the Humanities course is taught in small classes by language development specialists over one semester, with a total of fifty-two hours of formal class time. The course is orientated toward the social sciences. It is divided into modules that are centered around key social science concepts with a focus on issues related to identity. This focus enables us to engage in conceptual and language development work that articulates with students' other courses and helps them to explore the affective dimension of the transition to university. The emphasis on debate and comparing different points of view is important, given the students' background of rote learning and acceptance of authority.

The course is task based. Students work mainly in small groups on worksheets that guide them through processes of analyzing and constructing argument in the social sciences. In line with the genre approach, students are conceptualized as apprentices; and we use the principle of scaffolding, so that by the time they reach the final module, they are required to work at a greater level of complexity (in terms of content and form) with less intervention from us. While the course is fairly general, we try to create an awareness of disciplinary difference through our readings and our tasks.

After an initial introduction, which facilitates a discussion about the school to university transition and its implications, and which orientates students into the discourse of lectures, time management, and general study skills, we spend three weeks on a module called Language and Identity, followed by Culture and Gender. For the purposes of this chapter we will describe the Culture module, because its position midway in the course enables us to illustrate our method of scaffolding students into working out their position in the academic conversation through analysis and engagement with the other participants.

NEGOTIATING THE TRANSITION

As with all our modules, an essay topic frames the Culture module. Reading and writing skills are taught using debates about culture and cross-cultural contact. This is an important principle: content and skills are viewed as inseparable since the ways of knowing in the social sciences are inextricably linked to the forms of expression. As Berkenkotter and Huckin (1995, 4) point out: "Genre knowledge embraces both form and content, including a sense of what content is appropriate to a particular purpose in a particular situation at a particular point in time."

In 2002, the essay topic read: "Identify and analyse the notion of culture which you find most relevant to your experience of the transition to the UCT environment. Draw on your readings and classroom discussions of the different perspectives of the concept of culture."

The marking criteria for the essay are made explicit as a way of inducting students into our disciplinary expectations and drawing attention to the specificity of university essays (compared to the general ones written at school). Students are required to demonstrate an understanding of the concept of culture from different theoretical perspectives and an ability to apply theory.

In the preceding essay, on the relationship between language and identity, students have to develop a logical argument at its most basic level, that is, demonstrate that they can construct a position in relation to the different views in the debate. The Culture essay obliges students to move from the simple identification of different points of view to engage with theory at deeper levels of analysis, comparison, and application. The formal aspects of developing a logical argument through use of the discourse conventions are also dealt with at a more advanced level in this module through the teaching of what constitutes a definition in the various disciplines in the social sciences: coherence (the overall logic of an argument), cohesion (logic within a paragraph), introductions and conclusions. These formal aspects of the genre are all explicitly foregrounded in the marking criteria. Skills initiated in the first module, such as essay title analysis and referencing, are reinforced through tasks.

The essay simultaneously asks students to grapple with a concept central to the social sciences and provides the space for them to engage in critical reflection on their own processes of transition through dialogue with established positions. It provides students with an opportunity to discuss their struggles to come to terms with UCT institutional culture and to explore their defensiveness about the new environment. The following extracts from their preceding Language and Identity essays illustrate students' perceptions and feelings when they first arrive:

"People they can speak another language but they cannot forget their background or their identity" (S'busiso).

"People around you might influence your behaviour but they cannot influence your identity. . . . It is clear that that language a person chooses to speak can only influence his or her actions. The identity remains unchanged" (Sizwe).

"The fact that I am in an environment that requires of me to communicate in another language does not give me another identity but asks of me to change my behaviour to accommodate everyone" (Michael).

"I still strongly believe that the language you choose to speak cannot reveal your identity. It would take decades and decades for me to change this point of view, I can even publish a book about it. The other languages you choose to speak have nothing to do with your identity" (Vuyani).

Students' authorial and autobiographical selves are very strong in these early essays. The essay topic did not refer directly to students' transition to the UCT environment; however, it is evident that students draw on the prescribed readings only minimally, and have used their current experiences of "difference" and diversity as the basis of their arguments. The "you" in the essays is invariably self-reflexive.

It would be easy to dismiss these as the clumsy first efforts of the novice writer unable to find an appropriate register. Bartholomae's (1985) now-famous article illustrates the difficulty students have in trying to take on an authoritative role, slipping instead into "a more immediately recognizable voice of authority, the voice of a teacher giving a lesson or the voice of a parent lecturing at the dinner table" (136). Indeed, this is partly the case in these extracts. However, taken as a whole, the identities constructed in the essays also provide us with evidence that students are struggling with who they are, as well as with their writing. The essays reflect an overwhelming desire to assert a consistent, singular identity: that of students' home environments. In many cases identity is conflated with ethnicity; in others it is distinguished from the "white," "English" environment of UCT. We see in these statements a desire to preserve, not to "lose" or "forget" an original identity. Moreover, cultural identity is intrinsically connected to students' home languages. What emerges in many of the essays (and in our interviews) is the notion that it is possible to assume certain roles, to "behave" in certain ways in one's environment without any consequent effects on one's core identity.

The essays also reflect the shock of students' transition to a completely different environment. Even though the UCT student population is now over 50 percent "black," its faculty are predominantly white and the architecture, codes, and rituals are still markedly "English" and upper class in character. For some "black" students, the transition also represents their first encounter with "black" people from other ethnic and class backgrounds. As a consequence of the apartheid policy of "separate development," many students still grow up and go to school in environments that have homogenous ethnic and language identities. Students are socialized into the need to defend traditional boundaries, the result of the apartheid emphasis on preserving such division, consequent postapartheid competition over resources and power, and the perceived threat of assimilation to "Westernization" in the form of Anglicization.

Herrington and Curtis (2000, 35) write: "When we attempt to learn a new discourse, particularly as writers, we are entering a subjectivity, and how we experience that subjectivity depends on how it fits with our private/personal sense of identity and values. When the fit seems natural, we may take on a particular orientation without critical awareness that we are doing so. At the other extreme, if we are asked to take on an orientation that violates our basic sense of self, then we may feel assaulted."

There is a danger that the desire to preserve and defend "difference" may prevent students from entering into the academic conversation as critical participants. They may suppress their own views and experiences, engaging instrumentally with the views they encounter in the academy. They may also remain trapped in "commonsense" assumptions and rhetoric, based on their own experiences. A good example of this occurred when a "colored" student proclaimed: "I have no culture," because he associated "culture" with the traditional ceremonies and rituals that characterize "African" communities.

It is for these reasons that we begin the module by using case studies and visual evidence to challenge students to review their assumptions in the light of historical and contemporary evidence to the contrary. For example, we show students photographs that illustrate that people do change how they live and identify over time. This is dramatically illustrated through the life histories of people who experienced the regulation of work and physical dislocation that characterized apartheid. Through discussion of these shifts, and of students' own life experiences of change from an apartheid context to the "new" South Africa, and of moving from home to university, we are able to broaden their notions of what constitutes culture beyond static conceptions of culture as tradition and ethnicity. Like Scott (2002, 127), we want to help them "to hear the voices of past experience so that the new voices of the University can become audible by recognizable echo or by contrast." Engaging students in verbal debate and exploratory talk in which they view their experiences and commonsense understandings alongside other perspectives, thus also constitutes an important part of the "acquisition" process: articulating and clarifying ideas that may be difficult to express elsewhere.

Britton, whose work is often associated with process approaches, stresses the value of helping students to connect what they know with the unfamiliar through exploratory talk. He writes about students using their "inner reflections upon experience" as a means toward "interpreting the new and re-interpreting the familiar" (1986, 108). By the time students reach the Culture module, they are sufficiently comfortable with each other to engage in this kind of exploration. This is significant because, as our interviews showed, even students who were quite confident in our small-group discussions seldom spoke in their other classes during their first semester. In S'busiso's words: "If maybe I raised my hand in class, there was something beating fast in my heart" (first interview).

After these discussions, we ask students to write a definition of culture. They are told to regard these definitions as tentative: there will almost certainly be changes in the light of new readings and new understandings. This is the start of their process writing. At this point, we are still stressing exploratory thinking and writing. We purposefully do so before they are introduced to the module's theoretical reading, anticipating that they may otherwise be overwhelmed by the weight of authority.

DEFINING CULTURE

Our next step is to move into genre analysis. We introduce the class to the role of concept definition in social science argument construction. Students' schooled understandings are that a definition is an uncontested, one-line explanation, elicited from the dictionary. We discuss (through illustration) the limits of the conventional dictionary for the purposes of defining concepts such as "culture" in the context of the social sciences. Students are presented with a range of definitions taken from different disciplines in the social sciences in order to draw attention to the centrality of definition to meaning making and to articulation of point of view in the construction of argument. Students confer over these in groups, answering the following questions:

- What does each definition emphasize about the concept of culture?
- Who is the writer addressing? Provide evidence.
- Are there similarities in the definitions? What conclusions can you come to about the "ingredients" of a good definition?
- What do you think of each of these definitions?

The aim of this exercise is to illustrate how writers articulate their membership of particular discourse communities. We show how point of view is embedded in definition and how the type of definition relates to disciplinary context. Students are introduced to the specialized vocabulary (e.g., "norms and values") and conceptual distinctions (e.g., between "society" and "culture") that are particular to the social sciences. We also illustrate different styles of explanation (e.g., the use of metaphor or case study exemplification).

The definition exercise foregrounds the social nature of text construction and is key to establishing a metalanguage about the genre of the social science essay. At the end of this session, students return to the process of developing their own definitions by taking into account those that they have read (in terms of both form and content). This is crucial to our belief that they can disagree with, but not ignore, the new discourses and ideologies with which they are confronted. In order to be acknowledged as a legitimate voice inside the debate, students have to engage with its multiple points of view, using the linguistic conventions that characterize the genre.

READING AND WRITING CULTURE

We see reading as underpinning the writing process—one reads for a purpose, and reading plays a crucial part in "acquiring"/ "learning" the discourse. In Dias's (1994, 194) words: "[W]e need to talk of students finding themselves in the language of the texts they must read, of living in that quiet tension between exploring and defining what they know and recognising what the texts offer towards clarifying, shaping and extending that knowing."

We use articles written in Africa that illustrate different views of culture and different written genres. Our major theoretical text is Robert Thornton's (1988) "Culture: A Contemporary Definition," a difficult article both in terms of the conceptual terrain it explores and its language level. It is used as a theoretical basis for analyzing the notions of culture in the autobiographical, anthropological, and political texts that follow, and as a vehicle for teaching students the skills to read and analyze a demanding text.

Thornton explains contemporary notions of culture in South Africa by tracing the term's intellectual history to romantic and modernist conceptions of culture and nation. He explores when, how, and why boundaries are created, and traces processes of socialization and constructions of "self" and "other." Thornton's contention that the boundaries of race, class, and gender are a construction, existing only in the imagination, as well as his challenge to the contemporary ideology of multiculturalism, provide the focal points for heated discussion. Invariably, we find our own understandings challenged by students' perceptions and interpretation of their cultural environments.

Because the Thornton article is such a good example of the genre, we use it to model social science argument. Through an exploration of subheadings, the introduction and conclusion, the use of evidence to substantiate claims, as well as sentence-level analysis of the use of modals, pronouns, conjunctions, and citation in the article, we are able to illustrate how writers define their positions within the debate and create coherence. Critical language awareness at the sentence level is crucial because, as a result of an emphasis on oral proficiency and a lack of focus on close, critical analysis of texts at school, students have very little meta-awareness of how grammar works to create meaning. In addition, the often instrumental approach to referencing in their "mainstream" courses results in students viewing citation solely as a display of reading or as proof that one has not plagiarized, and not as a process of tracing tradition and establishing authority (Angélil-Carter 2000).

The Thornton article is carefully scaffolded by us, but students then move on to reviewing three other texts (Achebe 1975; Biko 1987; Ramphele 1995) in groups, using worksheets that reinforce reading skills. Thornton's metaphor of "boundaries" is used as an analytical tool. An important part of the discussion is an analysis of each writer's position on cross-cultural contact in terms of its historical and social context. As they progress, students are reminded of the need to develop and refine their definitions and think through their own positions in preparation for their essays. We teach mind-mapping tools to enable them to plan their essays by identifying, summarizing, and comparing the different views of culture. We also revisit the essay topic and marking criteria. Thus, in preparation for the first drafts of their essays, students engage in a process of "learning" the genre, alongside process exploration through talking, reading, and writing. They move through a recursive process of analyzing the arguments of others and composing their own, and are constantly reminded of their roles as critical participants in a debate.

After the first drafts of the essay have been written, we engage in further close linguistic analysis and awareness raising about the genre by modeling good practice through analysis of extracts on "culture" by published authors and novice writers. We look at how coherence and cohesion are established in writing, paying particular attention to linguistic markers of cohesion such as conjunctions and pronouns, because these pose particular difficulties that relate to transfer from the African languages. Students review their own drafts in the light of these tasks and comment to us on their analysis of their own essays. This is part of establishing a metalanguage, which enables them to analyze and talk about their own writing. It is also part of reiterating that writing is a process. Improvement happens through self-reflection and dialogue with their teachers and their peers.

The concept of dialogic feedback on writing is unfamiliar to most of our students. Students tell us that at school they often handed in essays without rereading and teachers handed them back having marked only the grammar. We mark students' drafts, using the metalanguage of the course and the explicit marking criteria to draw their attention to how they have defined, used authority, and to where coherence has worked or broken down. We also engage in verbal feedback where appropriate.

CROSSING THE BOUNDARIES?

Our analysis of the 2002 Culture essays revealed that some were still written in a mainly oral register, and some students wrote personal narratives that avoided the theory. However, most essays grappled with argument construction, and though students' efforts to use the discourse conventions were often overly self-conscious, for the most part there were marked shifts from the first essay, both in the ways that students position themselves and in their fluency in the discourse. In her first essay, Noluthando had written: "I only learned their [whites'] culture and language to adapt not to adopt and I did not lose myself in their culture for I practised theirs only in the school vicinity to suit the environment."

In the Culture essay, her shift is typical of many of her classmates. She starts by anchoring her discussion in the language of her first essay and identifying with the black consciousness sentiments in an essay by Steve Biko (1987): "I found it very difficult to adopt and adapt to the UCT society, because I thought that by doing that I would lose myself into a foreign culture."

She goes on to discuss her fear of becoming a "coconut," which she defines as people who are "black by race but behave like whites." Then she says: "[B]ut as time went on, I found myself not interacting and became an outcast. It is only then it occurred to me that culture is not stagnant, and that I needed to cross these boundaries (Ramphele 1995). . . . I found myself at the crossroads of cultures, my own culture and that of UCT, which is like two different worlds to me (Achebe 1975), for I enjoy some things that are done in both cultures."

The influence of the ideology of the Language in the Humanities course is strongly evident here. Although we present the Culture module as a debate, together with the current rhetoric about building a unified South Africa, the theoretical framing of the module makes it very difficult for students not to engage with the notion that South Africans share a common culture and that boundaries can be crossed. Noluthando had indeed been quite isolated and withdrawn partly because of her anger about not being accepted into the School of Law, and because she found UCT culture "somehow white" (first interview). She seemed to feel that she must protect herself from being assimilated. Achebe's (1975) metaphor of the potentially liberating and enriching effects of existing at the "crossroads" of Western and African culture and choosing which aspects of each to adopt allows her a way to "enjoy some things that are done in both cultures." The discourse of the Culture module opens up a way of rationalizing changes in her style of dress and allows her to relax her defensive behavior toward fellow students and the institution.

Our interviews revealed that, particularly for some of the students from rural backgrounds, the Thornton (1988) article was liberating, allowing them to see how boundaries of gender, race, and tradition have been used to control and limit. Noloyiso writes about the policing of tradition by the "elders" in her rural community: "They created boundaries by saying 'you are this kind of a person in this kind of culture' and they used to tell us what must be done. If you ask why, they tell you that 'it is our religion.' Sometimes they say 'you will die' and in that way they try to stop us from mixing our cultures with other cultures."

In her interview, Noloyiso talks about how "free" she feels at UCT. The discourse of the Culture module provides her with the resources and the language in which to express this. Another example of this is Garth, the elected class representative, a "colored" student who was extremely popular in class and seemed to connect easily across boundaries of gender, race, and disability (there were two blind students in the class). Both in class and in his first interview, Garth revealed that he had been taught to despise "black" (African) people by his "white" grandmother who had raised him in his rural village: "I remember that my grandmother used to say blacks stink, they never wash and you are not supposed to eat [food that comes] out of their hands."

In his essay Garth writes: "Coming to UCT represented a lot of things that I was socialised against. . . . I am proud to say that unlike Ramphele (1995) who 'stretches across the boundaries,' I can freely cross the boundaries of another culture and find commonness within that culture with which I can communicate. . . . Culture does indeed change, because it is not organic but social, which means it can be unlearned and redefined. Culture changes and its boundaries are crossed daily, by people who are brave enough to find out more about the 'other' (DOH101F, Course Reader, 2002) and who are willing to accept differences and also acknowledge the sameness that is found within the other culture."

For Noloyiso, Garth, and others, the Culture module seemed to have the effect of questioning the "taken for granted." In her first interview Sisanda says about the course: "The themes we learn about made me search deeply within me to find out who I really am and how I came to be that person. . . . I enjoyed the culture essay because it is asking me about my own experience, things that I've always taken for granted, my everyday life I'm encountering at UCT."

For these students the Culture module had achieved its goal of not only teaching the discourse conventions, but of helping students to move beyond the defensive positions in their first essays toward exploring their "becoming-selves" in relation to the discourse (Clark and Ivanič 1997, 134). However, it was also evident from the interviews that a number of individuals who had written of embracing diversity and "crossing boundaries" in their essays adopted a stance contrary to their beliefs, and were in fact uneasy (or in the case of Bulelwa, deeply alienated) in the environment. In her essay Bulelwa writes: "I have certainly settled in the UCT environment without any huge problems. . . . Although I seem to have adapted well here, I still remember the way things are done back home."

When asked (in the first interview) how she would describe UCT culture, Bulelwa replies:

> It is different from where I come from. Even if you were not a student, back home you would feel warmth. You would be part of the group and even if we would have visitors they would end up friends with everybody. There would always be warmth and here you don't see that. . . .
>
> *Rochelle:* And have you managed to make friends here?
>
> *Bulelwa:* Not the way I would like. I used to have friends, I mean everyone was my friend and I didn't have a specific friend. But here it so difficult and you can't even choose who you would like for a friend.

Similarly, Sizwe spoke passionately in his interview about how Steve Biko's notion that "we are throwing away our culture and being influenced by Western culture" had had a powerful effect on his thinking. When asked why he did not use Biko in his essay, he said: "I didn't know how I was going to put it clearly in the essay, so I chose the other writers" (first interview). In informal conversation with us about his experiences in other courses, Andrew spoke of how he often took positions with which he disagreed "for fear of being judged" or because essay questions did not always make allowances for other positions: "the structure is determining you." He had experienced particular difficulty expressing authority in part because of the very different messages he was getting: in psychology he was told to avoid the use of the personal pronoun, while in social work he was writing personal reflective essays. An analysis of his psychology essay revealed that his response was to mimic the discourse, skillfully paraphrasing the views on gender violence without any attempt to assert an authorial presence despite the fact that he comes from a community context of extreme violence and is a community activist. His essay reflects conscious distancing through phrases like "society out there." His efforts were rewarded with an excellent mark.

Clark and Ivanič (1997, 144) write: "Writers consciously or subconsciously adjust the impression they convey to readers, according to their commitments and what is in their best interests. These two forces may be in conflict, especially in situations like writing an academic assignment for assessment purposes. Writers often find themselves attempting to inhabit subject positions with which they do not really identify, or feel ambivalent about."

This is an important point. We believe that the process of learning/acquiring the discourse must include space for students to explore who they are and who they are becoming. However, for a variety of reasons, students may choose to distance themselves from such exploration. This also constitutes an acceptable position. Our task is to help students develop meta-awareness of the image constructed by their "discoursal choices" (Clark and Ivanič 1997, 231) and of the constraints and possibilities within their disciplinary discourses. We are quite open about this in our discussions with students. While it is not possible to teach this kind of nuanced analysis outside of the disciplines, we believe that, through feedback, we can make students aware of the effects of their discoursal choices and remind them of the importance of their own experiences and points of view.

On the basis of our second interviews, conducted after students had returned to the university after midyear trips home, we concluded that the contradictory positions in students' self-representation are often the result of their own ambivalence about who they are and where they belong. It is also the result of an anxiety produced by the negative feedback they receive on their writing. Many feel that it is easier to assimilate to the dominant discourses than to try to be critical participants. In the face of this, it seems important to acknowledge the extent to which students make strategic choices based on their own agendas (see also Thesen 1997; Herrington and Curtis 2000). By the end of her first year, Babalwa still wanted to be told the correct answer and was frustrated by her philosophy course, where "you keep on debating because there's no answer. . . . They say they don't look at the outcome, but in a way you are because you are using education as a means to go."

We found this statement fascinating because Rochelle's ethnography of Western Cape township schooling traces a trope where certain students are identified by teachers as "going": they are the students who are classified as achievers, who are expected to have a future outside of the confines of the impoverished, violent townships (Kapp 2000). Babalwa is one such student, classified as "at risk" by the university, yet frustrated by being held back, not being given the "means to go." Because of financial pressures from home, university education is a means to an instrumental end for Babalwa, and the academic debate is far removed from the reality of needing to pass in order to earn a living.

After the Culture module, we move on to the last module of the course, which focuses on the concept of gender. We reduce the scaffolding substantially and students have to work through the reading and writing process far more independently. This is part of reinforcing the need to internalize the methods of the course and to transfer and apply this knowledge to their other learning contexts. Students engage in exploratory talk on the nature/nurture debate, drawing on their earlier discussions on identity and cultural boundaries. They use their metaknowledge of genre to engage in close critical analysis of the readings and to present their observations to their peers. The process of analyzing the essay topic, producing drafts, and writing final essays is similarly informed by peer dialogue. We assist with guidance and feedback only when asked to do so.

By the end of our course in 2002, we felt that students were, for the most part, grappling with their roles as critical participants in the academic conversation. They were able to articulate and demonstrate metalevel understanding of the genre of the social science essay. The practice in exploratory talk and writing had also enabled them to become a lot more confident and, by the second semester, almost all reported that they were active participants in tutorial discussions and were less daunted by the writing process.

However, we are aware that there are distinct limitations to what can be achieved in a short course. Students "learn" quite quickly how to make many of the discoursal moves that characterize academic language. "Acquiring" ownership of a position takes much longer. In part, this is a factor of their educational backgrounds, their hesitation about whether their views will be valued in such a culturally different environment, as well as the multiplicity of discourses that they negotiate in their first year and the negative feedback they receive on their essays when they write outside of the accepted ideology. But it is also the result of their own identity transitions, the complex tensions between home and academic discourse, and the resultant ambivalence.

CONCLUSION

In attempting to illustrate our use of genre pedagogy, we have shown how process approaches that stress "doing" and exploration can be placed alongside genre and academic literacy approaches that focus explicitly on the nuances of form. A genre approach is a key resource for providing initial generic access to the discourse. However, acquiring the deep structure of the disciplines and becoming critical members of the discourse is a process, and has to be continually addressed within the context of the disciplines over time.

The students we teach have often experienced crime, violence, and abuse closeup and have had to battle through tough ethical choices with little adult guidance. In this sense, they may have lived experience of many of the social issues that are central to the concerns of disciplines in the humanities. The fact that they have had to move between radically different discourses (when they enter UCT) is a valuable resource that may enable comparison and critique (Gee 1990). Providing the space and the tools for students to explore their own sense of self in relation to disciplinary discourses has the potential to open up an affective and cognitive space, as well as creating the opportunity for mutual learning within the academy. In Thornton's (1988, 18) words: "to discuss culture is to be a part of culture, to have an effect on it, and ultimately to change the very nature of the 'object' itself."

ACKNOWLEDGMENTS

We wish to acknowledge the considerable contribution of our colleagues Lucia Thesen and Stella Clark in sharing ideas, codeveloping and teaching the Language in the Humanities course over many years. We are grateful to Anne Herrington and Charlie Moran for their invaluable comments on our early drafts. This material is based upon work supported by the National Research Foundation (under grant number 2054167) and the Spencer Foundation. Any opinion, findings, and conclusions or recommendations expressed in the material are those of the author(s) and therefore the NRF does not accept liability in regard thereto.

NOTES

1. It is impossible to contextualize fully the imbrications of South African language and educational backgrounds without using the apartheid system of racial classification ("African," "colored," "Indian," and "white") upon which they were based. However, to signify our own beliefs that these categories are, to some degree at least, artificially constructed, we will use quotation marks. In this essay we use the category "black" inclusively to refer to "African," "colored," and "Indian" students.

2. In the South African system of tertiary education, students enter into disciplinary specialization in their first year. In the humanities at UCT, all students are required to take at least one disciplinary-orientated introductory course. Students who are deemed "at risk" are also required to take Language in the Humanities. For the most part these are students who come from disadvantaged home and school backgrounds who are also second-language speakers of English.

3. Gee (1990, 146) makes this useful distinction between "acquiring" and "learning" secondary discourses by drawing on Krashen's description of second-language learning.

7

"GETTING ON THE RIGHT SIDE OF IT"
Problematizing and Rethinking the Research Paper Genre in the College Composition Course

Carmen Kynard

My first teaching assignment at my current college was the infamous freshman research paper class. To my then pleasant surprise, my students expressed a familiarity and ease with "the research paper." They explained how they wrote such papers for almost all of their classes. Some of their courses even required two research papers per semester along with essays, short-answer tests, departmental midterm/final exams, and homework assignments. When I asked to see samples of these research papers, I understood more clearly how they were able to accomplish so much "formal" writing in one semester for one class. After reading about three papers, a pattern was apparent. It was as if these papers had been written by the same person. There were no real distinctions in any of the twenty or so papers in the ways that positions were assumed, counterarguments constructed, types of evidence gathered, voices incorporated, perspectives presented, formal and rhetorical choices made, structural and organizational techniques used. There were no autobiographical accounts, poems, interviews (published or done by the student), or survey data. There was never an explicit acknowledgment or understanding that students' sources were at best secondary ones, representing someone else's opinion, and hence, students never really analyzed why authors thought a certain way. Each source was projected with the fact-laden "objectivity" that encyclopedias seem to convey. Unlike many of my colleagues with whom I have shared this experience, I do not automatically accuse these students of plagiarism. I believe very much that they wrote these carbon-copy papers themselves. This is what and how they had been taught and they had indeed learned their lesson well. What I suspected was that the context in which the "research paper" as a genre had always been presented to them, from high school on up into even freshman composition, was so consistent that now all they had to do was churn out a standard, stagnant form.

That these were the kinds of papers produced in the name of the college research paper is of course no coincidence. It is part and parcel of the problematic politics from which "documented writing" gets reproduced by students who are regarded as mere tabula rasa–typed "initiates" at the university. In 1982, in his landmark essay for *College English*, "The 'Research Paper' in the Writing Course: A Non-Form of Writing," Richard Larson warned of the widespread tendency to teach and conceive of the research paper as such a "separately designated activity" (814). He described the way that instructors approach the research paper as if it were a type of generic writing that incorporates the results of research and then differentiate that writing from other rhetorical and discursive plans for writing. Just as with the students I describe here, students heed this message and reproduce in mass number this type of "nonwriting" that Larson castigated two decades ago. To this end, Robert Davis and Mark Shadle, in their CCC article "Building a Mystery": Alternative Research Writing and the Academic Act of Seeking," argue that research writing textbooks still reinforce this kind of writing by giving students a "standardized concept of how academic research writing should look and sound" (2000, 418). Given what Davis and Shadle see as the omnipresence of the research paper as a linear, contrived, and templated collection of detached facts,[1] the assignment itself teaches students "little more than the act of producing, as effortlessly as possible, a drab discourse, vacant of originality or commitment" (419).

According to Larson (1982), we undermine our teaching by compromising the very goals of why we might want students to do research: to familiarize themselves with ways of gathering information; to draw upon and acknowledge the data from outside themselves in their writing; to become comfortable with using in their own writing the citation of other sources as a way of identifying, exploring, and evaluating issues; and to incorporate a thoughtful, perceptive examination of their sources and the contribution that those sources have made to their thinking. Since I agree with the ways Larson describes the purposes and goals of students doing research, I must also concur that this type of thinking and writing is undermined by the ways in which we, as instructors, often construct the genre of the research paper in our classrooms. For me, there was very little in the paper samples I collected that represented any of Larson's goals. There was no evidence of students exploring, analyzing, or connecting to their topics and sources. In fact, none of these students could engage in dialogue or debate with me about the content of their papers,

why they chose their topics, or what they learned. They were merely playing "the school game" and had learned how to do it well. The rules of
the game required exactly the kind of "unwillingness or inability to think
imaginatively and originally" as Davis and Shadle describe, alongside
the acquisition of an apolitical notion of writing and its social purposes
(2000, 425). In the end, this is what set the stage for me to question my
own notions of topic generation, form, and genre when teaching "the
research paper," notions that I believe situate writing and the politics of
academic work quite differently. That semester essentially became, for
me, the first draft of my vision of such a classroom, with ongoing revisions
going into the next year.

As David Russell shows in *Writing in the Academic Disciplines, 1870–1990:
A Curricular History* (1991), the research paper as a genre and how we
even think of research has a very specific history in American schools.
This history and its current manifestations hardly make the research
paper a value-free, apolitical exercise in which students simply learn to
write better and more fluently as they move onward into their other
classes. The problematic nature of this history was what I encountered
when I first taught the "research paper" at my current college; my second
semester, what I am calling the revision stage, represents ways my students
and I revised those encounters.

THE FIRST DRAFT: ENCOUNTERING AND COUNTERING PRIVILEGED
FORMS AND PRIVILEGED STUDENTS

> Are we arguing that facts are useless, or that the discourses of expository
> intent, such as the modernist research paper, be abandoned? No. We are sug-
> gesting, however, that facts and expository writing have limits; they only allow
> certain types of inquiry to take place. What we envision, finally, is a discourse
> that will not have limits, that will allow for various kinds of inquiry to echo,
> question, and deepen one another.
>
> —Robert Davis and Mark Shadle

In that first semester of Comp II, my own ability to push students to
rethink what they saw as the research paper was limited. The most "successful" students in the class at the college, the two women with the highest cumulative grade point average (and they made sure to remind everyone of it), were unsurprisingly the most resistant. At the onset, Nellie
routinely questioned my desire for her and her classmates to choose their
own topics. She wanted an assigned topic with every class focused solely

on explicit guidelines for "the" thesis statement, each topic sentence, and APA style. Anything outside of this simply was not a writing class. She struggled to write any analytic response to the articles (she merely summarized the works) we read in the course and could not understand why we were reading so many "inconsequential" Caribbean and African authors anyway. All that was required to her was a summary of the main points of a text. That those points carried varied, socially situated messages or meanings for the reader and writer was irrelevant for her writing. Meanwhile, she prided herself on being able to speak "properly" and "intelligently," unlike her "ignorant," "slang"-burdened classmates who, she told me during office hours, should not be permitted to speak so much in class. She also made sure to inform me on many occasions, undoubtedly feeling comfortable with me as a fellow light-skinned woman, that the "light-skinned people" in the Brooklyn neighborhoods of her youth had simply informed her that she was being raised better than "the brown people." I assume she did not appreciate my comments to her about people like "us" choosing to stand outside of the black community and take on anti-black racism in order to "pass." She dropped the course right after, never having produced any piece of writing that articulated her opinion on something other than being better than the "brown people."

Meanwhile, Alice, a light-green-eyed native of Trinidad, also prided herself on her ability to speak "proper" English with a "perfect British accent" (in fact, neither of the two students actually possessed the phonological systems they claimed). Alice consistently (but never with success) tried to impress upon her classmates that her homeland of Trinidad was a most inviting and racially harmonious place and that it was tragic that no one else had been brought up there as she had (usually making references to the family's maids and expensive private schooling). In the end, the challenges that I posed to her about her research papers largely went unheeded. Her final paper focused on the disciplining of children in Asian countries. The question that framed her paper was: what is it about Asian culture that makes people not want to discuss openly the issue of child abuse? I suggested that she could also be self-reflective in her paper as to why she had chosen this topic—introducing her to the notion of the researcher's standpoint—and thus, perhaps, even ask herself: what was it about her own current culture that assumed it could and should frame such a question and answer it about someone else? I also raised issues about sources: were they Asian writers? Were they "Americanized"? She insisted that such issues were not pertinent to the writing of a research

paper. As far as she was concerned, she had transitions, a clear and con-
cise thesis statement, strong topic sentences for each paragraph that did
not begin with articles; furthermore, she had used APA style flawlessly.

It is no coincidence that *these* students resisted so strongly, as they
were simply valorizing an academic form that had rewarded them. They
had no need, then, to engage a type of writing that would, as Davis and
Shadle propose in their work, question falsely dichotomized boundaries
of the academy, "logos-dominated arguing," and the dominant notions of
depersonalized writing as "academic" (2000, 422). Alice seemed unable
and unwilling to analyze her own interests in her project. Thus, she could
not situate academic work as always socially and politically situated, even
though each question she framed and every sentence that she wrote in
her paper were loaded with her own assumptions and perspectives. Just
as problematic in these cases was the fact that these two students' privileging coincides quite obviously and directly with race, class, and skin-color
positions.

Interestingly, the students in that first semester most clearly willing to
take risks seemed to be those who had very negative experiences in their
previous writing courses. One such student, Gail, waited until her last
semester to repeat this particular course requirement. Her final paper
took its inspiration from an assigned text by the highly acclaimed socio-
linguist Geneva Smitherman (2000), who described being left back in
elementary school and later being placed in a college remedial speech
class because she was an Ebonics speaker. The text goes on to historicize
linguistic and structural racism as well as important research on black
language varieties. Gail had an elementary school–age daughter in the
New York public school system who was placed in speech classes because
of her Caribbean "accent," and after reading Smitherman, she seemed
to have a new charge and connection to language politics and education
(and I imagine her fire was also sparked by the class's two light-skinned,
light-eyed "dream children"—as Toni Morrison [1970] names such a
character, Maureen Peal, in *The Bluest Eye*). In her paper, Gail described
her daughter's growing silence, distaste for school, and propensity to
"correct" the English of everyone in the house. Gail's paper turned out,
then, to be an examination of her daughter's classroom, research into
black language varieties, a collection of published black scholars' views
on language and literacy for black students, and a sampling of creative
writing that incorporated the use of these language varieties. It seemed
that Gail was wrapped up in informing her ideas about language and

culture, while she was also deciding what she should do with her child at the school she was attending. At the end of the course, she even wrote me a note and came to see me about my writing an article about language. She said she would take on her child's school and that I, in turn, should write something to enlighten her professors and my colleagues. She criticized these professors for not making her sensitive to her daughter's situation earlier and called these people "black dread on the outside but white on the inside," especially because they thought they were doing something positive by ridiculing every student aloud in class for using black language varieties.

Another student, Kesha, wrote about drug addiction, inspired by an assigned text by college professor and noted writer Megan Foss (1999), who was once a drug addict and prostitute. As a working-class woman, Foss focuses a large part of the purpose of her essay on addressing class politics and writing. As someone who had witnessed firsthand the reality of drug addiction in people's lives, Kesha wanted to talk about the experiences of black women with prison records and drug histories. In her final research paper, she interviewed addicts in a rehabilitation center as well as the staff who worked there. She then did one case study of an individual she knew. Kesha seemed to work with more ease than Gail, who seemed to struggle with how to incorporate her and her daughter's own narratives alongside the texts she was reading. Meanwhile, it seemed that all I needed to do was explain briefly to Kesha what a case study was and it appeared in her paper. Similarly, all I had to do was suggest that she place her interviewee's narratives alongside information that focused on the experiences of blacks in the criminal justice system and reasons for drug abuse. I simply asked her: What was the social and racial context of all of this? She was then off and running, and eventually decided to shape this writing into a piece of literature, an actual brochure, that the rehabilitation center would be able to use. In Kesha's case, I just showed her examples of models that I was sure she had not seen before. Because she was clear about her purposes for this brochure and whom she wanted to help with it, simply showing her a few models was all that I needed to do. She was always clear from her initial reading of Foss that she wanted to center black women's voices, and so she revised the interview models I showed her according to what would be most appropriate for her brochure. For a large number of students, however, rethinking what they thought a research paper could be was an easy enough process, but the actual writing proved to be an excruciatingly confusing task.

For Elva, writing her paper was frustrating, albeit beneficial (or so she said). She struggled throughout the writing of her paper and in the end, there still seemed to be large gaps and holes. She was very caught up in male-female relationships and wanted to show that black culture exhibits a different type of interaction via romance, body/beauty preferences, and so on from what goes on in mainstream white culture. She decided to interview young, single, heterosexual black men and women. She knew what she wanted to do and whom she wanted to interview, but designing questions was very challenging for her. She found this difficult and so consulted her classmates, whom she tested questions on. I thought this was brilliant and told her that this was called a "pilot study," a tool that she clearly understood. After we looked at her "pilot," she collected data from at least forty people. The next and most difficult process was "aggregating" the data. Designing questions, disseminating questionnaires, and then categorizing responses took an exacting amount of time for her and she interpreted this as incompetence. It did not seem to comfort her when I insisted that what she was doing was, in fact, quite difficult because it was very sophisticated. Throughout our many e-mail exchanges and meetings, she continued to run into moments where she was frustrated. No matter how much her writing group and I thought her frustrations were natural (very few people sing and dance with utter joy as they write), she saw herself as incompetent. I even explained (and offered her the opportunity to work with a partner) that scholars often undertake such research in partners and teams and that researchers who collect data for their dissertations might take years to aggregate it, but she still seemed to interpret her struggles as defeat (and this is not even to mention the difficulty she encountered in using texts and personal experiences to define what she meant by black culture and romance). In the end, what interested her most were the differences that occurred across generations. Although the actual written paper was still far from finished, I gave her a good grade on the final project based on her very tedious and time-consuming journey into collecting and aggregating data alongside textual resources. She would need more practice and time with writing up data such as hers, but as a first attempt at such writing, I thought she showed a sharp skill, maturity, and sophistication akin to what my own peers in graduate school were doing in their pilot studies. She, however, never seemed convinced of this.

It was largely through working with Elva that I began to question more rigorously the nature of the research paper in terms of what counts as "evidence." The type of data that Elva was collecting and her attempt to write it up should not have been a new endeavor for her. She was in fact focusing in the social sciences and was well into her major. None of what she described as her previous research papers, however, seemed to fall outside of the typical library-go-fetch process. Larson (1982) also commented on this phenomenon in terms of the dangers of allowing students to think that research relies primarily upon books. He notes that only one or two fields of study represent disciplines where the corpus of its research protocols rest on book collecting alone. He argues that much research regarded as "humanistic" takes place outside of the library, just like the very field in which Elva was concentrating her coursework. More importantly, facts—which Elva collected quite well—take on meaning only inside of cultural debates and disciplinary, interpretative networks within which they are framed (Booth, Columb, and Williams 1995; Crowley and Hawhee 1999). Likewise, the very notion of the thesis/support format that had structured Elva's entire freshman composition experience (with its final culminating expression in the research paper) has always already been questioned also. Davis and Shadle (2000) go on to point out the central thinking of scholars such as Paul Heilker (1996), Lydia Fakundiny (1991), and Bruce Ballenger (1994) in questioning our notions of the research paper and essay writing in the ways that we limit students' thinking and disengage students' work from theories central to social epistemology and rhetoric. The one stock essay form seems the easiest to teach and grade, requiring thus only a mechanical reflex on the part of students and a counterreflex from the teacher's pen. This, however, does not mean that this is the only way to teach writing, that this is a worthwhile assignment for teachers to give or students to complete, that there is only one kind of essay and one way to write it, or that there is only one kind of information and one way to dump it into writing.

Ann Johns's work is particularly helpful here. In her essay "Destabilizing and Enriching Novice Students' Genre Theories," (2002a), she points out that teachers simplify and generalize text production to such an extent that many features of texts and contexts are distorted or simply discarded. What then happens is that we lift those genres and discourses out of the communities of practice that gave rise to them in their particular purpose, place, and time. The dynamism is wiped away and instead a generic, absolute template for only one type of task is embraced. To this end, Johns reminds us that the genres in which we write "are mental abstractions, perpetually subject to change, socially situated, and revised to respond to varied audiences or purposes" (237). She thus advocates a pedagogy that destabilizes students' notions of academic texts, enriches them by embracing the contestation and negotiation through which academic discourses and disciplines are constituted, and then expands students' notions' of their writing by inviting them to participate in this work. She cites five goals in her work: (1) to evoke student interest, since motivating students to perform is a crucial element; (2) to draw from students' own life histories, including their pedagogical histories; (3) to provide experiences, especially in the context of students labeled as "remedial" and discriminated against because of their bilingualism and ethnicities, that allow students to experience themselves in powerful roles during their reading and writing in the classroom; (4) to destabilize students' theories of history and their theories of genre as static and preexisting; and (5) to provide sufficient scaffolding or assisted performance for students to be supported, critiqued, and encouraged as their theories are destabilized. In this way, students not only become writers but also genre theorists, a process that can be well applied wherever they write. This to me seems the purpose and goal for the freshman research paper class.

While it was easy for me to be critical of the dominant, traditional approaches to the research paper that my students had encountered, what I needed to take on was the more difficult project that Johns describes, which would involve a critical examination of writing in my own classroom. What I needed to do, then, what I had failed especially to do with Elva, was provide a type of scaffolding in the classroom where students would not only be engaging alternative forms of research writing but would also be looking at why, how, where, and when they are used. In that first semester, I was making it up as I went along, trying to understand the context of the place I was in and how it structured students' notions of what the research paper genre was. But what had really happened in my own classroom? How and why did students define and redefine research, its purposes, and its methods? How did students make their decision about the structures and forms of their research writing? What difference did it make in a final research paper if students spent the semester reading and writing (high stakes and low stakes) in a variety of forms, genres, voices, and language varieties? Which forms of writing did students themselves privilege? The exploration of these questions was sparked in that first semester and would continue a year later, when the infamous research paper class would meet my students and me again.

"THEN BRING IT ON": THE REVISION STAGE—THE SELF AS TEXT

Criticism, contestation and difference is not a genre, not a skill, not a later developmental moment, not a reading position. It is, according to Voloshinov, a constitutive and available element of every sign, utterance and text. It can be, following Bourdieu, a principal strategy in realizing, converting, and contesting economic, cultural, and social capital. That is, unless dominant cultures and pedagogical practices, however intentionally or unintentionally, silence it.

—Allan Luke

In the second year of teaching "the research paper," I began the semester by asking students to reflect on their prior research experiences. I wanted these reflections to fulfill two purposes: (1) to find out exactly what students had written before; and (2) to discover what students defined as the "research" genre based on their prior experiences. Interestingly, the student with the most extensive and varied experience was a young woman, Bjana, who had gone to one of the established small alternative high schools in New York City. It is no coincidence that she always seemed to have no hesitation to take on what I thought were very sophisticated and challenging writing topics. Her final paper was an examination of the impact of colonialism on a people's culture and language. Early in the semester, Bjana wrote about Ngugi wa' Thiong'o's *Decolonising the Mind: The Politics of Language in African Literature* (1986) and made plans to read other work by him. In the end, her paper used Ngugi's arguments about colonialism robbing the language and culture of Africa to contextualize American imperialism in Puerto Rico. Unlike Alice, who had been reluctant to do so when examining what she defined as Asian culture, Bjana explained her own researcher's position as a black person in America. She saw U.S. racism against blacks as constituting their colonization, thus making the United States a country that robs other people abroad of their culture and language at the same time that it does so for blacks here. I was immediately fascinated by the multiple levels of her argument. It made sense to me, though, given her prior experiences in high school, which included a research paper on the Vietnam War using interviews with black veterans, a position paper on education after studying the differences and similarities in the historical debates between Booker T. Washington and W. E. B. DuBois, neighborhood studies interviewing longtime residents and the history of white flight, and histories investigating the conflict between blacks and Jews in Brooklyn. Writing and its social purposes had been a central force in her high school experience, and she could articulate connections to writing, empowerment, and black culture and history that few other students could.

Along with collecting information about students' prior research experiences, I decided that I would ask students to think about the research topics in each of their journal responses, where they were asked to explore what, if any, issue was emerging that they would like to think more extensively about. In this way, I was hoping that the notion of choosing their own topic would not be such a daunting task as it had been in the previous semester. In that way, by the middle of the semester, I hoped we could focus instead on what kinds of data could inform the topics and, in turn, how to write about them. I wanted to encourage students to define and invent their own means of informing their topics while simultaneously deciding the genres in which they would construct the meanings of their subject.

The topics that students would be exploring did indeed take shape early in the semester, all somehow sparked by discussions in class around the texts we were reading and the issues students raised. Each of the topics represented personal connections for the students that were explicitly explored in their papers, pushing forth new understandings of the genre of the research paper in comparison to what they came in with. In fact, I was a bit surprised by how personal their writing was, although that was never an explicit requirement of the research paper. Perhaps what I saw as students' willingness to really "lay it all down on the line" resulted from the journal guidelines, where I attempted to center personal introspection. Along with articulating research possibilities, students were asked to respond in writing to a central set of questions for every text read in the course:

- What for you is most important in this text? Why? What is important about this information?
- What quote or parts of the texts (key words, favorite phrases, etc.) do you find most compelling? Why? (Please keep track of page numbers for later citations in papers.)
- What personal experience(s) can you connect to this information? How? Why? Think of this as opportunity to really delve into looking at why you think what you think, why you respond the way you do. What is triggering your response? What do you think is impacting the way you see/think about something? Explain.

- What other readings, music, conversations, proverbs, granmomma's wisdom, gossip, etc. do you connect to this information? How? Why?

The formal writing assignments throughout the term always asked students to compare any two or three texts in the set we had just finished reading. Students were guided in class through writing to choose their own texts and the topic they would decide for their papers. In each of these cases, "the self" could serve as one of their chosen texts. "Reading the self as a text" was a phrase I used a lot that semester, and it made sense for students because of our extensive discussions that began after reading excerpts from Keith Gilyard's *Voices of the Self* (1991). This meant that students had to explain a specific, personal story while also analyzing its larger social and political dimensions as the substance of a comparison to a reading from the course. Of course, not all students chose to do this at all times and often compared two readings to one another. Some typical paper topics throughout the term consisted of the following:

- comparisons of living in poverty as a black child in the Caribbean or as a Caribbean American in the United States to excerpts from Dick Gregory's (1964) autobiography about the same topic (an African American in the United States)
- comparisons of Geneva Smitherman's (1999) elementary school experiences with language discrimination to their own educational experiences
- comparisons of personal issues and experiences of assimilation, language, and cultural identity to Richard Rodriguez (1983) and/or Amy Tan (1991)
- comparisons between Haki Madhubuti's (1990) politicization of racism and the experiences of black men to short stories and narratives written by former students (included in the course packet) and by themselves
- comparisons between Patricia Hill Collins's (1990) politicization of racism and sexism and the experiences of black women to short stories and narratives written by former students (included in the course packet) and by themselves

There was never an instance where a student did not, at least once in the course, use "the self as a text" in a formal writing assignment. Thus, by the end of the term, choosing one's own topic and texts, while also socially and politically interrogating one's personal connection to the topic, were nothing new. I was fascinated with the kinds of topics students chose, topics that I could never have created:

- issues of identity and culture for a "hip-hop cultured," black Panamanian man in Brooklyn
- how and why Brooklyn teenagers choose historically black colleges and universities
- racism as experienced by black women in corporate America
- disciplining methods of Caribbean parents in the United States and the Caribbean
- the case of reparations for slavery
- black motherhood as defined by black women historically and currently
- autism and the experience of black children and parents
- negative perceptions and stereotypes about Haitian vodun
- the role of the black barbershop in black communities
- police brutality and community response
- racism encountered by black students at historically white colleges
- differences in slavery in the Hispanophone, Anglophone, and Francophone Caribbean
- low self-esteem as a barrier to school success for black teenagers
- differences between Catholic high schools and public high school in the Brooklyn Flatbush area
- oral history of the "Lafayette" projects in Brooklyn (the pseudonym here is created by the student)
- AIDS in Africa

Before students produced any of their own writing, however, many wanted to test me in the very beginning. Did I really mean what I was saying? And what would I do when they did just what I was asking for? This was especially clear with Malcolm, who always seemed to be taking my temperature by asking me if I was really going to let him write about the "real" issues of *his* life. He even asked me if I really valued Ebonics like Geneva Smitherman and if I could get "down" like her. I told him that I didn't think I could get down quite like Dr. G. but that I do try a "lil sumthin, sumthin here and there," as Smitherman's work was important to me. At this point, he assured me that he could "throw down" just like her and could "drop lines just as good." I couldn't help but laugh and gave what I thought was the most appropriate response to this very curious student: "Then bring it on. I ain't skeered," and he laughed. I was, in fact, quite impressed by his line of questioning because it showed that he understood Smitherman's work, *Talkin That Talk: Language, Culture, and Education in African America* (1999), very well as well as how to assess his own professor's politics of writing and academic work. He was simply testing me to see if I walked what I talked. In the text that we had read, Smitherman herself describes the resistance she faced when she decided not to put the g's on her critical text *Talkin and Testifyin*—a story that I felt was very important to students' understanding of what happens when new stuff comes through old, rusted pipelines. I stress to students, as I did with Malcolm, that Smitherman's science and the way she drops it were not always welcomed but she stayed true to the game and did it anyway. I can't make that kind of decision for students, but I can and will support them when they strike out for something that is new on the page in both content and form (since they really do hang together, like beans and cornbread, is what I usually say). I also point out, based on the texts that we have read, that they are simply following the trajectory of a long-standing history and politics of many socially conscious black writers. Mixing their genres and forms does not mean that they have not achieved what has been "standardized" but instead have moved past it and its purposes (again, Smitherman's story is an important lesson here: she herself talks *not* about the difficulty of achieving a standardized form, but of self-consciously hybridizing an academic style, a style very few writers successfully achieve). I'm not sure who was more surprised at the end: Malcolm, by my "allowance" of his writing; or me, by what and how he actually wrote. Malcolm's first paper, "Love, Hell, or Right," was a personal comparison to "Love Letters" by Megan Foss (the same essay that had sparked Kesha's research paper the previous year). Foss was once a prostitute and drug addict who learned to write in prison by writing love letters to her then pimp-boyfriend. Her piece opens with an autobiographical/memoir account of her life and then moves into questioning the academy's choking of what she regards as her working-class life and language. Malcolm's piece was also about his love letters and literacy in prison and he opened with the following:

> As I sit here in my eight-by-ten urine scented cell, I pray that the pale correct officer yells my name on the mail call. Although I am not a Muslim, nor a Christian, I plead with Allah and Jesus to send mail from my baby girl, Nichole. . . . behind these iron vines I learned that pain is love. . . . In here my clock moves like a handicapped turtle. My nights are filled with traumatizing noises from the man in cell five getting burned to death, the guy in cell nine trying to strangle himself with wet sheets and the soft fellow from Queens getting his anus ripped open Louima style with no grease. This is where I had to find love. In hell, now you know that is not right.

Mama never said that it would days like this. I have to put a sheet over my transparent bars to defecate or piss. Somewhere out there I know that there is a better life for an intelligent thug like me. A life filled with less tears. A life filled with more smiles. I hate this place like I hate the cops who killed my father. I hate this place like I hate drug dealers who sold cooked up cocaine to my struggling mother. The only thing that keeps me ticking is the love letters that I receive when the pale-faced men call my name. In this hellhole these love letters make me feel all right.

The substance of his essay looks at how his literacy was driven by the love letters that he wrote to his girlfriend and also to his boys (what he called "thug love letters"). Foss had inspired him to think of his literacy being shaped by these letters. Malcolm's letters kept him connected to the outside world where he could be free. The beauty of the essay is obviously connected to the way that Malcolm situates his literacy, especially in the way he recaptured his experiences alongside a re-creation of the love letters that kept him emotionally and spiritually alive. I was blown away by his writing—the content, the form, the language, the flow—and I told him so. He had an essay that needed to be heard and read by more people:

Malcolm. . . . A beautiful and passionate piece. Although, perhaps presumptuous of me, I want to hear more—probably me needin to mind my own business, you know how I do. Nevertheless, you got a story/autobiography here that needs to be put in print just as is Megan Foss's. . . .

That first paragraph wrapped me right up in your writing! The metaphors and images on the first page—the clock moving like a turtle, pale-faced men, hell-hole, iron vines, thug love letters, thug love style. I could go on here. The words escape me to describe the power this had for me. Beautiful and terrifying all at the same time! Let's talk about this piece, about it being your final project for this class. You could use the Foss piece as your model—notice what she does in the beginning and then how she ends her piece. Her political commentary/analysis is just like the science you always droppin in class. . . .

So yeah, you had it right: you can get down like Dr. G and now I see what you mean that some folks just ain't ready for this. Yet and still, I hope the space of this classroom is a place where you can to write what you gotta write, no matter who ain't ready yet.

Malcolm did not follow my suggestions regarding the Foss model because he did not need to. His paper had it its own historical, political context. He called his final paper "Issues of Black Folks"; he wanted to model it after W. E. B. DuBois's *Souls of Black Folks* as a genre in which to create his own "auto-sociographical text."[2] He created various mini-chapters where he would write about personal experiences, observations, and historical information about being a black man in America. His first chapter was this quoted piece that he wrote in response to Foss, "Love, Hell, or Right." His second chapter, "Miseducation Continued," examined issues of race, curriculum, and education in urban schools. His final chapter, "Black Men's Gender," was an attempt to be in dialogue with writers such as Haki Madhubuti (1991) alongside key black feminist thinkers like Patricia Hill-Collins (1991) in order to critically represent what he saw as issues of gender oppression in the lived experiences of black men. He ended the course by writing and talking to me about his desire to start writing more stories about his life that could someday become a book. It was obvious to me in his first paper that he had tested the waters and started swimming across after he saw what kind of water-moves I was making. He even insists now that he will be visiting my future classes to make sure that his writing is in my next course reader. The purpose of Malcolm's project, then, was not to copy a predetermined genre, not even W. E. B. DuBois's. What was equally important and impressive to me was the way that he could engage the way that DuBois's genre emerged out of a particular social, historical context intimately connected to the politics of post-Reconstruction. That moment was not necessarily Malcolm's but it held lessons for him to learn as he went forth with his own genre in his own "second post-Reconstruction moment."[3]

Like Malcolm and many of the other students whom I have met, personal interrogations are neither a stylistic issue, where they merely pepper the opening of their writing with a good story, nor are they simply a self-therapeutic maneuver. Students took on themselves as texts and really pushed the boundaries of the research genre for themselves and for me. Students like Malcolm were an integral part of that process. In small groups, students read each other's proposals, drafts, and final papers and were thus a part of each other's entire process—from the generating of topics to the final writing. They also gave each other feedback in a whole-class format where all students had to informally present their research. Thus, in taking on the kind of writing that Malcolm did, he also set the tone for how writing could and would look that semester.

As Davis and Shadle have argued, when students use and mix multiple genres and mediums as well as disciplines and culture, their work can move directly up against the false opposition that happens in composition studies and academic culture: "academic and expressive writing; fiction and nonfiction; high, pop, and folk culture, and [research methods across disciplines]" (2000, 418). This, in turn, helps students to reconstruct the purposes and processes of academic work while also helping them to understand that there is a variety of information and discourses, modes and genres. That a student like Malcolm's empowerment rests with an ability to mimic preexisting genres denies the sophistication of his thinking and social consciousness, the ways in which he can and has already mimicked plenty of forms already, and most important, his uncanny and straight-up approach for analyzing the politics of the teacher who expects and wants nothing more from him than static writing formulas. We would do well here to heed the work of Allan Luke (1996), who questions whether "technical control" offers success in what is now the generic, overused trope of the "culture of power." Such theories often focus little on helping students read and analyze structures of oppression and domination that are never static or fully transparent. There is an assumption that power can be gleaned through direct transmission provided by teachers solely through text types used in the classroom. Luke calls this an analytical separation of ideology from function instead of a close reading of the site of contestations of difference, a reading that Malcolm was clearly able to form in his understandings of not just what DuBois wrote but *how* he wrote it (and, as with the case of Geneva Smitherman, we would do well to remember, as Cedric Robinson (2000) points out, that DuBois met extreme opposition with his work form the "culture of power" but did it *anyway*).

Luke's work illuminates the ways in which texts are always formed inside of powerful forces of ideological struggle about what will count as knowledge. Thus, texts become a type of technology whose structures and effect *cannot* be simply learned and mimicked without investigating their ideological origins, current locations, and consequences. Such generic tropes about "cultures of power" and showing it to students are neither historically informed nor socially illuminating, and they reify and essentialize power more than dismantle it. To this end, Luke argues: "Whether viewed in terms of mastery of genres, mastery of reason, mastery of the self, or mastery of skills, power is treated as something which can be identified, transmitted, and possessed. By investing power in particular genres, texts, skills, abilities, competences, the range of educational interventions tend to reify power: that is, to turn it into an object which can be

(semiotically, pedagogically, institutionally, psychologically) deconstruct-
ed and pedagogically reassembled and transmitted" (1996, 321).

As Luke argues, these types of notions of power that rest solely in terms
of control of text types actually match well with traditionalist, instrumental approaches. What is achieved, then, is a "purely instrumental and
technical (and hence economically beneficial) terminology" that depo-
liticizes notions of culture and curriculum rather than explicates their
political workings and ramifications (1996, 325). Luke's position, where
genres are "political sites of contest," is very different from what I see as
the dominant Oz model: all one needs is one pair of dress shoes for the
"power culture" ball, click the heels, and then go anywhere at any time.
What Malcolm and his classmates thus need is not a demonstration of
how to take apart the genres of their disciplines so that they can readily
reproduce them but an approach, "a critical social theory of practice,"
that centers examinations of how and why a particular writer did what he
or she did, when, and why (332). In this way, writing becomes a "social
strategy" located in a particular history and network of power relations
that students can and often will choose to participate in (333).

"CAN'T GET ON THE RIGHT SIDE OF IT": CONTINUING THE REVISION STAGE—OLD GENRE PRESCRIPTIONS AND NEW INVENTIONS

It was the students majoring in the social sciences who made me think
back on the events and activities in the course that had supported the
kinds of writing that students like Malcolm were undertaking in their
research papers. Yet, it was also these students who made me think more
about how the genre of the research paper takes shape and shapes writing
and thinking.

The social science students all seemed very interested in the topics
they had chosen for themselves. The topics of their papers in Comp II
were the same as the topics they were doing for their social science classes.
While I thought there were obvious connections to the writing they were
doing in both classes, none of them seemed to think so. The only connections they saw were the APA format requirements. Ideally, I had hoped
that students would use the space of our composition course to write an-
depth paper for their social science work. I even argued that the carrot
to this approach would be the "killing of two birds with one stone," so
to speak. None of the students, however, chose to do this. The students
wrote completely different papers. There was nothing explicitly stated in

the requirements of their social science papers that matched what I saw as the traditional research paper format in its collection of a detached list of "facts." Yet the students wrote exactly these types of essays for their social science classes.

One student, George, chose to write about manic-depressive disorder. His essay for the Comp class opened with a story about his favorite and closest cousin, who became his sole support when he moved to the United States from Jamaica. All of a sudden, she had an explosively violent episode, which he described with extensive detail so the reader could grasp the terror it must have inflicted and the pain George felt watching his cousin's life: "It has been over ten years since A—— has been diagnosed with this illness, and life has continued to be a thin line between sanity and insanity for my dear cousin and, in some ways, me as well." This story and that of his family's responses never made it into his other class's paper. For our composition class, George included general information about manic depression from his other paper but he also used online sources for his composition research paper derived from large health organizations. His paper also included information about support groups and descriptions of the current research and controversies in the field where he discussed his own opinions and experiences. While it may seem positive that George satisfied the expectations of his other course with the writing that he submitted, that writing represented a "non-form of writing"(Larson 1982) that did not allow him to engage the multiple and competing perspectives in the field. His accumulation of facts for his social science paper was so general and inconsequential as to make the content almost juvenile. What he produced, in fact, did not represent the type of discourses and research methods that are currently happening in his field and his writing in our composition course clearly indicated that he was more than ready to do as much.

I link George's paper here to the ideal of research in the late nineteenth century, which created what David Russell has called a very "narrow view of the production of written knowledge" for the modern-day university (1991, 72). He links these early writing models to an Enlightenment project whose goal was to present "an unproblematic recording of the facts in correct language" (73). Knowledge consisted in one form that could be readily sought and replicated, not socially negotiated and changing. Though Russell's work describes the history of the late nineteenth century, George's paper for the social science course makes me suspect that some contemporary classrooms may be no different in the ways in which fact and expression are regulated, ways that were interestingly and not coincidentally designed at a time when his presence at the American university would have been "legally" barred under the same Enlightenment project.

Russell also documents the way that this early research ideal influenced the infamous research paper and as such, has played a central role in mass education today. In this new model of the research paper, the professor represented a disciplinary community with the student as the disciple. However, this research paper industry was itself created at this moment when the research ideal was expanded alongside a large, more impersonal university where students were not expected to draft and revise their papers and faculty did not discuss the social processes and methods of writing in their courses. As the research paper became a routine, the focus moved away from an apprentice model to a mode of production. Knowledge in the disciplines was not regarded as politically constructed and actively situated by conflicting social agents. Thus, the research paper as a genre was really akin almost to an exam—students were simply expected to display facts that they had learned and not enter the "rhetorical universe of a discipline" and thus, the emphasis was on form, length, and sources (1991, 91). Given the responses of students like Alice and Nellie, it would seem that very little has changed in more than fifty years of faculty assigning and grading research papers. Russell goes on to further document the work of George Arms in 1943, whose examination of textbooks' model papers gave examples where no writing had a communicative or rhetorical purpose outside of the classroom or addressed a problem that did not have clear-cut, ready-made, and factual solutions. What is interesting, then, about my social science student George's paper is that he turned a serious issue, one that was complex and situated for him, along with his acute awareness of his audience and purposes for writing, into exactly the same kind of paper for his social science class that Arms was reading and critiquing decades ago. One can't help but wonder what Arms would say if he knew this kind of paper that he abhorred all those years ago got George an A today.

Rhonda was another student who was working on a research paper for her social science class who wrote a very similar paper to George's and also received an A. Her topic was incest. She knew early on that this would be her topic for both courses. I assumed that she would want to use the same paper for both classes and offered her the option. Like George, however, she did not do this. Her social science paper focused mostly on

the prevalence of incest in statistical terms and ended with two concluding paragraphs: one on the psychological trauma incest inflicts on families, another on the kinds of therapy available to survivors. Although she
described her paper for the composition class as interesting, the paper
for her other class was something she said she could "not seem to get on
the right side of." She came to talk to me particularly about the issue of
how she was instructed to create the social science paper. She needed
an introduction paragraph with a thesis statement that named her three
arguments. In her body she could have one argument that could be
extensive while the other two arguments could be confined to one paragraph each. This formula confused her. She understood it, but for some
reason she found herself struggling to get it down on paper. In the end,
this paper consisted of very different explorations and conclusions form
her composition paper, which focused on female survivors who have used
writing and social consciousness to combat and heal histories of incest
both socially and individually.

After Rhonda submitted her draft, I noticed that she was absent from
class for a few days. This was very much unlike her so I assumed she must
be really sick. I didn't, however, place a call or e-mail to her at that point.
I also didn't get a chance to read the pile of drafts from students until a
week later. She had, I now believe, prodded me to find out my reactions,
just as Malcolm had done, but I didn't really get it at the time. In her
process and reflective writing that I assigned with the submission of the
draft, she wrote about getting carried away with "the story" at the beginning of the paper. She felt she spent too much time there and that she
needed to analyze the writers more. I reminded her that it was just a draft
and that we would have to sit down and look at this together and decide
what she might do.

"The story" that she was warning me about was a recounting of moving in with her mother, who had left her with her grandmother until
she could find work, at the age of eight. "A real hell started" when her
stepfather began to molest her. Rhonda screamed in agony one day and a
neighbor heard her cry and came to the house. The stepfather, realizing
his trespasses would no longer be allowed, accused Rhonda of trying to
stab him soon after. She was then sent back to live with her grandmother.
This is where "her story" ends. At this point in her paper, she moved
abruptly into four paragraphs in which she discussed four authors' experiences with incest. It was as if she were playing it safe and using the same
strategy that she was instructed to use in her social science class.

I had suspected that Rhonda was an incest survivor all along but had not expected that she would situate herself and her experiences in her writing in this way. On the back of each of the twelve pages of her "story," I wrote her a note where I commented as to how her writing had impacted me and connected to my own personal "story." I made sure to communicate clearly that my bottom line was that she need not stop "her story" but go deeper into looking at it and the role her own writing had in that process (she had described herself as a writer and as someone who needed it in her life on the very first day of class). I told her that I liked where she was going with her analysis of the women writers/survivors. If she so chose, I thought she could make this be a central focus as a crucial variable in how female incest survivors have opened a space for this type of sexual oppression to be dealt with socially. But most important, I really wanted her to make sure that this was a paper that she would be able to "get on the right side of" in terms of the way she was shaping her arguments and purposes rather than following some arbitrary formula. I thought she should continue to situate herself and her own healing in these writers' stories by constantly asking, and thus writing: What am I learning about myself by reading these women—what are the similarities and differences? How does it impact me and my memories to read this— when and where in the text do these responses occur for me? Where does this all take me? Where does this take me as a writer? What does this mean for women writers generally? What does this show about the psychological and social aspects of incest?

The morning that I did finally read Rhonda's draft, I made a mental note to call her if she did not show up for class. She did come to class that day and I apologized that I had not read her work earlier and that I supported everything she was doing in her writing. The following day we met again to talk about her other incest paper, the one she said she couldn't write. Mostly she asked me for ways to organize it "better" because she just did not like it at all (and still doesn't, though she scored high on it). Had Rhonda's paper in the composition class made the seemingly "objective" nature of her other paper more difficult? What are the consequences when students are not really interrogating the personal and instead just present the "factual" information, even though they are deeply connected to what they are writing about? When I think back on Rhonda's two papers, I can't help but think about the two very distinct titles. One essay was called "Incest and Treatment." The other was "Surviving to Write: A Story of Women Who Determined Their Destiny." I am struck by how nested form, content, and the social analyses of the personal really are. In Rhonda's paper for her social science class, she did not find a space in the confines of that genre that would allow her to examine writing and social issues of gender oppression in relation to the topic of incest. Just like George, her conclusions about "treatment" for incest survivors were very narrowly and minimally defined (not even mirroring what actually exists and is discussed in the literature of the discipline), as it had to be contextualized within a narrow range of writing options.

It seems to me that what we often do in the name of the research paper buries more possibilities than it unearths. Exploring a multiplicity of genres, then, encompasses more than just offering numerous modalities. It expands our understandings of the problems and solutions that our fields can offer at the same time that it can sometimes uncover intersections of identity, social structures, and writing. Ironically, Nellie and Alice, two of the most resistant students I have met, have reaffirmed my commitment to situating the politics of writing, genre, and academic work. Their resistance to rethinking the genre of the research paper and their identity as writers was mixed in complicated ways. Perhaps an approach that prompts an interrogation of those identities will encourage them to "unearth more," a process that I now believe may have been more fruitful for them that I initially thought.

Neither of them has fared well at the university due to the very issues surrounding race, class, and identity that were there on the surface when we met. Nellie, as it ends up, dropped out the semester after we met as her oldest son was being pushed into special education and was very angry with her. Ironically, I know about all of this today because she visits me intermittently, not to discuss her being better than "the brown people," but to rediscuss those issues that politically, she just was not ready to face at our first meeting. Meanwhile, Alice stayed in school a little longer but eventually dropped out also. She found herself overwhelmed with having to take care of a large family whose wealth in the Caribbean was not what it once was and hence were forced to migrate to the United States. The rising costs of tuition made attending college more and more difficult for Alice, although she had a fairly well-paying full-time job. This is especially the case since she advances very little at her job, now hating how everyone moves past her on the promotion line, but telling her how much they love her "little British accent." I was floored in both cases when the students began talking to me about all of this and I am still unsure if this means I opened up a space for them that they did not find anywhere else or if I failed them miserably. Perhaps it is both. However, when I meet students like them today, I know to be more patient, to dig deeper into those places that they are reluctant to visit. Even when it seems that students would rather retreat into that comfortable "non- form of writing" that Larson describes (1982, 811), where they have to say and question very little, they are hardly safe there.

NOTES

1.   Davis and Shadle explain in their article that in a 1982 survey, 84 percent of all freshman composition courses taught the "research paper" (2000, 417).

2.   I borrow the term "auto-sociographic" from Sylvia Wynter (1981), who uses it to describe the writings of C. L. R. James, particularly regarding his text *Beyond a Boundary*. She argues that the nature of what he had experienced and the purposes of his writing required a new and different genre with which to capture this. For more about this, see Cedric Robinson's *Black Marxism: The Making of the Black Radical Tradition* (2000).

3.   I take this term "second post-Reconstruction" from Manning Marable. Scholars such as Marable regard the post-emancipation moment of Reconstruction as a major site in U.S. history where social relations would be reconstructed. Following this moment, however, came a backlash, referred to as the post-Reconstruction, which framed Jim Crow and legalized racial apartheid in the United States. The second moment of social upheaval, created by the civil rights and black power movements, is referred to as the second Reconstruction. I am here calling the current backlash in social equity the second post-Reconstruction. For more about this see Marable's anthology with Leith Mullings, *Let Nobody Turn Us Around* (1999) and his *Reform and Rebellion: The Second Reconstruction in Black America, 1945–1990* (1991).

8

THE RESUMÉ AS GENRE
A Rhetorical Foundation for First-Year Composition

T. Shane Peagler and Kathleen Blake Yancey

In the last fifteen years, questions about the role of genre in the development of writing have increasingly informed both theory and practice in the composition classroom. David Jolliffe (1996) has observed, for example, that the most frequent genre that we ask students to compose is the "genre" of the school essay, noting that too often that genre doesn't connect to the genres of life or workplace. Anne Beaufort (1999) put a face on such a claim in her landmark study, *Writing in the Real World: Making the Transition from School to Work*, which demonstrates how the genres of school don't in fact "transfer" to those of the workplace very well. At the same time, however, some genres *do* seem to operate as an interface between multiple cultures: for instance, the resumé, that document where writers represent themselves to others, in the context of carrying forward what we are now, in one site, to a new site where we may become anew. Put differently, the resumé functions, in part, to assist a writer in securing a job, and as such it is itself a site of transition, a new discursive space where writers represent their past in the context of aspirations, the future. And for students perhaps especially, the appeal of the resumé—with its seemingly obvious format, with its templates, with its slots that we only need to fill in and out—is that it seems to be such an "easy" document or writing, one grounded in rules and thus simple to author. Naturally enough, human beings tend to like rules. Rules are explicit; they signal us as to what's right and wrong; and on the basis of rules, we can create clear expectations, so we can predict what will happen to us—which is pretty comforting in a postmodern, fragmented world. Rules, in other words, can seem to make life—and writing situations—easier to navigate.

By definition, however, writing isn't rule bound, but rather convention governed, rhetorical, even (perhaps particularly) when it comes to writing a resumé. Thus, the resumé, precisely because of the common misperceptions surrounding it, provides an interesting rhetorical site for composition instruction. Students often think that if we just give them the slots, they can fill them in—and as an emblem of writing, if we allow such misperceptions to continue, the picture of writing that students create will likewise be fundamentally flawed. In English classes, it's all *just rhetorical* (with the negative baggage that expression entails), but in the real world—the world where writing gets something done!—it's by the rulebook, after all. If, on the other hand, we introduced the resumé as a genre—with Shane teaching the class and Kathleen participating as an external reviewer—we thought we could articulate some of these misperceptions and address them. In such an approach, we also thought that we could address some of the identity issues that accompany any practice in genre. As Freedman and Medway point out (1994, 14–16), discursive practices position certain forms of identity that can be at odds with the identity of the student, and in the case of the resumé, there is the tension between the still-in-formation student and the fully formed professional. As a genre, the resumé would allow us to speak to that tension in helpful ways. Not least, we hoped that the attention to rhetorical situation that we would build in would provide a central concept that would lead to and frame the rest of the course. Including the resumé, then, seemed to offer considerable promise: as a task, as a site for identity construction, as a way of understanding.

How we might go about such instruction and with what result: these are the questions we address in the following chapter.

THE RESUMÉ AS GENRE: WHY AND HOW

Like other genres, resumés are a means of social action, as Carolyn Miller (1984) suggested twenty years ago. And as Joe Comprone (1993) explains, any genre is itself the place where writers balance two sets of needs at least: on the one hand, the needs of a writer to express an intent; on the other, the needs of one or more audiences. Somehow, Comprone says, we must balance these competing needs.[1] To illustrate this argument, he briefly outlines the resumé as a genre of social action, arguing that the key is to balance the impulse for personal expression with the needs of a socially constructed world. "It is useful to think of writing not as entirely socially or individually motivated, but as a mode of discourse particularly suited to learning how to manage information, ideas, conventions, and intentions. Only with effective management techniques can individuals use writing to find and place their voices in the ongoing conversations that are generated by rhetorical situations; only with effective management techniques can individuals use writing to change the direction of these conversations.

The concept of genre can be an effective means of approaching the strategies for directing this management process" (106).

Comprone further suggests that the resumé is an ideal genre to teach: through the concept and the practice of genre, writers complete a writing task and understand more generally about the art and practice of composing itself. He suggests, in other words, that the resumé, precisely because it is an overlooked and untheorized genre, provides a particularly interesting introduction to both the construct and the processes of writing. That was our hope as well, as we used an approach founded on genre as a means of introducing writing, rhetoric, and genre to a class of English 102 students.

Clemson's English 102 course is very like other English 102 classes around the country: it asks students to read carefully; to interpret and evaluate research of various kinds; and to write to and from that research, often within the genre of the academic argument. Our new unit on the resumé as genre, then, needed to "fit" with these general outcomes, which it would do, we thought, if we used it explicitly and early on to introduce both the idea and practice of genre. In fact, we thought as a writing task, the resumé would provide an excellent introduction to the course. Specifically, it could locate our vocabulary of writing—writing, processes, practice, genre, rhetorical situation, and so on—and it could highlight in particular the rhetorical situation and how every writing, even the apparently formulaic resumé, is situated within and informed by it. This last point merits some explanation. Because they appear so formulaic, much like the ubiquitous five-paragraph "theme," resumés are understood as mechanical texts; give me the slots, students say, and we'll fill them in. Interestingly, seen this way, not only are they not Carolyn Miller's genre as social action, but they are also not rhetorical in the simplest terms. Intended to secure a job, they aren't written *in the context of* any rhetorical situation. The person who might read the resumé and the need of the employing institution (be it school, lab, government, or firm) for certain kinds of employees: these are absent for most students. In other words, writing the resumé, for many, is a fundamentally *arhetorical* activity.

To help students rewrite that (mis)understanding, to help them see that resumés are rhetorical, we adapted two concepts borrowed from Gunther Kress (1999a, 86–88): critique and design. In terms of critique, we focused on analysis, asking students to gather resumés, read them, and review them together, in part to make the point (experientially) that resumés do vary. No template will suffice. And because students themselves gathered the materials of the exercise and conducted the work, the insights likewise belonged to them. And as a principle of design, we built in a reiteration: we asked students to recategorize the resumés, looking at them from another vantage point: what does the reiteration teach us about resumé-as-genre? In other words, though this iterative analysis, students "invented" their own genre of resumé as well as some of the more general conceptual understandings of genre. With this foundation created, students then "designed" their own resumés. Such was the logic of our curriculum, or, in another language, the "delivered" curriculum.[2] Within the framework of the syllabus, the resumé was the first formal assignment, and it counted, as did the other formal assignments, for 15 percent of the final grade. Students also created a culminating digital portfolio, worth 20 percent of the grade. From their work samples, their portfolios, and their reflections, we have learned about the "experienced" curriculum: what, after all, did students learn in this approach?

TEACHING THE RESUMÉ AS A GENRE: THE CLASSROOM CONTEXT

The term began with an introduction to rhetoric; thus, before beginning with the resumé, Shane maintained a dual focus. On one hand, he introduced his class to the basic concepts of classical rhetoric, using Aristotle as a touchstone for his teaching. The students engaged in discussion, classroom activities, and homework assignments related to ethos, pathos, logos, as well as the concepts behind the rhetorical triangle, and as is the case with most of Shane's students, many commented that this was their first exposure to such ideas about communication.

To introduce students to genre, Shane used several classroom and homework assignments where students examined persuasion in the context of different "types" of writing such as newspaper editorials, Web pages, poems, and academic papers. This allowed him to introduce the basic idea of genre as well as the ways writers use different genres to communicate both in school and outside of it. At the end of week two, Shane also used a class period to discuss the formal concept of genre, pointing out that the previous week's assignments called for the students to explore a variety of genres with which they were already familiar. This familiarity with "real-world" genres invited students to contrast their new understanding of genre with their previous experiences with the concept—which often involved associating it with static literary tropes instead of with active, rhetorical endeavors.

In the midst of this discussion, a clear pattern emerged: most students were using the discussion of genre as a means of disparaging their experiences in high school English courses. Many felt that a central problem with their past English instruction was that they were either asked to study passively a specific genre, such as the sonnet, so as to "fix" it, or they were asked to mimic a genre and create a work consistent with the "rules" governing the genre. Not surprisingly, students associated this discussion of genre with their own struggles in conforming to other generic "rules" such as those governing the five-paragraph essay. In examining their past experiences, the students realized that most of their work had been constructed as a result of a prescriptive definition of genre. This, then, was the remembered curriculum of genre that students brought with them into class. Asking students to articulate it allowed Shane to use that context as he pointed out the differences between the students' experience with genre and the more rhetorical one that would inform this writing class.

My three most interesting communities are Work, Family, and Friends. I navigate within my Work community differently in each of the jobs I have had. When I was a soccer referee, I had to talk a specific way to each of the different kinds of people I encountered. This included other refs I was working with, team coaches, players, and spectators. In my Family community, I give a certain kind of respect and love to different members. Sometimes, I can talk to my brother and sister in a different way than I can anyone else, and they understand things about me better. Some things are easy to discuss with my parents, and some are not. I understand some of their knowledge and what I must know when talking to them. My friends group is split into people from Clemson (that I more recently met) and older friends from Maryland (where I moved from). I spend more time with my Clemson friends, but my Maryland friends know a lot more about me and we go farther back. I have known and trust them longer, and these reasons mean I can tell them certain things and talk in a way with them that only we might understand. I know them more, and I therefore can tailor my discourse with them specific to this.

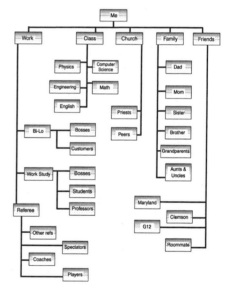

Another key lesson involved helping students understand discourse communities. Again, to draw on the students' own experiences, Shane asked them to create two representations of their discourse communities:

a verbal explanation and a visual map. As the example above suggests, when asked, students are quite articulate—both visually and verbally—in locating the social spaces of their communicative lives. What's also interesting is how students understand the relationship between and among the many factors in rhetorical situations: audience, broken down into *the different kinds of people;* what the audience knows—*their knowledge;* attitude, here of *love and respect;* familiarity, as with some family members like a *brother* and *sister;* and *ease* of topic.

With these kinds of activities and discussions as a backdrop, we began the resumé.

RESUMÉ ASSIGNMENT: THE CRITIQUE AND DESIGN OF THE DELIVERED CURRICULUM

The analytical part of the resumé assignment was divided into three parts. First, students were asked to locate five resumés from within their field of study. These ranged from engineering to nursing to art, and the resumés could be found online or obtained from mentors or advisors at the university or in the private sector. The students were then randomly placed in groups of five, with each group asked to coauthor a single review of all of the combined resumés. More specifically, students were asked to begin by reading all of the resumés from the group, looking for textual features that were of interest, either unique to certain resumés or consistent across all resumés, "textual features" referring here to anything on the page the students found relevant, from style to format to specific content or punctuation. As the students read, they were asked to compile their own list of salient features from each resumé. As the students finished with their own reviews, they were asked then to discuss their "findings" with the group, compiling a collaborative section where they consolidated their analysis.

The second part of the analysis assignment asked students to reorganize the resumés and place them in new categories of their own choosing. The students could invent their own categories here, based on the individual's major, college, interest, or potential job. In some cases, the students chose to organize the resumés based on layout and design. Other students chose to divide the resumés along stylistic lines. Yet other students chose to examine the stylistic choices made by individuals from certain colleges on campus. Most of the students in this particular class were from engineering or the sciences, and thus we wanted to resist the impulse for students to say "all engineering resumés are the same." Rather, students were asked to look beyond the discipline associated with

the particular resumé to examine the way that resumé functioned rhetorically. Here we provided some basic questions such as: In what ways is each
of your categories different? In what ways are these categories similar?
What do the resumés in each category tell us about the field they are
associated with?

The culminating part of the analysis assignment asked students to
make the connect between resumé and rhetorical situation: how, students
were asked, do the textual features you identified in the first part of the
analysis work within a rhetorical situation between a writer and audience?
How is meaning made in this situation? What do these textual features tell
us about the culture of the job market? In composing this collaborative
class exercise, our hope was that students would acquire knowledge and
critical distance that they would bring to the construction of their own
resumés.

Which—in the context of a writing classroom—is where it actually
matters, in the design phase of the curriculum. To help students with the
design task, we created a specific protocol.

- First, students were to locate an actual job listing.
- Second, they were asked to construct their own resumés based on the job
  listing.
- Third, the students were then asked to review their own resumés as well as
  the resumés from their peers in the class.
- And last, they were asked to revise their work and submit it.

In many ways, this process mirrors what we often do in writing courses,
whether they be business or first-year composition. Two features of the
assignment, however, seem unusual, at least in our experience and in that
of our students, if their accounts are accurate. First, we required students
to locate a real job that represented in some way their own professional
aspirations; this of course provided a rhetorical situation for the resumé.
(The class is, of course, the principal rhetorical situation, but the resumé
isn't targeted to the class but to the job and the person doing the hiring.)
Second, we used Kathleen as an expert external reviewer. She visited in
order to give a "reading" of the students' work, based in part on her experience as a member of several diverse hiring committees—in the academy
but outside it as well, involving faculty, Web designers, engineers, lead
administrators, architects, and executive directors. She visited on the day
the first drafts were due, and she read the resumés of three student volunteers, using a reflective reading practice not unlike a read-aloud protocol.

With the resumé projected on the screen, she reviewed each of the three resumés, commenting on what she understood from each, verbalizing the inferences and interpretations she was making as she read them, and explaining why she was drawing these conclusions. Our intent was that this "live" review by an expert of sorts would dramatize how resumés are rhetorical, enacting a social role and purpose.

With this modeling and with a fairly conventional peer review, students revised their resumés and submitted both copies with a reflection that asked students to respond to seven questions:

- What did you learn about the resumé?
- What did you learn about genre?
- Was that what you expected to learn? Explain.
- What was the hardest part about this unit?
- What was most interesting?
- How will your writing change because of what you've learned?
- Anything else?

THE RESUMÉ AS GENRE: THE EXPERIENCED CURRICULUM

When we review the resumés and the reflections from this class of twenty students, we learn as much as they. Specifically, students' observations fall into three categories:

- how surprising they found this approach, based on their earlier experiences
- how they used this approach in creating their own resumés and what they learned from it
- how difficult and yet useful they found the concepts and language associated with this approach

As explained earlier, teaching the resumé as a genre allowed students to revisit concepts they believed they already knew; this theme appeared in several student reflections. Several students, for instance, remarked that they found their earlier conception of genre too limited, but that they liked the "new" concept of genre and found it useful as a theoretical frame. And the earlier conceptions of genre included references both in and out of school: while often they were out of school—several students, for instance, thought of genre as a way to categorize types of movies—most of the observations were squarely located in school practices, and of those, most were reading rather than writing practices. For example, one student remarked, "I have learned about genre since fourth grade, but this put it in an entirely different perspective. All I used to be taught was what the word 'genre' means and different types of genre (like short story, essay, novel, etc.)" (Vanzo). Similarly, another made the connection to classical literature, and in particular to the language appropriate there: "I had always been told that genre referred to poetry and other classical literature. I was unaware of the fact that resumés could be a genre in themselves. [In this class] I also learned that every genre can have its own particular language style. Previously I was only exposed to flowery, Shakespearian language from my AP English teacher, and that was what I thought that everything you wrote in an English class should sound like, no matter what it was actually for" (Haynes).

What it was actually for, of course, is another way to talk about the rhetorical situation. For many students, using genre to talk about writing was a good thing: it brought to the use of language a kind of flexibility and rhetoricity that students sometimes had already intuited and that most of them appreciated.

The resumé itself was also located in familiar experience, and as in the case of genre as a concept, this was not altogether good news. Many students had written resumés in English classes previously, and for all of our students with this experience, it was an exercise in formula. The following comment summarizes nicely that common experience: "I took a course in high school that taught us how to write a resume, and they made it seem like every resume had the exact same elements in the exact same order. In this class we also addressed what the layout and word choice in your resumé says about you, and I had never been told about those things as part of the process of making a good resumé" (Haynes).

In general, what seemed to be missing, from the students' accounts of their previous experience, at least, was a *process* of making a good resumé. Or, they believed, if there is a process, it is completely formatted and mechanical: "I had done units on resumés before in high school but my teachers never took this approach to them. In high school the teachers mostly took a rubric approach where I was taught that this, this and this, need to be [on] a resumé and it was not a good resumé unless you had them" (Bingham).

School isn't the sole culprit, however, and it's equally possible that teachers presented guidelines and conventions, and students interpreted those as rules.[3] Even when school isn't invoked, however, the mechanistic nature of writing, and of the resumé particularly, is the unspoken context of writing:

I honestly expected that there was one and only one way to write a resumé, and that we would learn this correct way and the lesson would be finished; however, I learned that the structure and content of a resumé is more based on yourself, your accomplishments, and the job you are trying to obtain. Before, I never really thought of the resumé as such an important and persuasive document. I thought that if your experience and credentials were significant enough that it would not matter how you ordered or styled them. I now know that this is not true. I now realized that the structure and design of a resumé is an argument in itself. (Adams)

A NEW PROCESS

Since their earlier experiences were not a good index to the current composing situation, students needed to develop a new process. Not surprisingly, the process involved both analysis and design. For instance, several students talked about the role of the resumé analysis assignment in shaping their sense of what is possible in a resumé: "The hardest part of this unit was probably having to find the resumés and go through and critic [*sic*] them individually. I had a difficult time finding resumés to begin with, and then once I did find them I was not really sure what I was looking for. I also knew that my resumé was not set up anything like any of the ones that I saw, and they looked a lot better and more professional to me then mine did" (Haynes).

Another moment that over half the students found valuable was the external review: "The most interesting thing was when Dr. Yancey came to speak. She was very informative, and she was telling us things that will be helpful to us for a long time. No one else had ever pointed out to me that you could tailor your resumé for the particular job you were applying for, and she helped me to see the sense in that and how helpful it can be to your chances of getting a job" (Haynes).

The student here, like many, found valuable both the how—*you could tailor your resumé for the particular job you were applying for*—and the why—*she helped me to see the sense in that.* Without this how and why, it's easy to understand why students see resumés—and writing more generally—as they do: in part, because genre itself is presented as a static entity rather than as a participant in a recurring social situation, in part because they never actually see or hear anyone reading *their* work. Without an audience whose reading they have seen or heard and thus might be able to project, without a genre that permits tailoring, it's all too easy to think of writing as a message not to be constructed, but only to be delivered.

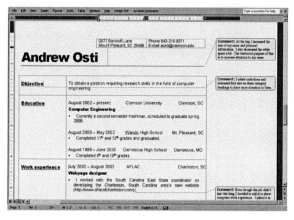

In drafting, all students were to take peer response and use it to improve their original drafts. Likewise, all students were required to submit two copies of the resumé, the before and after version. And most students, because we are a laptop campus, submitted a revised version that was annotated. The changes that they made included every dimension of the resumé, from amount of information and arrangement to font size and style and use of white space. As interesting is what they learned—about process, resumés, and genre—and why they made the changes they did.

In some cases, students created a new composing process for themselves, one requiring invention, and the invention itself is focused on both self and audience. "I have discovered that the resumé is not just a boring document that can be slapped together in a few minutes. It requires a good deal of effort and critical thinking. I learned that in order to make a resumé, you need to do invention to come up with a detailed list of all activities or discourse communities that you belong to. Then, you must determine which of those are relevant to your resumé. I also learned the importance of textual features in a resumé. Textual features play a huge role in the effectiveness and persuasiveness of a resumé" (Coonce).

Many valued what they had learned about themselves relative to the world represented by professional resumés: they found that the inventional process used to create a resumé was a useful heuristic for understanding the self: "From the past few weeks of lessons, I have not only learned a lot about resumés but also about myself. I have deeply considered my attributes and achievements, and how I could best present these to a potential employer to obtain a certain job" (Adams).

And in some cases, such an analysis helps students project into the future:

The hardest part about this unit was writing my own resumé. Since I am young and have very little job experience it was hard to find qualifications to put on the resumé. During my high school days I mostly concentrated on school work and had little time or need to get a job until late in my junior year and it, of course, had nothing to do with the field I plan on going into after college. I hope to get an internship or coop while at Clemson in order to gain some experience before I get out into the work force. I know if I do not get some sort of internship it will be very difficult to get a job with no experience. (Bingham)

And of course for other students, this projection can be ambiguous, uncertain, and anxiety producing: "Another difficult part was choosing a job to apply for. We were told to pick a job in our major or our area of interest. Well, this is a subject that is currently up in the air for me. I have no idea what I want to do for the rest of my life, and I am currently feeling a lot of pressure to decide as I approach my second year at Clemson" (Lee).

That's hard, of course, but it can also be a means of thinking about the future, a chance to rehearse a role.

More generally, another value of this assignment is that it crosses boundaries—from *high school days* to *Clemson* to an *internship* to the *workforce*—while it teaches central concepts and practices. And, as important, the resumé can function as a vehicle for professional self-analysis, and as a school document, it can function to represent and shape that out-of-school future: "Thinking back to the beginning of the semester I'm not sure what I was expecting to learn. One thing I know, I wasn't expecting to learn about resumés and writing resumés. I thought that this was much farther in the future [and I didn't need] to be thinking about it now. I realized that I need to start getting my resumé together because a resumé is something that is going to build over time and although now it may not be very impressive in a few years it probably will be" (Pohlman).

And, as hoped, many students claim that what they learned from this assignment has transferred to their writing more generally. "My construction of a resumé has changed greatly as seen by the alterations I made since Dr. Yancey's lecture. My writing in general has also changed due to our original discussion of ethos, pathos, logos, and discourse communities. The idea of sitting down and thinking about who your audience is and what they respond to before writing will now become a necessary part of my writing process" (Lee).

Some students cited specific examples of this transfer. One commented on rewriting a letter requesting an audition for a position as a placekicker on Clemson's football team and on keying to the audience specifically. And in some cases students make the connection between many different kinds of audiences in talking about the role of audience generally:

> Probably the biggest aspect I came to change (and improve) in my writing is the realization and understanding of the audience. I never used to pay attention to the audience I was writing to. I would just write my argument, pretty much ignoring everything else. In this class, we were taught to use invention to persuade. In order to use invention, all available means of persuasion for any given situation have to be understood. Our audience is a very important aspect to understand when persuading or arguing. For example, you wouldn't want to use slang or talk the same way you do to your friends if you are writing a letter to the president of a company or organization (this also relates back to the Discourse Communities assignment). You can see in Project 2 and Project 3 how I wrote in letter format. This is because they were each directed to a politician. I didn't want to write to a general public (ex. "All highway drivers" or "All American people") because these people can't do anything about the problem. I wrote specifically to politicians who can propose/pass a bill or vote to make a change. Considering my audience has brought another aspect to all of my papers, in and out of English class. In this lab report, written this semester for my Engineering 120 class, I noticed myself constantly thinking about my audience. I would say to myself things like, "Would my professor want me to say this?" or "Would this wording be appropriate here?" I took into account the way supporting graphs, as instructed by the professor, should go near the text that refer to them. The headers and most of the wording are also good examples of this. I wouldn't talk to most of my friends using the same words I did in this report. (Osti)

THE ROLE OF GENRE

Genre, as used in this approach, means both practice and concept. But over and over again, what students told us was that the concepts were new, were difficult, and were worthwhile.

Early on, students understood that genre has a wider definition than they'd understood: "I learned that genre does not just refer to types of books. Genre can be anything that is reoccurring in our composition. Before this class the thought of a resumé being a genre had never really occurred to me." And they were able to use this concept to ground other genres and to see them as social action as well: "This English 102 class has helped me to realize that a letter is not just a letter; it is a way of conveying your ideas to someone and getting them to act on those ideas" (Haynes).[4] And students were able, as well, to see in genre the flexibility that is rhetorical: "I learned that a genre describes a certain style of writing. It gives a broad definition of what format or tone should be used. However, it does not provide a template for you to just fill in. It is still vague and open to a variety of interpretations" (Coonce).

To be accurate, not all students found writing a resumé interesting or engaging: "To be honest, I found the actual discussion of resumé quite boring because it dealt with things that could be understood easily through common sense." But, according to the same student, the ideas matter: "The ideas underneath the surface that you were trying to teach us through the use of the resumé genre were the interesting ones." They were also, for some students, both unfamiliar and difficult: "The hardest part about this unit was the terminology. Learning new terms and ideas and being able to recall these terms in order to describe writing was difficult. Although it may have been difficult, I enjoyed learning about these things, being able to better express myself, and using them to more fully understand writing" (Coonce).

Synthesized neatly by one student, there was a lot to be learned:

What did I learn about genre? For all intensive purposes [*sic*] I have come up with a definition of genre in the case of our resumé building. I now think of genre as a rhetorical way of presenting information and/or facts such that it will have the effect planned or hoped. This is exactly what we did with the resumés (or were supposed to do). I learned that organization of information can be a key factor with different jobs, and that can also serve as the dividing boundary between information provided in a vacuum, and information provided that makes a person stand out.

Was this what I expected to learn? With respect to resumés, yes. I fully understand that one of the goals of this class is to change my method of thinking (if even in the slightest degree), and this assignment facilitated that process. With respect to English 102, this is not what I expected. I do not see my friends in their respective engl 102 classes working on resumés, which is bad for them. I view this class now as more of an application of English in the real world (i.e. resumés). (Krenson)

One test of whether this approach is useful, of course, is whether students can use these resumés in an intended rhetorical context; two students mentioned that they were doing just that, and one of them raised a technological issue that we will address in the future. As he narrates, "the first resumé is pretty plain looking. It lists my on campus address which probably isn't a good idea because that is going to change rela-

tively quickly. Additionally, it spills over to a second page, making it look somewhat unprofessional and cheap. Being in Microsoft Word format is also probably not a very good thing, since it could be incompatible with some systems and word is notorious for carrying viruses so it my deter some people from even opening it. Also, I neglected to list some of my better achievements and awards."

The second version, he says, required him to return and rethink, using what he had learned in the first draft.

> In this class I was able to formalize and sharpen both my understanding and use of these concepts. By this I mean that I learned not only the official terms but gained experience applying them to different situations. For example, the resumé project was interesting in forcing me to apply rhetorical skills to something that I don't enjoy. Unlike web sites and papers on topics I enjoy writing about, I found writing my resumé to be dreadfully boring and uninteresting. Consequently, I can honestly say that I just threw my paper together without much thought. However, later in the year I found myself having to assemble a real resumé for several internship opportunities. I went back to the resumé I created for the first paper and realized that, rhetorically speaking, it was not suited for the position I was looking for. So I went back to it and re-designed it, this

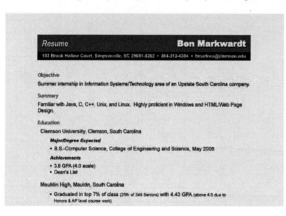

time using my enhanced understanding of rhetoric to make a better argument. As you can see, this version of my resumé is far more visually appeasing and better organized. To an employer looking for interns, this resumé not only fits the job description better but the added visuals dramatically increase my ethos and hints at other talents in addition to programming.

CONCLUSION

In *Collision Course* (1999), Russel Durst tracks the competing agendas of students and faculty in first-year composition studies classrooms. Durst's composition students want practical help; Durst's colleagues—along with many in the profession—want theory and critique as well. It's another version of the theory/practice divide, with faculty on one side, students on another, finding in first-year composition a site for a conflict between two impulses: on the one hand, students' "instrumentalism," and on the other, faculty theorizing. Durst's curricular reply to this tension is what he calls "reflective instrumentalism," which, he says, "preserves the intellectual rigor and social analysis of current pedagogies without rejecting the pragmatism of most . . . students. Instead, the approach accepts students' pragmatic goals, offers to help them achieve their goals, but adds a reflective dimension that, while itself useful in the work world, also helps students place their individual aspirations in the larger context necessary for critical analysis" (178).

In some ways, we have used an analogous approach. Appreciating students' interest in writing beyond the academy, we at the same time resist an instrumental approach that, we believe, is at odds with student growth and development as well as with what we know about writing. The addition of "reflective" to such instrumentalism, in our case, means that writing is useful, that it is conceptual and theoretical, that it allows both faculty and students to learn through reflection and in the exercise of writing.

In our resumé-as-genre approach, we focused on the concept and practice of genre within a rhetorical situation. Instead of looking to explain genres by talking about them in abstraction or by reference only to literary texts, or even only to texts in popular culture, we talked with students about genres operating in specific social situations and as rhetorical actions. We provided a definition of genre that functions as a strategy for responding to a reader in a specific context. And we asked: What happens when we start to think about a resumé in this fashion?

We moved away from the prescriptive notion of genre, so common to students, one where a genre is a document whose slots need only to be filled, primarily because it is not dynamic but static, and where the author is merely someone who inputs information. Rather, the resumé, as a genre, invites the author to make conscious, rhetorical choices, to question the nature of the genre, and to become an active participant in the social construction of the document.

For us, this was a novel exercise, and we have learned much: how what students bring with them influences what they can and will learn; about the value of building a curriculum that includes analysis and design woven together; about letting students hear and see a real reader outside of the teacher who is reading for that rhetorical purpose; about asking students to review, generalize from, and comment on what they are learning; about the power of the concept of genre as well as the practice. For most students, likewise, this was a novel exercise: the resumé, which had been merely a form, became a text with multiple dimensions—audience and genre, of course, along with typography and arrangement and information and tone. For most students, it provided a window into the curriculum of writing: the language and practices of inventing and representing the self for an audience.

And for some of them, it has already moved beyond this first classroom iteration as it connects rhetorically to other worlds: "I have already used this outside of English class. I applied for a summer job with this resumé, and feel my chances of getting the job are increased due to the rhetorical decisions I made" (Osti).

NOTES

1. This balance between representing self and attending to the needs of others is a common refrain for first-year students: see Yancey 1998, *Reflection in the Writing Classroom.*

2. For a thorough discussion of three curricula—the lived, the delivered, and the experienced—see Yancey 2004, *Teaching Literature as Reflective Practice.*

3. See Harris 1979 for a still-useful description of the kinds of conventions students "translate" into rules.

4. And, as our editors remind us, a letter is not a letter is not a letter: that Melissa Haynes here identifies *letter* as a genre is the good news, that she does not disambiguate letter types the less good. Such an observation suggests the value of a discussion about the role that genre might play as the central unifying concept in English studies today.

PART THREE

Mixing Media, Evolving Genres

9

TEACHING AND LEARNING A MULTIMODAL GENRE IN A PSYCHOLOGY COURSE

Chris M. Anson
Deanna P. Dannels
Karen St. Clair

Increasingly, teachers in courses across a range of disciplines are creating assignments that involve the intersection of oral and written genres. In the past, when pedagogical literature on writing paid attention to oral communication, it did so from the perspective of the support that speaking can lend to a writer's developing text (through one-on-one tutorials, small-group peer conferencing, or reading aloud; see Brooke 1991, 1994; Gere 1990; Murray 1982; Walters 1992; Zoellner 1969). However, until very recently there has been little written on the teaching and learning of multimodal genres that involve both writing and speaking.

In this chapter, we first briefly describe and theorize new genres of communication that bring together writing and speaking in common performative events. In such events, the spoken genre depends upon or intersects with the written genre or vice versa, creating new constraints and new—and often challenging—textual and rhetorical decisions for students. We then turn to an examination of a multimodal assignment one of us (Karen) used in an undergraduate psychology course. We were especially interested in the relationship between the oral and written parts of this assignment, and in the decisions students made about what to present in each mode. In exploring this case of multimodality, we explain Karen's pedagogical rationale for the assignment, analyze the results of students' work, and, through an electronic questionnaire, consider the ways in which the students interpreted and responded to the task. In turn, the results of this descriptive analysis provided the basis for moments of reflection in which Karen considered the implications of the assignment for the further development of her teaching.

MULTIMODALITY AND HYBRID GENRES

Newly emerging technologies are giving rise to unique, blended, "hybrid," and multimodal genres of communication, what Holdstein calls "a type of generic bordercrossing" (1996, 281). In some cases, features of orality are said to be influencing written discourse, as in the rapid-fire exchanges common in Internet chat rooms or Instant Messenger–like systems (Leverenz 1997). Published essays can take the form of a printed e-mail exchange (Spooner and Yancey 1996). New technologies for visual display, such as PowerPoint and Flash Media, are altering the experience (for both speaker and audience) of conventional oratory (Yancey 2001). And information is increasingly conveyed through multiple media. The genre of the repair manual, for example, may now include written text, still and moving diagrams and pictures, brief video clips, and sound or voice, all enabled by Web-based or CD-ROM technology.

In theorizing the concept of genre in such multimodalities, we are drawn to work that rejects static or form-based conceptions of genre in favor of seeing genre in terms of its functions and actions within particular rhetorical spaces (see Anson and Dannels 2004; Miller 1984; Mountford 2001; Russell 1997). As Amy Devitt (2000) has suggested, genre is "a dynamic social construct, a changing cultural artifact with rhetorical and social functionality. . . . Developing within groups of users, the new genres are also fluid categories that reflect and reify the ideology and values of their users" (18). Genres, in other words, are context-specific manifestations of discursive and rhetorical actions that become normative through repeated use. For this reason, they often emerge as "hybrids" or blends of other genres, simultaneously realizing different forms, functions, and characteristics.

Early work on such permutations typically examined the ways in which a specific communicative event—a speech or a piece of writing—takes on characteristics of another, similar event in the same mode, blurring and blending their two sets of features. Jamieson and Campbell (1982), for example, describe a form of political eulogy that blends two broad rhetorical categories: epideictic and deliberative. The first three parts of the eulogy—acknowledging the person's death, celebrating his or her work in the past tense, and consoling those living—are epideictic in nature. The fourth, bringing the community together in the memory of the dead, is deliberative, a political call to action that focuses on the agendas or unfinished legislation of the deceased. This fourth "subgenre," Jamieson and Campbell suggest, is not a component of a traditional eulogy; it represents a further manifestation.

In classroom settings, students often must complete assignments that similarly vary from canonical forms in ways that relate to a teacher's goals, experiences, and dispositions, as well as to the subject matter at hand. Some varieties of "journal writing," for example, constrain students enough in focus, style, and audience that the writing is no longer highly expressive as conventionally defined by theorists such as Britton, et al. (1975) and Elbow (1973). Students used to journal writing in its most expressive manifestation must reorient their assumptions about the genre to match the specific classroom uses of it in each case. Similarly, students used to "saying what they think" after a moment of reflection in a classroom must learn a new variety of this genre when they are the spokesperson for a small group of three or four students, reporting on what the group "thinks" after a breakout session.

This situation becomes even more complex with the addition of different communicative modes (spoken language, written language, visual representations both moving and still, three-dimensional objects, sounds, or other phenomena). Theoretical work in social semiotics suggests we make sense of the world using multimodal resources—not simply linguistic, but pictorial, gestural, choreographical, and graphical, to name a few (Kress and van Leeuwen 1996; Kress and Threadgold 1988; Lemke 2002a, 2002b). Especially in scientific fields, but increasingly in others as well, the communicative patterns of the disciplines are in and of themselves multimodal. As Lemke (1998) puts it:

> Science is not done, is not communicated, through verbal language alone. It cannot be. The "concepts" of science are not verbal concepts, though they have verbal components. They are semiotic hybrids, simultaneously and essentially verbal-typological and mathematical-graphical-operational-topological. The actional, conversational, and written textual genres of science are historically and presently, fundamentally and irreducibly multimedia genres. To do science, to talk science, to read and write science it is necessary to juggle and combine in canonical ways verbal discourse, mathematical expression, graphical-visual representation, and motor operations in the "natural" (including human-as-natural) world (89).

Perhaps to create a better match between the multimodalities in students' learning and the tasks they complete as part of that learning, assignments across a range of disciplines now increasingly involve such merged representations, which are further enabled by new technologies that bring together text, speech, and visual media. In a teacher-education course at the University of Sydney, for example, students must compose the equivalent of one page in a textbook to be used to teach a concept to students in a particular stage of development. This text must include both visual and verbal elements. In the second phase of the assignment the students are asked to construct a digitized version of the text—a PowerPoint, Hyperstudio, or Web page (Simpson 2003). The students (prospective teachers) engage in such mixed-media assignments so that they can be better prepared to teach the next generation of learners. As the course designers put it, "the literacies involved in schooling and in social life are complex social practices involving the interpretation, production and use of a range of meaning making systems, including language and image. These are negotiated in a range of formats from traditional page-based material to screen-based electronic multi-media."

Similarly, in a Design Fundamentals course at North Carolina State University, students are asked to create a studio book that is a visual, verbal, and written record of the semester, including notes or sketches from required lectures or exhibitions, reflections on required and recommended readings, drawings of ideas and images for the design process, and a scrapbook of handouts and objects or images the students think are important to their design (North Carolina State University 2003a). In a medieval literature course at California Polytechnic University, students are asked to give a presentation that provides a close reading of a particular text. The presentation must be accompanied by a pedagogical handout, which includes an outline of the presentation and any background information. Students are encouraged to be creative in this handout, using illustrations, visual representations of their presentation, and the like, as long as the handout serves pedagogical ends (California Polytechnic University 2003).

For students, performing well on such tasks requires them to understand and interpret these genres within their context of use. We speculate that to begin the process, students apply broad schematic representations to the genre first, placing it into the best-matching "meta-genre" category—general discursive types they have experienced before, often repeatedly. When students are told that they will be required to do an oral presentation on their group project in chemical engineering, for example, their schemas for the meta-genre of oral presentation provide them with some general expectations and conventions for their behavior: stand up in front of the class, explain the project, and so on. Acting on such generalized knowledge, however, is not enough to guarantee them a successful performance. As they practice the speech genre within its context, more specific behaviors or expectations become clear: in an engineering progress report, presenters are often interrupted by the audience (a small group of managers) with questions or requests for clarification, a process often modeled by the teacher in class. Students unfamiliar with this instantiation must learn to "suspend" the progress of their presentation briefly to answer questions, and then, finding where they left off, quickly adjust the remaining presentation to accommodate the information they provided in the answer. As students prepare variations on poster sessions, presentations with accompanying visuals, or Web-based, multimedia assignments, they often need new strategies for deciding what information to convey in what mode, or how to organize it in a compelling and meaningful way for an audience.

The assignment we explore presents specific variations on the meta-genres of the classroom oral presentation and the classroom handout, brought together in a single communicative event. The more specific characteristics and constraints of the assignment—the length of the presentation, the accompaniment of a maximum one-page handout, the goal of extending the course material and informing peers about new concepts and studies—created a unique multimodal form. Because none of the students had ever completed such an assignment, it presented an interpretive challenge that had the potential to reveal much about the need for new methods of instruction and support, and new avenues for research on student learning and performance.

Our exploration of this assignment mirrors the kind of classroom-based assessment procedures encouraged in a view of teaching as reflective practice (see Angelo and Cross 1993; Glassick, Huber, and Maeroff 1997; Rice 1996; Schön 1987). In such a process, faculty systematically collect information about their instruction in order to engage in a "scholarship of teaching," actively investigating the effects of pedagogical decisions and continually improving their instruction. As Angelo (1991) puts it, "the purpose of classroom assessment is to provide faculty and students with information and insights needed to improve teaching effectiveness and learning quality" (17). Consistent with principles of the scholarship of teaching and learning—asking a question related to student learning, gathering data to answer that question, making results public and peer reviewed, and incorporating reflective practice—we create here a collaborative and cross-curricular variation on the typical processes of classroom-based assessment (see AAHE 2003).

In our meetings as a group, we settled on two operative questions that would simultaneously yield some broad speculation about multimodal genres in teaching and learning, and specific, instructionally helpful feedback for Karen in her own postcourse reflections:

- What performative choices did students make when faced with completing a multimodal (combined writing and speaking) assignment?
- Given a carefully articulated, supported, and assessed multimodal assignment, what can we discover about students' learning processes that can provide principles for crafting, supporting, and assessing effective multimodal assignments in the future?

Because Karen played a central role as designer of the assignment in question, as teacher of the course, and as beneficiary—in a direct sense—of her own reflection, we found our roles to be productively mixed. In keeping with investigative designs that encourage such a blending of roles and subject positions (see Fishman and McCarthy 2000), we developed a specific structure for our analysis. Two of us (Chris and Deanna) took the lead in collecting information: Karen's course materials, videotapes of the students' presentations, copies of all their handouts. In her role as instructor, Karen judged the students' performances on the assignment, rating them on a set of criteria and incorporating the results into her final course grades. Chris and Deanna then gathered information from the students through a postcourse online questionnaire. The questionnaire asked students to choose "agree," "disagree," or "not sure" for nine statements about writing and speaking and about the assignment. The statements were followed by twelve open-ended questions focusing on how the student completed the assignment, what they thought Karen was looking for, and so forth (see tables 1 and 2). They also coded the videotaped presentations for three features related to successful oratory: strong or weak eye contact with the audience, an extemporaneous style in contrast to a text-bound style (when students read note cards verbatim, for example), and the presence or absence of audience appeals (such as when the speaker asks the audience a direct or rhetorical question at the beginning of the talk). Karen then sent Chris and Deanna her evaluation of the students, including scores on each of the four categories on her rubric, and they figured those results into their analysis. They then presented a summary of their analysis to Karen, who began thinking about the implications of the information for her own teaching and future use of the multimodal assignment.

Engaging in a little genre-bending of our own, we also chose a somewhat unusual way to present the results of this study. As Karen considered the impact of our analysis on her teaching, she wrote brief reflective statements, eventually creating a commentary that appears in italics toward the end of the essay. In this way, she played a kind of hybrid role, at once the coauthor of the main text and the sole author of pedagogical reflections emerging from the analysis.

EXPLORATIONS IN MULTIMODALITY: THE MICROPRESENTATION

The context for our explorations was a special section of Psychology 201—Controversial Psychological Issues. This general education course is designed, as Karen's syllabus explains, to introduce students to "psychology and contemporary topics to illustrate how psychologists address controversial psychological issues." Karen's course objectives were to:

- refine the student's ability to research, analyze, evaluate, and make decisions about the details of complex contemporary issues in psychology
- improve the student's ability to effectively express views about psychological issues in writing and speaking
- expand the student's knowledge of psychology

Karen's preparation for this section of PSY 201 was supported by two faculty-development initiatives: the First-Year Inquiry Program and the Campus Writing and Speaking Program. In an attempt to reform "transmission" or "conduit" models of education (see Reddy 1979) and give students a more supportive experience, the university enlists faculty to teach First-Year Inquiry (FYI) versions of their courses. The FYI program encourages more hands-on work, more activities and assignments, and greater attention to "guided practice in writing, speaking, listening, asking questions, looking for answers, and evaluating evidence" (University of North Carolina 2003b). Participating instructors engage in a series of orientations and workshops designed to acquaint them with principles and methods for active learning, student-centered instruction, and inquiry-guided learning. Section size is capped at twenty to support the more student-centered nature of the course. (In her FYI section of PSY 201, Karen allowed one additional student to enroll, bringing her class size to twenty-one: eleven men and ten women, almost all first-year students. The class represented a mix of fourteen different intended majors.)

Supported by her work in the FYI program, Karen's version of PSY 201 engaged students in small-group work and class discussions, and included numerous informal writing and speaking assignments (usually one for each class), which counted for 20 percent of the final grade. Frequent ten-minute quizzes and a final examination provided assessments of learning, and together counted 40 percent of the final grade.

Karen's inclusion of the assignment that is the subject of our inquiry had a more direct genesis in NC State Campus Writing and Speaking Program's faculty seminar, which Karen took during the semester before teaching PSY 201. The semester-long, biweekly seminar is designed to help faculty incorporate both formal and informal writing and speaking into existing courses, with special attention to learning goals, assignment design, and assessment. During the seminar, Karen designed a new, formal, multimodal writing/speaking assignment: the oral presentation and accompanying one-page handout, which earned students 20 percent of their final grade. Before taking the seminar, Karen had built brief oral presentations into many of her courses, but she had never paired those with a writing assignment in a way that represented a single discourse activity utilizing both oral and written text. Students had occasionally used the board or an overhead projector to punctuate their presentations with something visual, but Karen had not built this systematically into the requirements for the assignment.

In its final version, Karen's assignment description took up three single-spaced pages and included a set of three learning objectives, five recommended steps to complete the assignment, and half a page of suggestions and tips for success. Described throughout as a "formal writing and speaking assignment," it allowed many options for topic choice but placed relatively tight constraints on delivery: students were asked to prepare a micropresentation—a brief oral presentation delivered to the class in no more than four to six minutes—summarizing an article they had located in the psychological literature about a controversial subject such as parental spanking of children, the psychological effects of video-game violence, and the use of electroshock therapy to treat depression. An accompanying written text (only a handout was allowed) had to be no more than a single page in length, designed to highlight, extend, elucidate, or provide examples to support the oral summary. The assignment sheet explained that the handout "is not a written summary of your presentation, nor is it a copy of your presentation notes. It is a visual that helps the audience understand and focus on your presentation. The handout allows elaboration on points; this enables you to provide more information in less time." Students were asked to bring twenty-five copies of the handout.

In addition to the list of five instructional suggestions included in the assignment handout (which we have reproduced as appendix 1), various kinds of classroom support were also foreshadowed in the assignment description: informal writing and speaking assignments to "serve as practice for successfully completing the steps" in the multimodal assignment, opportunities to discuss the students' readings in class, and peer-group work that yielded feedback on the preparation for the presentation. In addition, Karen provided the class with a set of detailed criteria (see appendix 2). These criteria were designed to be formative (helping the students to prepare the assignment) as well as summative (helping her to apply clear, consistent criteria to her grading). Constituting one of four separately scored criteria, the handout category "refers to the quality of your accompanying one-page handout. How well does it accompany your remarks? If you need to add time to your presentation to explain the handout, then the handout is not supporting your presentation. The handout illustrates, elaborates, and clarifies your remarks. A handout riddled with errors, hard to read, confusing, or poorly laid out indicates incomplete work."

To score the presentations, Karen used a rubric matched to the categories in the descriptive criteria.

From the perspective of classroom research, the three of us were interested in how students would respond to this multimodal genre: what would they do to complete the task? How would they conceive of the relationship between their spoken words and the written text? Could we discern anything in their performance or reflections on the experience that would help us to prefigure some new areas for pedagogical development and research on genres in communication across the curriculum?

ASSISTED INQUIRY: CLASSROOM-BASED ASSESSMENT FROM THE OUTSIDE IN

As we reviewed the videotapes of the students' presentations, we were immediately struck by how they used the handout. The class was evenly divided between those who distributed their handouts before starting their presentation and those who waited until it was over. Because Karen had made no recommendations or requirements for whether the audience should have the handout for reference during the talks, we speculated that students construed its purpose differently. Those who provided it at the end were perhaps seeing it as a form of documentation for Karen, or as something the audience could refer to later, while those who began their presentations by circulating the handout may have understood it to be a visual gloss, providing additional detail or allowing the audience to "follow along" as the speaker worked through his or her points.

Survey results confirmed our speculations: students described the purpose of their handout in quite different ways, some to "keep [the] audience on the right track so they could easily follow [the] speech without getting lost or bored," some to "restate" what they presented, and some to "provide a visual aid." A few students clearly used their handout as the equivalent of their talking points, reading from it verbatim. Although 47 percent of students referred to their handouts during the presentation, as many as a third simply handed it out and did not mention it (see table 1).

This key rhetorical and pragmatic difference in the presentations—handout before or after—was mildly correlated to the students' overall grade (with a six-point higher average score among those who circulated their handout in advance of the presentation). In addition, our codings of the videotapes showed a strong relationship to the "before or after" handout order: students who provided their handouts first generally gave livelier presentations, connected more with their audience, and spoke more extemporaneously, sometimes starting their presentation with an audience-directed question. In contrast, students who distributed their handouts at the end were more likely to read their note cards (or the handout itself) aloud, make little or no eye contact with the audience, and use few audience appeals. In two such cases, the students remembered to distribute the handouts only as they were about to take their seats again after their presentation.

Although we might imagine a further connection of these features to questionnaire items that asked students to say whether they liked or thought they were good at oral presentations, we did not see a predictable pattern. Students' self-concepts as orators or writers did not appear to be related overall to these aspects of their presentations. In fact, as shown in table 2, two-thirds of the class indicated that they do not dislike giving oral presentations (with more of them disliking writing assignments), most believe both writing and speaking are important in their planned careers, and most desire more writing and speaking instruction. Yet table 2 (page 183) shows them to be almost evenly split between those who think they are better at writing versus speaking.

TABLE 1

Responses to open-ended questions (by percentage)

What was the hardest part about this entire assignment for you?	
Getting up in front of the class	40%
Doing the research	27%
Figuring out how to organize the information/what to present	20%
Nothing/overall it was easy	13%
How did you go about writing your accompanying handout?	
Focused on key points/made an outline of my talk	60%
Took facts from the Internet	20%
Tried to add more interesting information	20%
How did you go about preparing for the presentation?	
I read over the material and created an outline.	40%
I wrote/studied notes about my material.	20%
I practiced aloud (alone or in front of a friend).	26%
I memorized my material.	7%
I didn't prepare at all.	7%
Did you do the handout first, or work on the oral presentation first?	
I did the handout first.	33%
I did the presentation first.	67%
Considering everything that you presented to the class, what percentage of that information do you think went into the handout and what percentage went into the presentation?	
5% to 10%	40%
20%-50%	47%
80-90%	13%
What percentage of your time went into constructing the handout?	
5%-10%	27%
20%-40%	46%
50%-75%	27%
How did you use the handout in your presentation? Did you refer to it, read from it, etc.?	
I referred to it as I talked.	47%
I just handed it out.	33%
I read from it.	7%
I used it as a guide.	13%
What purpose did you want the handout to serve? Did it serve that purpose? Why or why not?	
Visual aid for the audience	20%
An outline/summary/restatement of my presentation	40%
Reinforce/back up my major points	13%
Provide information on my topic	27%
If you could decide how to give a presentation in a future class, would you use an accompanying handout or not? Why or why not?	
It would depend on the presentation/information.	33%
Yes (conveys info., helps class to follow, backs up my points)	67%

(continued on next page)

(table 1 continued)

What do you think your teacher was looking for in the presentation and handout? That is, what do you think a "successful" handout and presentation looked like?	
Good connection between presentation and handout	33%
Performance factors: clear, understandable, thought-provoking	33%
Informational factors: hard work, knowledge, evidence of research	33%
If you could have chosen to summarize your article either in writing or in an oral presentation, which would you have chosen? Why?	
Writing (not good at oral/less time to prepare/feels more natural/can revise)	60%
Oral (not good at writing/can explain better orally/fewer errors/hate writing)	40%
Are you better at providing information orally or in writing? Why?	
Orally (body language, easier than writing, can show emotion)	40%
In writing (easier to organize thoughts, nervous with oral, can revise)	60%

The handouts themselves represented range of styles, textual density, and use of visuals. For example, Alan's handout, shown in reduced form in figure 1 (page 184), is visually appealing, with mixed font size, sophisticated layout, and a large red and black bar down the left side. He includes a graphic of a brain, and the handout is organized as bulleted points answering a central question at the top of the page. Along the right side of the page, further bulleted points provide examples of the language of diagnostic labeling, the subject of the article he located. In contrast, Kelly's handout on ADHD (figure 2 page 185) provides far more text and no visuals. It is organized as bulleted answers to two questions ("What is ADHD?" and "What are the symptoms of ADHD?"). Information about the article itself appears at the very end of the handout, in a five-line paragraph. Most of the text is in the same font size.

The range of styles, formats, density, font types, and other textual and visual elements in the handouts appears to reflect the way that students constructed the relationship between the oral and written components of the task. Karen did not provide examples of handouts, nor any information (beyond what we have already described) about their expected form and content. Considering all the information and suggestions Karen's assignment offered about the presentation—give it a clear structure, don't read it verbatim, use note cards, practice in front of a mirror, and so on (see appendix 1)—this range clearly shows that unfamiliar genres require more instructional support than most teachers are used to providing in content-area courses.

An examination of Karen's scores on the rubric showed no strong or predictable relationships to features of the handouts. However, we noticed a tendency for handouts that began with provocative or

TABLE 2

Responses to yes/no questions (by percentage)

Questionnaire item	Yes	No	Not sure
I generally dislike giving oral presentations.	33	67	0
I generally dislike doing writing assignments.	47	47	6
Oral presentations will be important in my career.	70	15	15
Writing will be important in my career.	67	13	20
I enjoyed the formal writing/speaking assignment in PSY 201.	60	13	27
The handout helped my oral presentation.	80	13	7
The handouts added significant value to the oral presentations of other students.	67	20	13
I would value additional instruction in how to give effective oral presentations.	80	13	7
I would value additional instruction in how to write effectively.	73	7	20

interesting questions, followed by an "answer" to the question in the form of well-organized information, to receive higher scores than handouts that simply provided information. This recognition of audience appeals appears to match Karen's overall scores on the presentations as well as the students' presentational styles: students who made more eye contact and used extemporaneous styles and audience appeals in their presentations tended more often to organize their handouts around questions. However, Karen's scores on the handouts also indicate as much concern for the clarity of the information as for the visual appeal of the handout per se; one or two well-designed handouts that contained seemingly random pieces of information in "unparallel" form received somewhat lower scores than less visually appealing handouts that were more carefully organized. When considered next to the descriptive rubric shown in appendix 2, these specific aspects of students' performances are most explicitly tied to her suggestions about delivery: demeanor, being both "relaxed and professional," and delivering the presentation "in a way that shows you are interested in your work." Clearly, some students are able to act on these general recommendations and admonitions while others need more explicit or extensive help knowing what they mean and how to apply them to their own performances.

Questionnaire results also suggest few strong consistencies among students, although some general tendencies do emerge from the data. Most students agreed that the handouts helped their own presentations, but were somewhat less sure that they helped the presentations of others. It is not possible to tell whether students felt their own handout helped them as presenters (e.g., to organize information or stay on track) more than it helped their audience; however, almost half said its purpose was

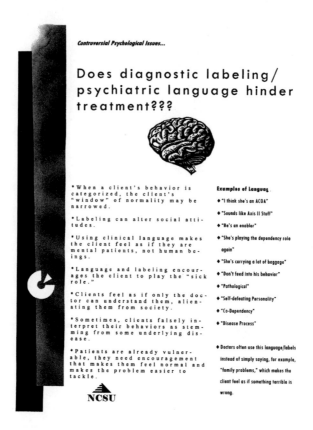

Figure 1: Alan's Handout

to provide an outline or restatement of their presentation, while about one-fifth referred directly to the needs of their audience. The students who saw their handout's purposes in this audience-focused way received the highest overall scores on their presentation, and were among those who connected with their audiences, spoke extemporaneously, and made eye contact.

Students' responses to the questionnaires provide a window into their learning processes as they completed the combined writing and speaking assignments. As shown in table 1, most students worked on the oral presentation first, before creating the handout (67 percent), and spent more time working on it than preparing the handout (73 percent spent one-half to three-quarters of their time preparing the presentation, while only 27 percent spent this amount of time on their handout). Students also

ADHD.........

What is attention deficit hyperactivity disorder (ADHD)?

Attention deficit hyperactivity disorder (ADHD) is the most common behavior disorder diagnosed in children and teens. ADHD refers to a group of symptoms that begin in early childhood and can continue into adulthood, causing difficulties at home, at school, at work, and within the community if not recognized and treated.

What are the symptoms of ADHD?

The three groups of ADHD symptoms are:

- **Inattention.** This is the most common symptom. In addition to having difficulty paying attention, people with this ADHD symptom often are unable to consistently focus, remember, and organize. They may be careless and have a hard time starting and completing tasks that are boring, repetitive, or challenging.
- **Impulsiveness.** People who frequently act before thinking may not make sound judgments or solve problems well. They may also have trouble developing and maintaining personal relationships. An adult may not keep the same job for long or spend money wisely.
- **Hyperactivity.** A hyperactive child may squirm, fidget, and climb or run when it is not appropriate. These children often have difficulty playing with others. They may talk a great deal and not be able to sit still for even a short time. Teenagers and adults who are hyperactive don't usually have the more obvious physical behaviors seen in children. Rather, they often feel restless and fidgety, and are not able to enjoy reading or other quiet activities.

Symptoms vary by individual and range from mild to severe.

Symptoms of ADHD can be similar to those of other conditions, such as:

- Learning disabilities.
- Oppositional defiant disorder (ODD).
- Conduct disorder.
- Anxiety disorder.
- Depression.

These conditions are sometimes mistaken for ADHD. They may also occur along with ADHD, which can make diagnosis of the primary problem difficult.
(information above taken from AOLHealth/ WebMD)

The article that I chose for my presentation was "ADHD, HUNTING, AND EVOLUTION: 'JUST SO STORIES'". In the article, the author is basically giving the reader many bizarre stories that account for ADHD and then he tells why they are faulty and untrue. He then goes on to tell what is the truth about those who have ADHD and why it is true and why the other "Just So Stories" are untrue.

Figure 2: Kelly's Handout

used specific processes to prepare the oral presentation and the handout. In preparing for the presentation, students typically read over their material or created an outline (40 percent), or practiced aloud (26 percent). When they created the handout, they typically focused on key points or made an outline for the talk (60 percent). The majority of students also estimated that much less information was provided on the handout than in the presentation. Yet all but one of the handouts provided more text than could be easily read aloud in four to five minutes. Students believe, in other words, that a brief oral presentation conveys far more information than a piece of written text with potentially equal informational and presentational value. These results suggest that, for the most part, students tackled this assignment with the perception that the handout was secondary to the presentation, rather than a tool for structuring or generating the presentation (see Yancey 2001).

Karen's weighting of the grading criteria toward the oral presentation (as well as the usual urgency of having to stand in front of one's peers) no doubt contributed to students' perceptions of its importance relative to the handout. Only one-third of the students explicitly connected the handout to the presentation in describing what they thought Karen was "looking for" in the assignment, in spite of Karen's including this as one of the criteria for success. Yet the majority of students agreed that they would use an accompanying handout for oral presentations in the future if given a chance. We see, then, a complicated relationship between the way that each mode in the assignment is weighted in the evaluation—in this case, not equally—and the overall rhetorical and pragmatic nature of the task. Professionals might understand that the quality of a handout is part of the quality and overall effect of the entire presentation, whereas students interpret this relationship using instructional cues such as how much each part counts, how extensive the suggestions are for each part, and the like.

Our analysis suggests that although students' performances variously interwove or kept separate the oral and written components of the assignment, generally they interpreted them as separate, familiar genres that they were asked to link together. Lacking schemas or operational knowledge for creating a single, multimodal genre in which the written/visual and spoken texts could strategically and artfully reinforce each other, they prepared each as a separate communicative medium. In a few cases, notably among the students who were most aware of the needs of their audience, the merging of the two modalities was fortuitous, but their success did not appear to be a consequence of the instructional support provided for the assignment.

From this perspective, we return to the design and nature of the assignment. In spite of the thorough, carefully presented information Karen provided to the students, and in spite of the direct and indirect instructional activities she crafted to support the assignment, the nature of its complex multimodality also revealed areas for continued instructional development. Certain language in the assignment description, for example, may have suggested the separateness of the two modes even while it was being presented as a single, multimodal task. Including the handout as a separate category in the evaluation rubric, even alongside an explanation pointing to the need for the handout to "support" the presentation, may have led students to divide their attention accordingly when preparing the assignment. Allocating fewer points to the handout relative to the oral presentation likewise suggests an instructional asymmetry between the two. Like the development of a creole from two separate languages, the "evolution" of this multimodal genre may be at a stage when both teachers and students find it easy to revert to more stable and canonical conceptions of each part.

ASSISTED INQUIRY: CLASSROOM-BASED ASSESSMENT FROM KAREN ST. CLAIR

After participating in the NC State Campus Writing and Speaking Program faculty seminar, I realized that when developing writing and speaking assignments, I need to consider several factors that affect the student's success in completing my assignments: the purpose of the assignments, my plan for guiding students through the assignment, my expectations when evaluating the student's performance, and the student's experience with writing and speaking assignments.

Consequently, for this section of PSY 201 I set out to mirror the course objectives in the formal writing and speaking assignment objectives. I believed the student should be able to apply a course-specific critical thinking process to an empirical or theoretical article concerning a psychological controversy, personalize the critical analysis by reflecting on how the controversy relates to his or her life, and effectively communicate this analysis and reflection. The term "effectively" is, finally, subjective, but specific criteria for evaluating the presentation introduced some objectivity: substance (accuracy and completeness of the information presented), coherence (clarity of the presentation), delivery (timing, evidence of rehearsal), and the handout (quality of support it provides). I prepared a detailed student handout describing the steps to take in completing the assignment, suggestions for successful completion, and how they would receive class support along the way. Reflecting on the analysis now, I recognize that the mixing of writing and speaking requirements in an assignment necessitates even more instruction and support along the way than I planned. Evaluation proved to be difficult; a greater consideration of the student's writing and speaking experiences offers some new insights that could translate into clearer criteria for evaluation.

The results focusing on the order of the handout—something that had not occurred to me to discuss—suggest the need for more time explaining the purpose of the handout (which was to support the information presented) and ways to prepare the handout (use of text and symbols, color and white space). When teaching this course again, not only would I provide stronger suggestions for incorporating the handout throughout the oral presentation, I would change the way I model this expectation by preparing one-page handouts that support or embellish some of my mini-lectures. I would distribute these handouts at the beginning of my presentation and "walk" the students through the points I make by referring to the handout.

The frequent opportunities over the semester for reading, speaking during class, writing informal assignments, and listening to others undoubtedly prepared the students for getting up in front of the group. Being at ease, however, does not necessarily mean skill in relating to the audience. Our analysis suggests that students have difficulty getting away from "doing something for the teacher." Even at the end of a semester, some students continue to "speak to the teacher" and ignore the classmate to whom the response is intended. Students are used to being "taught to" and, clearly, have difficulty making the rhetorical and interpersonal switch to "teach" their classmates. Expecting students to know intuitively the effect of delivery on the audience and to plunge into focusing on its needs and response is probably too high an expectation. Including effective communication as a course and assignment objective requires considerable guidance, modeling, and time for more practice in presentation. A practice I would like to explore further involves the use of "response cards." These small pieces of paper allow students to write comments about each other's presentations. The teacher reserves the editorial privilege to cull thoughtless or unnecessarily harsh comments, and delivers the comments the day following presentations. Perhaps an extension of this technique—using response cards following "practice" oral presentations and allowing for class discussion of specific aspects of presentation style—would provide peer support to reinforce the importance of one's audience.

It is possible, however, that students with less skill at audience appeal and less creative applications for the handout may have better understood their topics and prepared a more thoughtful presentation. My plans to manage the process of the assignment went awry when I set about to evaluate the presentation. Had I read each student's chosen article and carefully helped them work through their presentation outlines, I may have been better able to separate the evaluation criteria: substance, coherence, delivery, and handout. I did require that the chosen article meet my approval to avoid selection of a nonprofessional work. And I required each student to submit an outline of the oral presentation, but this was merely an exercise to keep them on track and avoid last-minute preparations. I found it impossible, however, to recall topics, articles, and outlines when listening to the presentations. Consequently, I was attracted to the delivery and use of the handout over the substance and clarity of points made.

The data also suggest some productive areas to consider when making fair comparisons among the students. Certainly, matching observable evaluation criteria *to assignment goals and objectives makes the grading task easier. And arranging for the formal writing and speaking assignment to be counted for only one-fifth on the final grade puts the value of the student's performance on the assignment in perspective. But my expectation for creative, unique presentations made fair evaluations difficult. The PSY 201 presentations were delivered over three class days. On the second and third day, I found myself grading less stringently than on the first day. In fact, I regraded the first two or three presentation to be fairer. I believe my gradual leaning toward being less stringent reflects my feeling of responsibility for the students' performances. This is not to say that many of the presentations were not what I would describe as "top notch." What I am suggesting is that when a student did not create an eye-catching handout, utilize the handout effectively, deliver the main point of the article, or present his or her reflection on the controversy, I recognized the need to provide a lot more guidance to students to help them through the preparation process.*

An ever-present course objective has been to prepare students of psychology for a variety of professional writing and speaking requirements. Although it is undoubtedly true that not all psychologists are skilled at writing and speaking in their work, I nevertheless feel an obligation to expose my students to what has been written and require that they write and speak about the discipline. With that obligation comes the need to state my objectives, guide students through the completion process, and prepare to evaluate what I ask for. All these and consideration of the students' experiences with writing and speaking would not only reduce my own frustrations, but would undoubtedly result in enhanced student outcomes. In the absence of formal study in composition and communication, many teachers in my position face sometimes daunting challenges when we incorporate writing and speaking—even as separate modes—into our classes. The help of experts like Chris and Deanna in "assisted classroom assessment" can reduce those challenges, as has been the case with my own multimodal assignment; but there is obviously much cross-curricular work yet to be done in the face of rapid change in communication, technology, media, and the goals of higher education.

CONCLUSION: GENRE, MULTIMODALITY, AND THE NEED FOR INSTRUCTIONAL DEVELOPMENT

Our limited results suggest that multi-modal assignments, although designed to help students to use new and increasingly important communicative strategies that stretch beyond the usual boundaries of canonical classroom forms, are often interpreted by students as separate genres that function to achieve similar goals. In essence, students seem to have difficulty seeing these genres outside of their traditional instantiations ("informative oral report," for example, and "accounting for one's read-ing in an outline of ideas to be turned in during class"). In this scenario, perhaps students are operating within an academic activity system whose scripts of "handout" and "presentation" position them in a contiguous, not complementary, relationship to one another (Russell 1997). Our informal data also suggest that students were only obliquely aware of ways they could enhance their presentation for their peer audience, perhaps by call-ing attention to interesting or relevant information in their handouts.

As we discovered in our informal exploration of a relatively simple mul-timodal assignment, students clearly need to be more fully supported in their acquisition of strategies and skills for communication in an increas-ingly complex world of discourse. The students' performances ranged from mediocre to excellent, yet almost all of them expressed a desire to receive more instruction in both writing and speaking. And if it is more likely that students will experience complex, multimodal assignments as they move out of general education courses like Karen's and into special-ized courses in their majors, the need to establish a base of support early on is clearly an issue for further consideration.

If Karen stands at the end of the WAC continuum where well-informed, diligent faculty reside, it is easy to see the scope of work that remains to be done in faculty development and orientation to communication across the curriculum. Our experiment in "assisted inquiry" finds some affinities with new processes in which peer or outside consultants can offer teachers formative evaluation that is sometimes difficult to collect on one's own; for example, a teacher can't simultaneously be an observer of his or her own teaching, nor is it possible to gather impressions from students that an outsider could using a procedure like small-group instructional diag-nosis (see Lewis and Lunde 2001).

But thankfully, not all such formative data collection needs to be externally supported. The process we used to explore and understand students' performances on this task is one that with little alteration could be fruitfully used by any teacher interested in how students interpret and respond to new kinds of assignments. Karen felt that her reflections were considerably enriched by an analysis that, with a few modifications (such as some additional categories on the scoring rubric in the absence of videotapes), could be used by teachers across a range of courses. Such methods promise to bring together the study of new educational genres with their principled application in courses across the varied landscape of higher education.

Finally, not only does our exploration suggest a need for support in students' acquisition of communication skills in multimodal settings, it also raises more complex questions about the nature of genre acquisition and performance. As they become more proficient members of their chosen disciplines where they are increasingly assigned multimodal genres, when do students stop performing within the frameworks of more traditional, single-mode genres? As they move from novice to expert in their disciplines, do they develop more complex and increasingly multimodal understandings of the communication genres that will face them in their professional context? Or are there other constraining aspects of the academic activity system that hamper the acquisition of complex multimodalities? Although our work does not fully answer these questions, our informal exploration suggests that when moving from single to multimodal genre pedagogy, the instructional complexities are also exponentially multiplied. Further research and pedagogy might benefit from increased explorations of these complexities.

APPENDIX 1

KAREN'S "SUGGESTIONS FOR SUCCESS"
(AS EXCERPTED FROM THE ASSIGNMENT)

1. Actively participate in class discussions about articles, the difference between theoretical and empirical research, and evaluating an article's quality.

2. Use information from class discussions on critical thinking, the scientific method, and psychology as guides when carefully reading the article to understand, identify, and critique the author's question, answer, and evidence.

3. Allow time for reflection about what you have discovered from study of the article. Do you agree with the author? Why or why not? How do you relate to the issue? What connections do you have with the author's stand? Do not rush to agree or disagree without being able to articulate why you agree or disagree.

4. Prepare an oral presentation of your work and a supporting handout for distribution by carefully planning and rehearsing.

    a. Consider your audience. Audiences show respect by paying attention to what you have to say; in return, respect them by keeping the focus on your assignment and not on your popularity. The audience expects your presentation to be more interesting than the article. Therefore, an engaging presentation style keeps your audience's attention.

    b. Typically a talk consists of introductory remarks, content or substance of the presentation, and a summary or restatement of the purpose. The substance of your presentation is an oral version of your work on the assignment: identifying the issue, the author's stand, and the author's evidence. Introductory remarks and summary of the purpose are "bookends" for your substance.

    c. No doubt you cannot memorize your presentation, but you are not to read a narrative to your audience. Prepare notes and record them on note cards. Insert talking points (key phrases, words, visual cues) into your notes to guide you through your presentation. Talking points include "check time," "refer to handout," "look at audience." A copy of the presentation notes are turned in to the instructor.

d.   The handout is no more than one page. You can have more than one page if you need to have a chart or diagram or an overhead. Make twenty-five copies of your handout (for each student, the instructor, and possible visitors). The handout is not a written summary of your presentation, nor is it a copy of your presentation notes. It is a visual that helps the audience understand and focus on your presentation. The handout allows elaboration on points; this enables you to provide more information in less time.

e.   Deliver your presentation for four to six minutes. When preparing the presentation, divide it into logical parts and make one note card (or two small) for each part. As you rehearse, time the parts of your presentation so adjustments can be made without sacrificing a whole part.

f.   Rehearse in front of a mirror, standing up. Do it alone until it is perfected. Once the wrinkles are ironed out, deliver the presentation to a trusted listener and ask for suggestions for improvement.

APPENDIX 2

ASSIGNMENT CRITERIA GIVEN TO STUDENTS

SCORING CRITERIA

1. *Substance:* This category refers to the accuracy of the information presented. Have you thoroughly and appropriately applied the critical thinking process? Have you correctly described the controversial issue and the author's stand on the issue? Do you completely and accurately present the author's evidence? Do not neglect to include your reflections on the issue and the author's stand. If you relate the issue, the author's stand, and the author's evidence but do not provide your reflections about the arguments, then your presentation is incomplete.

2. *Coherence:* This category refers to the clarity of the presentation. Your presentation should be clear enough for your audience to understand. How well does it hang together? Providing minute detail about the author's position and too little detail about your position renders your presentation incoherent or unbalanced. Consider providing context or introductory statements. Would the audience know which part of the assignment you are delivering?

3. *Delivery:* This category refers to the way you deliver your presentation. As you rehearse, consider your demeanor and professionalism. Running out of time (you will be stopped when your time is up, no matter where you are in the presentation), having too much time left, stumbling over your ideas, and losing your place indicate lack of preparation. Be relaxed but professional. Humor is acceptable within reason and when relevant. Delivering your presentation in a way that shows you are interested in your work will likely instill audience engagement and sustained interest.

4. *Handout:* This category refers to the quality of your accompanying one-page handout. How well does it accompany your remarks? If you need to add time to your presentation to explain the handout, then the handout is not supporting your presentation. The handout illustrates, elaborates, and clarifies your remarks. A handout riddled with errors, hard to read, confusing, or poorly laid out indicates incomplete work.

SCORING SCALE

Each criterion will be scored on the three-point scale of 3, 2, and 1, which roughly equates to the letter grades of A, B, and C, respectively. Each criterion is weighted equally. The maximum total score is 12. The scores for the criteria are totaled and divided by 12 and multiplied by 100 to yield a percentage score. The percentage score can be compared to the following percentage–letter grade scoring scale: 100–90 = A, 89–80 = B, 79–70 = C.

Any criterion scored 0 would equate to a letter grade of D or F, indicating that the criterion is met at a severely minimal level or not met at all. Should total scoring result in an assignment earning less than the equivalent of a C grade, the student would be obliged to redo the assignment. The new assignment score is subject to a "second-try" reduction in value.

10

THE TEACHING AND LEARNING OF WEB GENRES IN FIRST-YEAR COMPOSITION

Mike Edwards and Heidi McKee

The genres in which writers communicate evolve, and this evolution is now strikingly evident on the World Wide Web, where millions of people create documents for an ever-burgeoning number of sites. As teachers, the two of us have discovered that working with Web genres in the writing classroom is no easy task, largely because of the differing perceptions and experiences individuals bring to Web compositions. In this chapter we examine how the eclectic and changing nature of genres on the Web brought about a reconceptualizing and reorienting of our own expectations about teaching and learning writing, focusing on ways in which students adapted their writing for the Web and on the ways in which we tried (not always successfully) to adapt our approaches to the learning and teaching of Web genres. The complications we encountered in our teaching spring from a variety of sources. First, there are the institutional pressures of academic discourses and their intersections with non-academic discourses. Second, the Web itself is a vast and heterogeneous space, incorporating many different textual forms from which teachers and students might construct radically differing generic conceptions of Web pages.

The ways teachers and students work with Web genres are complicated by the diverse and often conflicting ways that Web pages have been defined and categorized. Just as print-based genres have been sometimes categorized by form alone, Web genres are sometimes described according to the technical aspects of sites, such as the link structures used or the coding or multimedia employed. For example, in an analysis of the research paper genre and its move to hypertext and the Web, Wendy Warren Austin classifies argumentative hypertext and Web genres by link structures, ranging from "primitive" to "true hypertext" (2001). Austin's classification of a Web genre based on link structures carries over from discussions of hypertext, a broad textual category of which Web sites are frequently seen as a subcategory (Golson 1999; Landow 1991, 1994a; Norton, Zimmerman, and Lindeman 1999). To take a more popular example, some of the more than thirty categories of sites listed on Cool Home Pages (http://www.coolhomepages.com) include "Audio/Sound," "CSS & DHTML," and "Flash," thereby focusing at least some attention on the technologies associated with the sites.

Teachers and students who work with Web genres must take into account the technical and structural composition of Web sites, because all sites share certain technical characteristics: they are designed to be read on-screen, they have the potential to incorporate graphics and sound, and they have the potential for linking. We also acknowledge the importance of including technical considerations in understandings of genre because, as Marcy Bauman has noted about working with writers new to the Web, "it becomes difficult to tell when literacy ends and technological proficiency begins"(1999, 279). But technical and formal aspects of Web sites are only one component of understanding Web genres.

Another component of genre on the Web is the content of the sites. Cool Home Pages includes other categories such as "Sports," "Corporate," "Travel," "Kids," "News," and "Personal." But simply calling something a personal home page or news site is an inadequate descriptor of genre, for a number of reasons. First, even within a genre that appears to be quite clearly defined according to content, there is a inevitably a great deal of rhetorical variation, as Anne Wysocki demonstrates in her analysis of two CD-ROMs of museum art collections (2001). Similarly, Gail Hawisher and Patricia Sullivan, in their analysis of women's visual representations on the Web, show that these representations are complicated by such factors as race, age, class, technical capabilities, sexual orientation, and professional status (1999). Given the complexity of genres on the Web, we feel it's important to develop in ourselves and in our students an understanding of genre that accounts for the interrelationships of form, content, context, and social purposes. In short, teachers must understand the heterogeneity of documents on the World Wide Web and the heterogeneity of possible responses to those documents, and maintain such an understanding in incorporating Web-based assignments into composition curricula. As instructors, our attempts to foster a contextual awareness of the workings of Web genres may sometimes not have the same results as our attempts to foster a contextual awareness of the workings of print genres, particularly because students' responses to assignments may often foreground previously unanticipated generic factors. Web pages as a genre preexist and transcend the classrooms into which they are incorporated as writing assignments, and so students often import nonacademic Web discourses into concrete, visible, and useful interactions with academic literacies. In our teaching, we were each surprised by Web discourses used by students that were unfamiliar to us.

We are both graduate students at the University of Massachusetts, Amherst, where we teach first-year composition courses in the writing program. The goals of the University of Massachusetts first-year composition course include that students "write for various audiences and purposes," "use various kinds of thinking and discourses," and revise their writing in "substantive ways" (University of Massachusetts 2002). While instructors are given some latitude in how to meet these goals, there are set essay assignments all instructors must include in the five-essay semester: a close, sustained engagement with a published essay, an essay incorporating library research, and an end-of-the-semester writer's retrospective.

Like all first-year composition instructors in the fall of 2000, we received at our orientation session Peter Elbow's "The Spirit and the Letter of the Writing Program" (2000), in which the goals for the course were explained. "The course is about the essay; it's called 'College Writing.' True, the goal of the course is not *only* academic writing, and the official description announces explicitly that the course is also meant to help students use writing in the rest of their lives during college, and after college too. Nevertheless, the most obvious purpose of the course is to help them do the writing they will need to do for other University faculty."

While we both incorporated Web-based writing assignments into our classes (with the full knowledge and support of the faculty and administrators in the program), we still sometimes felt pressure to ensure that the Web sites students created were somehow equivalent to an essay. The institutional pressure we felt for essay equivalence affected how each of us went about teaching and responding to sites and to the genres of the sites that our students created, as we will each explain in the subsequent sections.

Our reflections are drawn from a study we each conducted in spring 2002 (Mike's and Heidi's courses) and fall 2003 (Mike's course). Besides obtaining students' consent to keep and reproduce digital copies of their sites and their writings about their Web sites, we kept teaching journals and interviewed each other's students (face-to-face and via e-mail) about their experiences creating their Web sites.

As we will show in the following sections, the teaching and learning of Web genres are complicated both by the evolving heterogeneous nature of genres on the Web and by the differing notions we and our students hold about what Web writing entails. Mike will focus upon how differing conceptions of linking shaped students' and his own approaches to Web compositions, particularly in relation to understandings of essayistic literacy. Heidi will focus on the commercial discourses that shaped students' personal representations on the Web, making explicit connections between students' sites and the corporate models from which they worked. Although we each discuss individual students working on specific assignments in specific contexts, we feel that the disjunctions that occurred in our two classes between students' approaches to Web genres and our own approaches indicate issues that instructors should consider when incorporating Web assignments into composition curricula.

MIKE'S ACCOUNT: THE INTERSECTIONS OF INSIDER KNOWLEDGE AND ESSAYISTIC LITERACY

I introduced Web page instruction as a component of my writing assignments in the spring semester of 2002. I asked students to plan their third essay, a persuasive essay, as a multipage Web site incorporating links and graphics. Students made an initial paper plan for the site and then used Macromedia's Dreamweaver (a visual HTML editor and Web development application with powerful file management capabilities) to compose a multilinear Web site with at least four separate pages addressing a relevant and contemporary issue that was open to debate and could be argued on the basis of personal expertise and authority to an audience who needed to be convinced. The Web sites that students composed based on these requirements seemed to me to be largely successful as argumentative essays, although they did not closely resemble any documents I had seen in my five years of navigating the Web.

The following semester, in fall 2002, I approached matters differently. For a number of reasons, I moved from using Dreamweaver to teaching students HTML and having them edit their Web pages with a free, barebones text editor.[1] I began teaching HTML early in the semester and had students work with it in very small increments (first the concept of HTML tags, then the basic structure of an HTML document, then basic text-formatting tags, and so on), which were worked into each of their essay assignments. By the time we got to the fourth essay, students knew how to include links, tables, images, and complicated formatting in their Web pages. The fourth essay, like the third essay in the previous semester, was a persuasive essay; however, the assignment required students to use library and Internet sources, and document those sources on a multipage Web site, in support of their arguments. The planning stages for this essay were more complicated than they had been for the previous semester's third essay: students first composed annotated bibliographies and loose textual plans for their essays, and then drew crayon-and-marker visual representations of how they wanted their pages to look, as well as paper "maps" of their sites, to which their bibliographies and plans were indexed. Finally, students spent several class sessions synthesizing all these elements into their Web sites, with the more technically proficient students serving as peer coaches for their classmates.

Perhaps because the assignments in both semesters were nearly congruent—persuasive essays with multiple pages, links, and graphics, planned as Web documents from the outset—the documents that students produced in both semesters held some similar characteristics: sophisticated arguments that seemed to reflect what Douglas Hesse has called an "essayistic literacy" rather than a rhetoric more native to the Web (1999). In the most extreme cases, the essays felt alien to the medium in which I read them, as if their words were straitjacketed by the requirements of the assignment. In this section, I focus on two students, Ken and Bill—Ken from the spring semester, and Bill from the fall—to describe the disjunctions created by our differing expectations about the conventions of essays and the World Wide Web.

As many have argued, links and linking structures are the defining features of hypertext (Burbules 1998; DeWitt 1999; Golson 1999; Joyce 1995; Landow 1991, 1994a, 1997). Charles Moran and Anne Herrington have recently echoed this contention, suggesting again that the defining characteristics of hypertext documents, including Web pages, "are the internal and external links" (2002, 247). While it is useful to point out the existence of links as a characteristic that defines hypertext as a genre, as Moran and Herrington themselves suggest, looking at hypertext as a genre is looking from far too broad a perspective to be at all useful. It may be more helpful to examine what those links *do*, since, as Nicholas Burbules points out, "all links are not the same" (1998, 104).

George Landow (1991, 1994b, 1997), Michael Joyce (1995), David Kolb (1994), and others have focused considerable attention on concerns of unilinearity versus multilinearity in hypertext documents, and on understanding how the number of relationships any hypertext document is linked into (and its location among other documents) affects its meaning. Moran and Herrington use the adjectives "internal" and "external" to focus attention on where a document's links lead (2002). Burbules, in his argument "that selecting and following any particular line of association between distinct textual points involves an interpretation of the nature of the association this link implies," examines the relationships of rhetorical signification that links set up between documents (1998, 104).

I find all three of these perspectives on linking useful in attempting to understand the generic qualities of the Web sites students produced in the sections of College Writing I taught in spring and fall 2002. Burbules constructs what is perhaps the most systematic taxonomy of types of linking, and I would add to his point the contention that students in the sections I taught often interpreted the nature of link associations differently from the ways I did. I would also suggest that some of Burbules's characterizations obscure more than they illuminate, particularly the ways he lists links that enact the logic of cause and effect as being analogous to those that enact the logic of sequence, or, to quote Burbules, "Links that suggest 'this *and then* that' or 'this *because of* that'" (1998, 115). As I will show, my students were quite aware of the considerable difference between these two forms of linking, even if they might not have known the terms *parataxis* and *hypotaxis*.

These terms themselves, however, have been deployed in varying and sometimes conflicting ways in discussions of hypertext, by writers such as Marilyn Cooper (1999), Michael Joyce (1995), Richard Lanham (1993), and Jane Yellowlees Douglas (1998). Doug Brent goes so far as to assert that "hypertext . . . privileges infinite hypotaxis rather than parataxis" (1997), an assertion that I would strongly disagree with: perhaps, then, some clarifications and definitions are in order. Richard Lanham opposes hypotaxis to the "coordinate, rather than a subordinate, construction" of parataxis (1991, 108); Chaim Perelman and Lucie Olbrechts-Tyteca go further, and explain that hypotaxis "establishes precise connections between the elements of discourse," whereas parataxis is "characterized by the absence of precise connections between the parts" (1969, 157), with the emphasis being on the degree of precision. Hypotaxis, they continue, "controls the reader, forces him to see particular relationships, restricts the interpretations he may consider, and takes its inspiration from well-constructed legal reasoning" (158). Hypotaxis, in other words, is the explicit, rigorous, and carefully subordinated language of argument; the mode of connection favored, to my mind, by conventional essayistic literacy. As Douglas Hesse remarks, "One of the main responsibilities of the essayist is to point—at books, ideas, experiences, people, and so on. But essayists interpret their pointing" (1999, 44). Links on student Web pages can interpret their pointing, or they can simply point, and this distinction constitutes one of the generic qualities of Web pages.

Furthermore, hypotaxis and parataxis require different reading strategies. While the subordination of hypotaxis is highly explicit, it requires considerable attention to work through, as anyone who has read Samuel Johnson or Michel Foucault will attest. The "and/and/and" of parataxis is easier to digest, and has much more in common with the quick multipage browse of the Web, or what Burbules refers to as the "phenomenological orientation" of surfing (1998, 108).[2] Many students in the spring and fall 2003 sections I taught remarked that they had been using the World Wide Web since junior high school, and I believe, therefore, that their in-school understandings of Web page genres were strongly affected by their out-of-school understandings of Web page genres. This was particularly evident in many students' complaints in interviews that reading a sustained argument on a single Web page was unacceptably difficult. At the same time, when I would refer to "cohesion" and "unity" in my comments on their other essays, I was privileging precisely those sorts of sustained arguments; the same holds true for Moran and Herrington's suggesting "coherence" and "focus" as evaluative criteria for hypertext (2002, 250-51). Like me, students construct their notions of genre from texts, both print and Web, that they read: as Burbules suggests, "Reading is a practice, and as such it partakes of the contexts and social relations in which it takes place; significant differences in those contexts and relations alter the practice" (1998, 102).

Out of all the essays I received in the spring of 2002, I would argue that Ken's was the most influenced by out-of-school understandings of Web page genres. Ken, a self-described novice at making Web pages, produced a site that relied extensively on visual rhetoric and on humorous animated graphics in particular to supplement his explicitly audience-conscious informal tone. His site, "Don't Drink to Excess, Know Your Limit," begins not with text, but with two clipart pictures captioned "Before" and "After," the "Before" picture showing a smiling, cheering group of attractive college-age men and women at a bar with beer steins and wine glasses in hand, and the "After" picture a chiaroscuro rendering of a man sitting slumped on the edge of a bed, his face hidden, with his head in one hand and a bottle in the other. The site is divided into seven topical sections, with the links to all sections available at the bottom of each page. Each page contains a brief paragraph or two of text, frequently

Alternatives *(to doing this for weekend entertainment)*

Some people will say that drinking makes them more sociable, more pleasing, less timid and shy, more courageous, brave, inspiring, interesting, funny, smart, intuitive, poetic, and some people even say it makes them sexier. I don't know how something that damages your brain and a bunch of your vital organs can do all this for you, but if you think so then you are probably a few beers short of a six pack if you get my drift.
If you really have to drink alcohol in order for people to like you, which is what all of those things mentioned above are implying, then you must be a real zero. Self-esteem is low with you. There is no need for alcohol to do this, just being yourself and acting that way is what people should and will like you for, not because you can drink 5 beers in ten minutes or funnel three beers at the same time. That is a farce, and it will only hurt you in the end and bring you down even lower than you ever thought imaginable. Give yourself a chance to be who you are, don't mask it with a cloud of drunkenness or you will never really know what the people around you really think of who you are.

why you could do it

argument

excessive drinking   nvtech.com

background   All the way back to the flintstones

Figure 1: The concluding page of Ken's site

followed by a series of alcohol- or drunkenness-related animated graphics interspersed with sentences commenting upon or illustrated by the graphics (see figure 1).

Ken's site contains no external links; however, according to Ken, the site's layout, tone, and use of graphics imitate the UMassDrunks Web site (http://www.umassdrunks.com/).[3] Although I was not familiar then with UMassDrunks, many of Ken's classmates caught the reference: the UMassDrunks site (which included polls and games celebrating intoxication, a "party post" bulletin board, and a frequently updated gallery of photographs taken of and by drunk undergraduates) was highly popular with students. Ken's site, with its message urging students *not* to overindulge and its relaxed, forthright language, served as a highly effective parody of the UMassDrunks site, and carried an implicit exhortation to view its own graphics (as well as the gallery at UMassDrunks) as cautionary rather than celebratory.

While Ken's use of graphics causes the vertical length of many of his pages to violate Jakob Nielsen's no-scroll rule (1996), the chunks of text on each page are quite brief and easily scanned. His links, isolated at the bottom of each page and often separated from the page's main body text by one or more graphics, stand on their own without any indication (aside from the brief titles of the pages to which they link) of how they might be subordinated to the argument. I would thus characterize them as paratactic. Organized by topic, with links to every other page at the bottom of each page, the essay is multilinear in nature; the reader can take any route through Ken's site he or she desires.

Despite his essay's apparent multilinearity, Ken argued for the importance of what he called "flow." According to Ken, "If you just have a series of links that aren't really coordinated, or they don't go in order, then people are going to look at your essay and say, 'This isn't related to what I was just reading. So why am I reading this now; why aren't I reading this later?'" Ken pointed out that his pages were intended to be read in the vertical order in which they were linked at the bottom of each page, but he noted that he also tried to make sure that the pages could be read in any order. This is achieved by the frequent repetition of various forms of the word "drink" and the consistent use of humorous graphics and a casual, honest, witty, and knowing tone. Still, each of the pages stands well on its own, to the point where the site seems to comprise seven arguments against drinking too much. This is not to say that the site is not persuasive: by my standards, and the standards of Ken's classmates, it was highly persuasive. Rather, the site relies on a combination of factors that seem to stand in direct contrariety to the syllogistic reasoning and linear progression of thought that I typically associate with argumentation.

Bill's Web site, composed in the fall semester of 2003, relied on a much more linear, progressive mode of argumentation. His essay argues that the guidelines set down by the Recording Industry Association of America (RIAA) regarding explicit content in music are poorly thought out and should be either ignored or revised. The essay, after its introduction (a brief paragraph of text, followed by a collage of graphics), is divided into three main pages, labeled I, II, and III, and contains in-text links to other internal and external pages (see figure 2). The labels for his pages indicate that his essay progresses in a highly linear fashion, with each succeeding page relying on the arguments established on previous pages. In this sense, Bill's essay follows a mode of argumentation that seems to me to be much closer to the mode of conventional print-based essays.

Bill suggested that, while the assignment explicitly required multiple pages, the fact that he divided his essay into sections was also pragmatic: "Breaking it down makes it easier to think about. Say I have three sections with three points apiece. It's easier to think about than to discuss these nine things. It makes more sense to me to break it down." Echoing Jakob Nielsen (1996), Bill pointed out: "You get bored if you're scrolling down and down and down and down," and suggested that "you can't write big

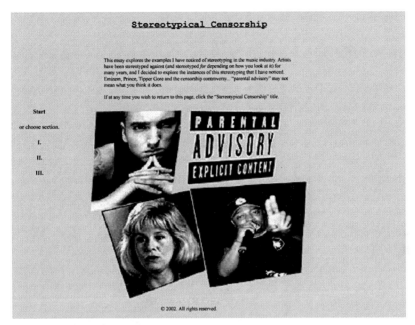

Stereotypical Censorship

This essay explores the examples I have noticed of stereotyping in the music industry. Artists have been stereotyped against (and stereotyped *for* depending on how you look at it) for many years, and I decided to explore the instances of this stereotyping that I have noticed. Eminem, Prince, Tipper Gore and the censorship controversy... "parental advisory" may not mean what you think it does.

If at any time you wish to return to this page, click the "Stereotypical Censorship" title.

Start

or choose section.

I.

II.

III.

Figure 2: Bill's introductory page

long descriptions and all this stuff and have your Web page go on for like eighteen pages. It just doesn't work." The links between the pages of Bill's essay appear, in apparent accordance with what seems to be a Web convention, on the left side of his text.

However, Bill also includes both internal and external links within the text of his paragraphs to material somehow supplementary to his argument, to citations, or to examples that often resisted or violated what I would think of as appropriate material for an essay. Clicking on the underlined title of the controversial gangsta rap song "Fuck tha Police," for example, plays an audio file of the song. I found this a fascinating strategy: while the song is clearly subordinated, hypotactically, to the argument of the essay, the audio file makes Bill's point far more forcefully than any textual example could have. Bill could have included a portion of the song's lyrics in text, which are themselves quite forceful:

> To the police I'm sayin fuck you punk
> Readin my rights and shit, it's all junk
> Pullin out a silly club, so you stand
> With a fake assed badge and a gun in your hand
> But take off the gun so you can see what's up
> And we'll go at it punk, I'ma fuck you up. (N.W.A. 1989)

But Bill's choice to include the song itself—its crisp beats, the sampled cymbal and funk guitar, MC Ren's aggressive snarl—places the example next to that which it exemplifies. Rather than having the language of his essay "tame" his example, it borrows from its power. In this sense, Bill's remark that "If I were going to do a personal narrative, I'd want to stick pictures of my friends, little links to [my hometown]," and his incorporation of the song, indicate that Web pages lend themselves to the concrete and particular.

Ken's and Bill's essays used links in radically different ways. The paratactic linking style of Ken's essay worked against my expectations of how an argument ought to work, and in fact I initially missed what was perhaps the most important component of Ken's argument: the parodic echo of the UMassDrunks site. Bill's essay was more linear and progressive, and his hypotactically linked examples also violated my expectations about arguments. However, in both cases, these were the most successful components of their essays: Ken's and Bill's Web pages were least convincing when they followed the conventions of Hesse's "essayistic literacy"—Bill's explicit, progressive, and dense initial prose describing the workings of the RIAA; Ken's attempt to tie his seven arguments together in an over-explained conclusion—and most convincing when they incorporated "unauthorized" modes of argumentation, or what Colin Lankshear and Michele Knobel call "insider knowledge" (2000).

Ken's and Bill's "insider knowledge" was knowledge about how discourse works on the World Wide Web, and it intersected in problematic ways with their positions as students in a classroom environment where they had already written several essays. Ken and Bill both had considerable experience navigating the Web, and both reported an understanding of the variety of genres that exist on the Web. As Moran and Herrington point out, "Students know this territory perhaps better than we do" (2002, 247), but they also know it *differently*. I was unfamiliar with UMassDrunks, and so missed the point of Ken's site; a site that Bill reported visiting on a daily basis, gamespot.com (http://www.gamespot.com), was one that I knew nothing about. At the same time, I would suspect that the number of undergraduates who visit *Arts and Letters Daily* (http://aldaily.com), the *Chronicle of Higher Education* (http://chronicle.com), or the *New York Review of Books* (http://nybooks.com) is relatively slight. My students do not read the same sites that I do, and so have notions about the generic conventions of Web sites that are different from mine—and I would suggest that *Arts and Letters Daily*, the *Chronicle*, and the *New York Review of Books* are all sites that favor Hesse's "essayistic literacy."

As teachers we need to understand that students will likely come into our classrooms holding much more familiarity with Web genres than they hold with Hesse's "essayistic literacy," and that any documents students produce will be influenced by this familiarity. Such an understanding is complicated by the fact that Web pages have a very brief and rapidly evolving history of generic characteristics. Web genres are overdetermined, shaped by too many different factors for us to be able to point to any one as the single determining factor. However, focusing on the way students use links, and the way those links position students and their Web pages within a social network, can help teachers to understand the ways in which students perceive their own positions. Heidi, in the next section, addresses the ways in which those perceptions play out within the commercialized context of the Web.

HEIDI'S ACCOUNT: SELF-REPRESENTATION AND COMMERCIALIZATION

For the past two years I have included a Web assignment in the College Writing sections I teach. Most semesters I have students convert an argumentative essay written about a current issue and for a particular audience into a Web site, with the guidelines being that students include multiple pages, incorporate images, develop link structures, and substantially revise their verbal text. In the process we discuss various design approaches to Web composition and rhetorical issues involved with the use of images, links, colors, text, and, for more technologically advanced students, sound and movement on Web sites. While this converting of an essay works well, particularly for students who have never made a Web site before and in the context of a course whose primary curricular focus is on print-based essays, in spring 2002, responding to numerous requests by students, I modified the assignment guidelines. Instead of stipulating that students convert an essay I gave them the option to compose something new for their Web sites.

Half of the twenty students chose to convert their argument essays, composing sites on such issues as the speed skating controversy at the Salt Lake Olympics, the proposed demolition of Fenway Park, and the dropout rate among UMass college students. Half of the students, however, chose to focus their sites upon topics they had not written about before in the class—at least not directly—thus creating what Billie Jones calls "native hypertexts" (2001) and what I prefer to call *Web-directed composi-tions*, which are composed exclusively for the Web. Of my students who chose to make new sites, most created what can broadly be categorized as personal sites, of which there are innumerable genres and subgenres evolving on the Web. One such genre is what Jay David Bolter identi-fies as the "gift page or site" (2001, 119), which is a site composed to be given to others, celebrating not only the individual(s) to whom the page is directed, but often the person creating the site as well. A number of students' sites from this class can be categorized within this gift genre. For example, one student dedicated her site to her younger brother; another student made a site about and for her friends at college.

Working with students as they composed these gift sites raised a number of issues for me that I had not encountered (or at least had not encountered as frequently) in previous semesters, including the domi-nance of visual over alphabetic imagery and the "fit" of these personal sites in the first-year composition curriculum. For my discussion here, however, I will focus on students' self-representations and my belated realizations of (1) the impact of commercialization upon my students' writing for the Web; and (2) the importance that an instructor learn as much as possible about the Web genres with which students are famil-iar and upon which they draw when composing their sites in order to engage students more critically with the rhetorical choices they make in their compositions.

In previous semesters when students converted essays into Web sites, they seldom made separate pages dedicated to explicit self-representa-tion; most instead opted for a few sentences describing themselves at the bottom of the main index page or an e-mail link. I realize now that my teaching of composing for the Web focused on issues of self-representa-tion primarily in relation to how design choices can build ethos, but I sel-dom discussed issues of explicit self-representation beyond what students might want to include on their index page. So when conferencing with students on earlier drafts of Web-directed compositions, I was surprised at the numerous pages with such titles as "About Me" or "Who I Am." Given that personal Web sites are so common on the Web, I should not have been surprised by these pages, but I think I was because I had not encoun-tered before such explicit representations of self in Web sites composed in the context of a composition classroom. What also surprised me—and eventually disturbed me—about these personal pages was the number of students who used lists to describe themselves.[4]

Jennifer

Height: 5' 3"
Weight: Again, like a girl is going to willingly give out her weight
Eyes: Dark brown
Hair: Dark blonde (I just dyed it strawberry blonde though)
High school: T. Regional Junior/ Senior High School
Year of Graduation: 2001
College: University of Massachusetts Amherst
Year of Graduation: 2005

Likes:

Sports: (To play) Softball/ Baseball, Street Hockey, Tackle Football, Basketball (To watch) Baseball/ Softball, Hockey, Equestrian, Football (occasionally)
Hobbies: Going to the beach, Hanging out with my friends, Rollerblading, Stargazing, Biking (occasionally), Being outside, Photography, Horseback riding

Dislikes:

Sports: (To play) Soccer, Golf (To watch) Racing, Golf
Hobbies: Shopping, School, Desk work (job wise)

Favorite:

Food: Chinese
Music: Almost anything
Movie: I like way to many to pick just one
Car: Not sure (as long as it's a stick-shift)
Author: J.R.R Tolkien, Terry Brooks, JK Rowling

Figure 3: Jennifer's section of her "Random Information" page

Jennifer, the first of two students I will focus on here, created a site titled "My Living Reflection" about her and her sister's experiences growing up as identical twins. As she explained in a reflective letter about her site, "I hope that [my sister] will enjoy the site. . . . I hope that anyone else who reads this site will see how twins are and aren't alike." Although her approach to writing this Web-directed composition was, as she explained, " kind of like an essay with pictures"—and indeed many of her pages are dominated by paragraphs of verbal text arranged with numerous images, creating an effect much like what Greg Wickliff and Kathleen Yancey call an "illustrated essay" (2001, 178)—her site included one page that is distinctly non-essay-like. She titled this page "Random Information" and it comprises lists of her and her sister's personal statistics, the activities each enjoys, and their favorite cars, food, movies, and books (see figure 3).[5]

I initially looked at this page with its list of likes and dislikes and its senior photos and thought about high school yearbooks, and I surmised that Jennifer was remediating a familiar print-based genre for the Web (Bolter 2001; Bolter and Grusin 1999). However, what I was eventually to learn was that Jennifer was not drawing—at least not consciously—from print-based genres, but, more problematically (I think), from commercialized Web-based genres.

Unfortunately I was not able to ask Jennifer about this page during a conference in the early drafting stages because at that point she had not constructed it. I first saw it at the final draft, where in a reflective letter about the process of composing her site, she wrote: "I like the Random Information page best" because "it was a lot of fun to compare and contrast what we like to do." I find it interesting that what Jennifer most liked about her site was what I least liked. Besides being bothered with the whole height/weight/eyes description, I also found the page an odd contrast to the rich detail, both visual and verbal, on the other pages. In her interview after the course was over, Jennifer explained: "Originally I was going to write a little essay about what we like to do and how we're different, but [my sister] said why not have a bio profile?" I have to admit that looking at the list above, I find part of me (the print-based English teacher who only in the past few years has moved to working with the Web and who teaches in a program that emphasizes the essay) missing that "little essay," a feeling that intensified once I learned what a bio profile is.

Briefly—I will describe in more detail below—bio profiles are lists of personal information that people are required to submit to commercial host sites such as AsianAvenue (http://www.asianavenue.com) or GeoCities (http://geocities.com), and they form the opening page of the "free" personal home pages people create at these Web hosting companies.

I first learned where to begin looking for bio profiles from another student, Kathy, who created what she described as a "couples site" about her boyfriend and their relationship. Judging from Kathy's description of her site, I surmise that couples sites form another genre of gift sites, serving many of the same social purposes. In her reflective letter accompanying her finished draft, Kathy explained (as I asked all students to do) the purpose(s) and audience(s) for her site: "My whole purpose of this Website is to give myself a chance to expand ourselves and was a gift for my boyfriend. . . . I hope after observing my whole Web page, he can have in mind that no matter how hard it is in life that I will always be there for him. . . . My main audience is, of course, my boyfriend. But also to those young adults or teenagers who may wander around surfing the net interested in couples' relationships."

Until I spoke with Kathy and viewed her site, I had no idea that couples sites existed on the Web. Kathy said she goes to them a lot to read about how other couples met and what they do together. From my perusal of some couples sites (do a Web search for "how we met" to see some), I realize that Kathy's site, while problematic for first-year composition (how many college papers are written for one's boyfriend?), is crafted solidly within the couples genre, and Kathy employed the social and textual conventions of the genre well—from the twinkling stars in the background of her pages to the "Him," "Her," and "Our" pages, and the many photos of her and her boyfriend together.[6]

Figure 4: Kathy's "Her" page

On both the "Him" page and the "Her" pages, of which I focus on the latter (see figure 4), Kathy had many links, including links to her online journal entries and to pages of more photos. She included photos of herself, her boyfriend, her friends, the Louis Vuitton purse she owns, and the Mazda car she drives. In the center of the page Kathy inserted a table listing information about her, categorized by such topics as age, nationality, occupation, and likes and dislikes.

When Kathy was asked in a postcourse e-mail interview "Did you have any other types of sites in mind when you were planning your pages?" she replied, "Actually, I do have another site in mind while planning my page. This site is the site I have shown already, www.asianavenue.com. I thought I could use some of the ideas I have on this page for the page in class." When I read her interview response, I remembered that in an in-class writing prior to working on Web pages (in which I asked students to write about their previous experiences with Web writing and their feelings about the upcoming Web assignment), Kathy mentioned that she had built a site on AsianAvenue, a point I originally missed following up on during class. My follow-up exploration of the profiles used on Web hosting services such as AsianAvenue and GeoCities heightened my concern about students' use of lists to describe themselves and made me regret the missed teaching and learning opportunities centered around students' appropriation of the generic features (and thus some of the social functions) of profiles.

Profiles, as I mentioned, are lists of required personal information that individuals fill out upon registering to receive access to Web space where they can then post a "free" personal site (see figure 5). While the exact personal information gathered in these profiles varies by company, in general they cover information such as "your birthday, city where you live, hobbies, and interests" (AsianAvenue) and "name, email address, birth date, gender, zip code, industry, and personal interests" (Yahoo, which owns and operates GeoCities). In user agreements and privacy policies, the Web hosting companies explicitly state that "Profile information will be used to create personalized content, service, and advertise [sic] on the Service. AsianAvenue.com may also use your profile to generate aggregate reports and market research" (AsianAvenue) and that such information will be used "to customize the advertising and consumer requests for products and services, improve our services, conduct research, and provide reporting for internal and external clients" (Yahoo). However, I wonder how many people, especially teenagers and young adults, actually read the companies' policies and thus can contextualize more fully the factors influencing the lists of personal information that dominate the portal pages of individual sites.

I see these lists like the one in figure 5 of likes, interests, and hobbies and then return to my students' pages, and I no longer see a high school yearbook format, which is how I first read Jennifer's and Kathy's lists, but rather a reduction of identity and self-presentation for marketers, advertisers, and other "internal and external clients," to use Yahoo's obfuscating phrase. Profiles are a feature of personal Web pages created for marketing purposes, and it disturbs me that this translation of identity into commercially viable categories seems to have been internalized by students who then, in representing themselves through lists, perpetuate their own commodification.

The dislocations created by moving writing and the teaching and learning of writing to the Web exposed more fully for me the ways in which students bring modes of expression shaped by corporate culture into the classroom and into both their print-based and Web-directed compositions. The commercialization of the Web is so pervasive, inducing what Michael Joyce calls a "commercial glaze" (1995, 167), that no matter what genre students write in for the Web, instructors need to be prepared to discuss more fully with students the ways in which their prior experiences reading the Web shape their approaches and their ideas for the sites they compose. Although in a subsequent semester of College Writing I

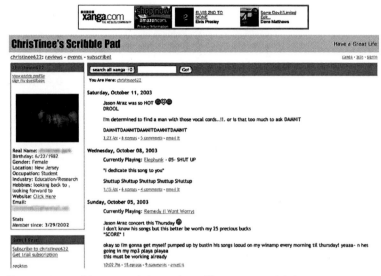

Figure 5. A portal for a personal page hosted by a commercial site

returned to having students convert an argumentative essay for the Web, I also included assignments focused on more explicit analysis of Web-based genres, including the rhetorical structuring of various sites students identified as ones they frequently visited and, of course, personal sites at Web hosting services like GeoCities.[7] My goal is to ensure that students look at the rhetorical constructions of Web sites, rather than through them (Lanham 1993, 72–83) in order that students may pay attention to how a site's generic features position them and thus contribute to what is said, how, in what context, and to whom. Only by engaging students and ourselves in ongoing discussions of the evolving Internet genres will we be adequately prepared to help them compose for the Web.

IMPLICATIONS FOR TEACHING WEB GENRES

While we have discussed the teaching of Web sites in just two instances in two specific contexts, we both feel that our experiences indicate significant issues for instructors to consider when incorporating Web-directed compositions into course curricula.

1. *We should acknowledge students' expertise in understanding, navigating, and composing in Web genres while also sharing our own expertise in analyzing and understanding genres.* In the attempts we both made to bring Web assignments into our classrooms (and in the turmoil of teaching students how to do such things as change background colors, design layouts, insert

images, format text, create links, manage files, and so on), we discovered that we had missed opportunities to engage with students in critical discussions of how Web genres get constructed, circulated, accepted, and altered. So, too, we discovered that we had overlooked students' cultural expertise with the Web, an expertise that helped them to produce rich, nuanced, and rhetorically sophisticated documents, and an expertise that could have helped us to earlier and more completely understand the complex nature of Web genres. Gail Hawisher and Cynthia Selfe point out that because so many instructors today "have come of age in a print generation . . . we often find ourselves casting about for effective ways to educate students for a world with which we ourselves are unfamiliar—and about which we remain uncertain" (1999b, 3). Yet even if we are unfamiliar with the evolving Web genres that influence our students' compositions—even if we don't have sites hosted at GeoCities or visit student-oriented sites like UMassDrunks—we do possess the critical, rhetorical, and theoretical knowledge to facilitate students' analyses of both the Web sites they visit and the Web sites they create.

2. *We should cultivate an awareness of and receptivity to hybrid, changing genres both in ourselves and in our students.* Both of our experiences have demonstrated the problems inherent in attempting to narrowly categorize Web texts by an attention to link structures, content, or technical considerations. We would argue for an understanding of Web texts that recognizes their evolving and hybrid nature, particularly because of the rapidly changing nature of the Web. With the Web even more so than with print-based genres, we find the perspective of Bill Cope and Mary Kalantzis instructive: "As genre theory evolves, however, it becomes obvious that more and more text is generically problematic. To describe this, we need to move beyond categorizations of the generic, towards using genre as an analytical tool for engaging with . . . multigeneric, intergeneric and heterglossic texts (1993a, 16)."

Employing genre as an analytical tool requires that we not only recognize the multigeneric nature of Web texts, but also develop strategies for helping students—and ourselves—identify and analyze the origins of our frequently differing conceptions of Web genres. The changing nature of the Web only serves to heighten the exigency of asking such basic questions as:

- What is the purpose of your site?
- For whom is it composed?

- Are you modeling your site—or features of your site—on other sites you have seen on the Web? What do you think of the values and power relations associated with those sites?
- What design decisions (e.g., links, graphics, sound, backgrounds, font, layout, color) have you made to achieve your purpose for your particular audience(s)? What sorts of texts, Web and print, influenced those decisions?
- If you were to categorize your site by genre, into what genre(s) would you say it fits?

These apparently fundamental questions take on new nuance when considered in relation to the Web. Addressing such questions in our classrooms can increase both students' and our own understandings of the diverse factors shaping genre expression and evolution.

But more than classroom inquiry is needed. We also need, as Colin Lankshear and Michele Knobel (2000) remark, "to get beyond research/ study of familiar genres." We particularly need to investigate the hybrid nature of Web genres using a variety of methodological and theoretical frames and researching a variety of contexts. In short, we need more knowledge to better understand and to better teach writing on and for the Web.

3. *We should foster awareness of the multiple, overlapping influences on the composition of Web texts.* First, and perhaps most obviously, the technology upon which the Web is based profoundly influences the texts and thus the genres of Web-directed compositions. For example, bandwidth (the amount of information that a user's link to the Internet can handle per unit of time) determines how quickly or slowly a user can send or receive files.[8] Our students, working with the university's broad bandwidth, often composed pages that, when they looked at them at home on dial-up connections, took "forever" to load. Some students decided to revise their pages to make them more accessible to lower bandwidth connections, while other students were less concerned with accessibility and more concerned with having flashing animations and including a large number of images.

Second, Web authors' access to and familiarity with various software resources profoundly shape the sites they create. Whether a Web site contains only text; text and static images; or text, static images, sound, and visual animations shapes the positions and interactions of readers and writers. Web sites that include sophisticated multimedia elements require a great deal of knowledge to create using code, but authors with relatively little Web experience can use visual HTML editors such as Macromedia's Dreamweaver to include multimedia elements in their texts. As writers incorporate more multimedia elements into their Web compositions, the nature of writing changes, and as teachers we need to be prepared for this.

Third, instructors need to acknowledge the institutional considerations shaping the teaching and academic expectations of Web assignments. As we both have discussed, we should have acknowledged further the pressures we felt to ensure that students' sites were equivalent to essays, and we should have recognized more fully that students' goals for their Web sites did not often align with our goals. Unlike their print-based essays (which, despite our best efforts, students still often saw as being for the teacher), students' Web sites were frequently directed to an audience outside the classroom. Although we were very much aware of the context of College Writing, many students bypassed considerations of this context altogether. Working within a curriculum highly focused upon print-based essays led us to impose constraints upon Web assignments and thus upon how we responded to and evaluated students' Web compositions, and such constraints and responses may have been simply inappropriate to the online genres students created.

CONCLUSIONS

Students, when composing Web documents, often draw their primary influences from the Web; as obvious as such a statement may seem, our experiences indicate that it bears repeating. Because of the millions and millions of pages on the Web, and with more being added every moment, each person can explore only a small portion of the Web. For these reasons, individual students will bring unique perceptions of Web genres to the classroom, perceptions perhaps even more idiosyncratic than those we may associate with print genres. Furthermore, the Web is just as saturated with influences and interests—corporate, commercial, or otherwise—as the rest of our culture. These influences explicitly and implicitly shape how individuals read and write online, and we believe it is essential that instructors and students situate individual approaches to Web composition within the broader contexts of these influences.

Our attention to the changing nature of the Web and its association with technological and corporate influences can usefully foreground the ways individuals bring societal influences to bear upon their texts, in ways that are often transparent to us when associated with print media. In teaching more traditional academic genres, teachers often bring in other works for analysis and discussion. In working with Web genres in the classroom, teachers need to engage students in specific cultural and rhetorical critiques of the Web sites that *they* most frequently visit, in addition to focusing attention on more conventionally academic Web sites, and the societal influences shaping both. We can learn much from studying such sites as UMassDrunks or the personal pages at Yahoo.

When we read, analyze, and compose Web texts with students, we need to also expand our own understandings of genre. As Marcy Bauman has noted, "In this time of unprecedented change, the genres we can invent and the genres we allow ourselves to use as a profession will determine the ways we can act in the world. We owe it to ourselves to draw the parameters as broadly as we can" (1991, 281). By initiating and sustaining disciplinary and classroom conversations centered around explicit analysis and discussion of emerging Web genres, including the diverse genres with which students are most familiar, we will be able to shape most fully how we can act in the world. We owe this to ourselves and, more important, to our students.

NOTES

1. Some students remarked on the sophistication and complexity of Dreamweaver as an editing tool. While using Dreamweaver gave students considerable flexibility in composing their Web pages, it also required sustained and intense instruction over more than one class session. A number of students struggled with the technology and worried out loud that their writing had suffered as a result. These concerns, along with concerns about the availability of Dreamweaver, led me to start reconsidering the ways I taught students to compose Web pages.

2. This is where the effects of parataxis on reading begin to blur with the effects of brevity. In his May 1996 "Alertbox" column, usability expert Jakob Nielsen asserted: "Only 10% of users scroll beyond the information that is visible on the screen when a page comes up." While Nielsen (1997) has since tempered this advice, suggesting that "the argument against scrolling is no longer as strong as it used to be," the no-scroll rule seems to have become accepted as conventional wisdom by many who design for the Web, and has led to the phenomenon of sites such as *Salon* and the *New York Times* breaking up their online stories into chunks of roughly 750 words. How do we separate out the sequential "and/and/and" of these chunks from the "and/and/and" of parataxis?

Part of the confusion over parataxis comes from the perception that the term merely means having multiple pages.

3.   Since Ken wrote his essay, the UMassDrunks site has been taken down in response to pressure from the university, only to be put back online in a different form.

4.   After teaching the course upon which my discussion is based and after researching and drafting this chapter, I read John Killoran's (2002) essay "Under Constriction: Colonization and Synthetic Institutionalization of Web Space," where he reports on his study of 106 personal home pages. He found, as did I, that Web authors frequently modeled their sites on institutional models and that eleven home page authors used lists or forms to identify themselves. Killoran briefly examines those lists for how they position individuals as "domesticated innocuous subjects and objects of a capitalist and bureaucratic order" (27), but he does not make the link to specific corporate Web models shaping the use of lists as means of representation.

5.   The Web sites of the students I focus on here were (and may still be) available on the Web, and all students gave permission to show screen captures of their sites. In these screen captures, I have changed students' names and blurred the photos.

6.   Responding to and grading Kathy's site was difficult for me because I resisted reading her site within the rhetorical frame she constructed. Whereas she saw this project as existing solely on the Web for her and her boyfriend and for other couples interested in their relationship, I was very cognizant of the more immediate context of College Writing.

7.   Since spring 2002, I have taught College Writing just one other semester, and I returned to having all students convert a current issue essay. I did this in part because I think it's easier for students to attend to issues of Web composition, including learning the technology, when they are revising text, not composing anew (especially for students new to Web composition, as most first-year students at UMass are).

8.   Greater bandwidth is often more expensive, making economic factors not only a determinant of access to the Internet, but also a determinant of what a user reads and writes on the Internet.

11

WRITING IN EMERGING GENRES
Student Web Sites in Writing and Writing-Intensive Classes

Mike Palmquist

Writers are living, in the fullest sense of the ancient Chinese proverb, in interesting times. Not since the fifteenth century, when Gutenberg perfected a workable system of movable type, has there been such a change in how information and ideas are exchanged. In the late fifteenth century, Gutenberg's technological innovations resulted in the widespread availability of printed work in vernacular languages, a factor that scholars such as Eisenstein (1979) argue contributed to the Protestant Reformation, the expansion of the Italian Renaissance, and the rise of the scientific method, among other movements. In the late twentieth and early twenty-first centuries, the Internet, and in particular the World Wide Web, has had what appears to be a similar effect on the means through which we communicate with each other. Whether the rise of networked communications will result in the widespread social, political, cultural, and economic changes attributed to the printing press remains uncertain, although numerous scholars have argued that it will (Dertouzos, 1997; Dewar 1998; Kaplan 1995; Negroponte 1995). What is certain, from a writer's point of view, is that the rules of writing have changed. Publication is no longer assumed to be linked to a printing press. Nor is it necessarily linked to well-defined print genres. As the Web has grown to encompass literally billions of sites and, despite the best efforts of Google and Yahoo! countless billions of pages, the range of expression has grown as well.

That range of expression poses opportunities for experienced writers. In much the same way that writers of English prose in the fifteenth and sixteenth centuries viewed the printing press as an opportunity to experiment with genre, contemporary writers have been experimenting with forms of expression made possible by network technologies. Unfortunately for readers, those experiments—like many of those of the Early Modern period—have been far from universally successful. Readers have found it difficult to anticipate the structure of and locate information within hypertextual documents published on the World Wide Web.

Consensus has not yet been achieved among Web developers about the functions and format of particular design elements, such as buttons and menus. And the frequent changes in the style and design of online documents, despite the best intentions of their authors, have often left readers frustrated and bewildered.

Like writers in the fifteenth and sixteenth centuries, we are in a period of transition. Despite the rapid growth of the Web, it remains very much a place of experimentation and adaptation. As de Casiol and Dyson argue, digital documents "have not yet developed a complete set of conventions that enable us to characterise them into genres" (2002, 165). Nonetheless, although stable genres are yet to emerge (Siddler 2002), other scholars suggest that some genres are in the process of emerging, such as the home page (Dillon and Gushrowski 2000), digital broadsheet (Watters and Shepherd 1997), resource list page (Crowston and Williams 2000), and discussion list page (Bauman 1999). Each of these emerging Web genres can be seen as arising from a recurring social situation: the personal home page, for example, as the presentation of self, or subject, in a highly condensed form to a large, likely unknowable audience. Concurrently, a number of print genres, among them the magazine article, scholarly journal article, the press release, and the opinion column, are being successfully adapted—or, to use Bolter and Grusin's (1999) term, *remediated*—for publication on the Web (Crowston and Williams 2000; Rho and Gedeon 2000). It is clear, however, that much remains in flux—and is likely to remain so for years to come.

This poses significant difficulties for writers new to the Web. In particular, it poses difficulties for student writers, whose efforts have been confined largely to print genres such as essays and reports. It also poses difficulties for teachers who ask students in writing and writing-intensive courses to create Web documents. Unfortunately, we know relatively little about the difficulties students face as they attempt to negotiate the complexities of writing documents intended for publication on the Web. Although much has been written about the use of hypertexts and Web sites in writing and writing-intensive classrooms (Chapman 1999; Mauriello, Pagnucci, and Winner 1999; Walker 2002; Williams 2001), the published literature reveals little about how student writers learn to negotiate the challenges of writing such documents. Wickliff and Yancey (2001) offer one of the few reports of students writing Web sites for the first time. Although their discussion of the efforts of university honors students to create a classwide Web site focused primarily on the students' use of visual elements, their conclusion—that these gifted students "performed much like basic writers when challenged with acquiring a broad set of new visual and computer literacy skills" (177)—suggests that even our strongest students will encounter difficulties as they move from composing genres that are typically published in print to those typically published on the Web. This conclusion is echoed, to some extent, by Edwards and McKee's description in chapter 10 of this book of their efforts to support the writing of Web sites in first-year composition classes, although Edwards and McKee report a greater degree of success in their classes than did Wickliff and Yancey and offer a more comprehensive set of recommendations about teaching Web writing.

In this chapter, I explore the efforts of students in three writing and writing-intensive classes to create Web sites. These Web sites served as the final project for each course. Drawing on interviews with the students and their teachers as well as analysis of the student sites, I will chart the efforts of students to understand the constraints and possibilities of emerging Web genres.

WEB GENRES: EMERGING CONVENTIONS

Web sites have been assigned for several years in writing and writing-intensive courses. And scholars have considered the constraints and possibilities of such documents—and, more broadly, of hypertexts—for decades (e.g., Bolter 1991, 1993; Bush 1945, 1967; Conklin 1987; Kaplan 1995; Nelson 1983; Slatin 1990). Yet the quickly shifting technological landscape of the Web, and the tools used to create documents distributed on the Web, have worked against the creation of stable genre definitions for Web documents.

In large part, this is because the defining characteristic of the Web—the link—allows writers to compose documents that have little resemblance to the linear print documents with which readers and writers are most familiar. The ability to create links has resulted in new ways to conceptualize transitions between and within Web documents. Footnotes and endnotes, for example, can be replaced with links to pop-up windows containing notes or with links to source documents. Although footnotes and endnotes are used in a number of remediated Web documents (Bolter and Grusin 1999), such as publications in online scholarly journals, writers are seldom *expected* to use them. Instead, footnotes and endnotes have become another linking strategy that writers *might* use.

The ability to create links has worked against the development of standardized organizational structures for documents published on the Web. Consider, for example, the wide range of organizational structures for scholarly articles published in journals housed on the Web, such as *Kairos* (http://english.ttu.edu/kairos), *Across the Disciplines* (http://wac.colostate.edu/atd), and *Enculturation (http://enculturation.gmu.edu)*. Unlike scholarly articles published in print journals, which rely almost exclusively on a linear (page 1, page 2, page 3) structure, scholarly articles published on the Web might adopt structures that are

- linear: navigation is restricted to adjacent pages (e.g., next, previous)
- hierarchical: navigation is possible only up (to a "parent" page) or down (to "child" pages)
- interlinked: navigation is possible between all pages
- combined: navigation is possible using a combination of the three other structures

Figure 1 provides an example of a combined structure that uses linear, hierarchical, and interlinked structures.

Document structure is closely related to the organization of documents. However, because individual pages can have specific organizational patterns, such as chronology or cause-effect, it is typically distinguished from organization per se. Recently, scholars such as Vaughan and Dillon (2000) have begun to refer to the structure of documents published on the Web using the term *shape.* Noting that the widely divergent structures of such documents can be difficult for readers to easily internalize and predict, they suggest that some shapes may be more appropriate for specific types of documents—such as news articles—than others. If so, and if some consensus can be arrived at concerning appropriate document shapes, we might find that certain shapes will become associated with emerging Web genres.

The ability to create links also affects a writer's choice of navigation tools—the means by which readers move through a Web site. Web developers typically provide readers with navigation support, such as menus, tables of contents, navigation headers and footers, site search tools, and graphical site maps (see figure 2). Even relatively simple Web sites tend to display navigation menus or headers, since these aids will allow readers not only to move to specific pages, but also to understand the content and purpose of the site. Over the past several years, navigation tools have become somewhat conventionalized. Side menus—often in the form of

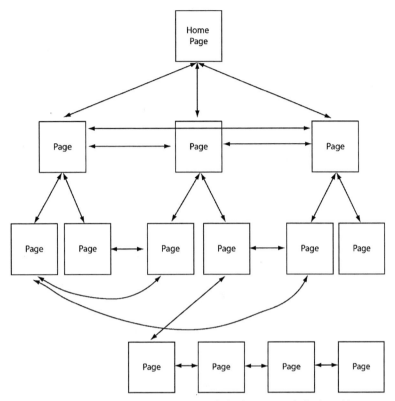

Figure 1: A combined document structure includes linear, interlinked, and hierarchical elements.

lists or buttons—have become a standard part of most complex sites. And a growing number of sites have begun to provide top menus that expand in a manner similar to the menus on word processing programs and other commonly used software applications.

The ability to link to and embed in Web documents a wider range of illustrations than is possible in print documents also increases the range of possibilities with which Web developers can work. In addition to the images, tables, charts, and graphs frequently used in print documents, documents published on the Web can include audio and video clips, animations, java applets such as mortgage calculators, embedded program files, and links to information stored in a database. Spreadsheets, tables, or charts, for example, can allow readers to better understand a topic or to engage in "what if" scenarios by changing the information or sorting on various categories. An image, such as a map of the western United States, can be transformed into a clickable map so that clicking on a

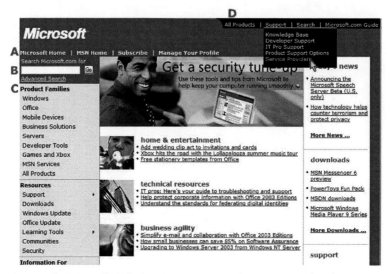

Figure 2: The Microsoft Web site, circa 2003, provides a navigation header (A), a search tool (B), a side menu (C), and a drop-down menu (D).

particular city or state would allow readers to obtain information about that city or state.

The expanded choices concerning document structure, navigation tools, and illustrations have worked against the quick emergence of genre conventions for Web documents. However, in the area of page design—the layout of text and illustrations on a Web page—conventions appear to be emerging. Page design typically reflects the social and commercial purposes of a Web site, with Web portals, such as Lycos, Yahoo! and MSN.com favoring a design that literally crams as much information as possible into a page and search sites such as Google and AllTheWeb.com opting for designs that highlight their primary function (see figure 3). Similarly, a number of commercial sites—including both news and information sites, such as CNN.com and the *New York Times Online*, and corporate sites, such as Microsoft.com and Sears.com—have adopted a design consistent with the digital broadsheet genre that Watters and Shepherd (1997) identified several years ago (see figure 4). This design mimics the front pages of newspapers and the tables of contents found in many mainstream magazines, allowing them to provide a large amount of information in a small space. In general, pages within Web sites, in particular those that provide "content," are increasingly adopting a design that sandwiches text and illustrations between page banners, navigation menus, and navigation headers and footers. Salon.com provides an example of a design adopted

Figure 3: The simple, uncluttered design of the Google home page calls attention to its primary functions and search types.

Figure 4: The CNN.com site uses a design consistent with the digital broadsheet genre.

Figure 5: A widely used Web page design. The page banner, navigation header and footer (not shown), and side menu frame the main content of the page.

by a number of Web sites, with the text and illustrations—in this case, of an article—placed within a column bordered by links to related information, advertisements, and other pages on the site (see figure 5).

Although attempts have been made to define genres among Web documents, the pace of technological change works against their definition. It remains uncertain whether the conventions that are beginning to emerge will withstand the continuing pace of technological development.

SIX STUDENTS WRITING FOR THE WEB: AN EXPLORATORY STUDY

To better understand how student writers learn and adapt to writing in the shifting landscape of the Web, I interviewed six student writers (all identified pseudonymously here): two each from a speech communications course, an undergraduate Web development course, and a graduate Web writing course, and examined the Web sites they created.

- Jessica was a senior speech communications major. She planned to attend graduate school in communication theory. Her site focused on forms and effects of propaganda.
- Reid was a senior speech communication major who planned to pursue a career in a communications field. His site focused on the history and varieties of contemporary Christian music.
- Ellen was a senior writing major. She planned to seek a career in grant writing and public relations. Her site focused on the work and life of Emily Dickinson.
- Kathy was a nontraditional student who was completing her junior year. A writing major in the English department, she had decided to establish a small business that facilitated the formation of student book groups. Her site supported that business.
- Callie was a second-year MFA candidate focusing on fiction and nonfiction. A former accountant, she had enrolled in graduate school in her mid-thirties to pursue a career in writing and literary publishing. Her Web site consisted of a collection of linked nonfiction vignettes and short essays about her family.
- Paul was a first-year master's candidate who had enrolled in graduate school after a successful career as a small businessman. He intended to pursue a career as a writer and consultant. His site consisted of a collection of essays about a bicyclist following the Lewis and Clark Trail.

I selected students from the three classes to increase the likelihood of obtaining findings that were not influenced by the genre conventions suggested by a particular faculty member. The speech course was taught by a faculty member who had been working with the Web since the mid-1990s. The undergraduate Web development class was taught by an instructor with three years' experience designing and editing Web sites and four years' experience teaching composition and creative writing. I taught the graduate workshop, bringing to the classroom seventeen years of experience teaching writing and seven years' experience teaching Web design. I recruited students from the speech communication course through a class presentation. I recruited students in the writing courses via electronic mail. I waited until the semester was completed and grades had been submitted to recruit students from the graduate workshop.

The three classes introduced students to Web design by teaching HTML coding. The two writing classes allowed students to use WYSIWYG (what you see is what you get) Web editors, such as Macromedia Dreamweaver or Microsoft FrontPage, after they had demonstrated proficiency with HTML code. The instructor of the speech class did not allow students to use a WYSIWYG Web editor.

In the interviews, I asked students to reflect on their experiences reading and developing documents for the Web, to discuss issues that I hoped would allow me to estimate their understanding of the Web as "genred," to describe the writing processes they had followed to create their Web sites, and to reflect on how those processes differed from those they used to write print documents. My questions directed their attention to the four issues discussed above—document structure, navigation tools, digital illustrations, and page design. My examination of their Web sites focused on those issues as well.

RESULTS AND DISCUSSION

In general, students in the three classes produced effective Web sites, with the graduate and undergraduate writing students, predictably, producing more polished and usable sites than those in the speech communication course, and the graduate students producing the most polished and best-written sites. In part, these findings stem from the amount of instruction provided in Web development in the three courses.

The three courses represent a spectrum of instruction. The speech communication course focused on exploring the theoretical differences between face-to-face, group, and mediated communication. As is the case in most writing-intensive courses, the Web assignment served as one of many activities covered in the course. As a final project, it received significant attention throughout the second half of the course, but it was not the only activity to which the students and instructor devoted their class-related time. The instructor provided a general template for the assignment: a minimum of five pages, including a home page and a works cited page, and some sort of navigation support for readers. The intermediate Web development course focused on the theoretical and practical differences between print and digital documents. Students were required to complete three academic essays, which focused on the analysis of Web sites and online communities, and two Web sites, a personal home page and a larger topical Web site. The instructor introduced Web design approximately four weeks into the sixteen-week semester and spent roughly equal amounts of time on the print and Web assignments. The graduate creative writing course required students to create a single Web site containing a portfolio of work written for the class. Projects included a poetry site that used Flash animation to create dynamic poems, a script for a play, a novel adapted to the Web, and collections of nonfiction. The course focused on Web design and development throughout the semester. Students were introduced to basic coding techniques and design issues on the first day of class and, by the middle of the semester, had gained familiarity with HTML, cascading style sheets, and JavaScript. Full-class workshops of individual projects took place during the last seven weeks of the sixteen-week semester.

Students' Experience with the Web

Prior to beginning their work in the three courses, the six students had used the Web for personal and academic purposes. These purposes included using Web-based communication tools to chat and participate in discussion forums, using search sites such as Google and Yahoo!, conducting research for courses using Web-based library resources such as online catalogues and databases, and viewing documents for aesthetic purposes (e.g., reading fiction or poetry on the Web).

Three of the four undergraduates, Jessica, Reid, and Ellen, began using the Web as a communication and research tool while they were in junior or senior high school—roughly the mid-1990s. Kathy, in contrast, began using it in 2000, shortly before she began her undergraduate studies. Ellen pointed out that she "started using the Web in junior high school and was introduced to the Internet in a group format, which consisted of the entire class circling around a few computers in my school's computer lab." At roughly the same time, her family purchased a computer and obtained an America Online account. "My concept of the

Internet was really jaded after I started using AOL," she said. "I thought that the purpose of the Web was to 'chat' and meet people." Reid, who, like Jessica, used the Web largely for research until enrolling in his speech communication class, observed that he used the Web only casually until his senior year of high school, when he realized that the Web was "a lot bigger than I thought."

Like the undergraduate students, Callie noted that she had used the Web for informational purposes for several years. Since beginning her graduate studies, however, she noted that her use of the Web had grown. "I also go to the Web to read or look at art or experience a Web design," she said. "I guess I'm trying to say I see the Web as more of an artistic outlet now."

Only two of the students brought experience of developing Web sites to their classes. Kathy, the undergraduate student who had used the Web for the shortest amount of time—beginning in 2000—had worked for a year as a Web site editor using Microsoft FrontPage, a WYSIWYG Web editor. "Eventually the time necessary to maintain this site was no longer worth what they paid me, so after about a year, I quit," she said. "At the time I began [the class], I had only been using the Web to check e-mail or to surf around for information." Paul, a graduate student who had enrolled in the English department's master's program after three decades as a small-business owner, began using the Web as a business tool in 1997 to support just-in-time buying and eventually directed the development of a site for his company. "Around 1999 I had a site built for my own company," he said. "I used it as a marketing tool, sales catalogue, and all-purpose conduit for business-to-business communications." Paul noted that he made significant contributions to the overall content and design of his company's site, but he did not do any of the development or maintenance of its pages.

Individually, the six students brought different conceptions of the Web to their work in the three classes. Paul saw the Web largely through the lens of business, Callie considered it at least in part as a place for artistic expression, and the four undergraduates, to varying degrees, saw it as a communication and information-access tool. Although two of the students had experience developing Web pages, that experiencewas limited: neither had written text for the Web and neither had coded Web pages.

Students' Understanding of Web Documents as Genred

Even after completing their courses, the idea that documents published on the Web might be classified into discrete genres would likely come as a surprise to the undergraduates who participated in this study. In their interviews, they refer to Web sites in a fairly monolithic sense. Even the two writing majors, who had more than a passing familiarity with the notion that print documents can be classified by genre, tended to refer to Web sites as an undifferentiated set of documents—as though one Web site might be much like another despite differences in site structure, design, navigation tools, purpose, and audience.

In part, this reflects a lack of emphasis on genre in the two undergraduate classes. Although Kathy and Ellen were required to write an essay that evaluated and reflected on a Web site, and were encouraged by their instructor to explore Web sites and share in their class discussion forum links to interesting sites, their instructor noted in an interview after the course ended that she felt some ambivalence about addressing the issue of genre during the course. "I don't think I addressed this type of writing specifically as its own genre," she said. Instead, she focused on the need to produce well-written Web sites: "I was asking the students to first think about their writing and second to think about how they could put their writing into a 'Web structure' —to turn it into that genre of writing we might now call Web writing. So, yes, I think Web writing does then become its own genre, for better or for worse depending on what assumptions and applications are at hand."

Similarly, the instructor of the speech communication course did not address the issue of genres. Nor did he require his students to explore and discuss among themselves other Web sites, a decision that may have also limited Jessica and Reid's awareness of genre differences among Web sites. "I should have," he said in an interview following the completion of the course. "And I have in the past. But I tried some new things [this semester] and deleting this component was a mistake."

In contrast to the students in the two undergraduate classes, the graduate students showed a more nuanced understanding of genre in Web documents. Callie, for example, discussed her interests in exploring creative and informative Web sites, suggesting an awareness of different document functions and genres on the Web. "I would say the whole writing experience was somewhat liberating," she said. "Creative hypertext—hyperfiction, etc.—is still so new to the Web that I felt I could do whatever I wanted. The biggest challenge to me was to try to leave the linear structure associated with printed text." In part, Callie's awareness of genre emerges from class discussions that explored the implications of writing for the Web in genres normally composed for print media. The ten students in the course, who had the freedom to write in any creative genre, produced short and long fiction, nonfiction essays and vignettes, poetry, and a play. Callie's awareness of genre, which is matched by Paul's, also reflects the more extensive experience as readers of print documents that they brought to the course.

Despite their comparative inexperience as writers, and despite the lack of focus on genre in their courses, the undergraduates articulated issues closely related to the idea of genre on the Web. Their focus in their interviews on site structure, navigation, ease of use, and general design features of Web sites suggests an emerging notion of features that should be present in effective sites, and to some extent this suggests an emerging notion of genres on the Web. Kathy's focus on sites that accomplished a purpose similar to the one she envisioned for her small-business Web site, for example, come closest to a sense of differing genres on the Web. "I spent lots of time looking at similar sites searching for the best way to organize mine," she said. "Also, I was concerned about the look of my site. Colors and the overall feel were important. I learned from other sites what I did not want, in addition to what I might try to emulate. If a site didn't do what I thought it should, I asked myself what I might do differently."

The other undergraduates expressed similar concerns about site structure, ease of use, and navigation issues. "For me, it's mostly navigation [that concerns me about Web sites]," said Jessica. "Design matters. But not being able to find something I want, especially when I know it's in there, is really frustrating." Reid expressed similar concerns about Web sites, noting that his recent searches for information about graduate programs had brought him to some "ridiculous" sites. "It really bothers me when I come to a site that's unfriendly—that you can't figure out," he said. "You don't know where you're going. You don't know what you're doing. It's totally illogical to me to be able to figure out what their strengths are academically, what they offer to students, things like that."

Had the undergraduate students been asked directly about differences among types of Web sites, such as search sites, portals, news and information sites, educational sites, commercial sites, and so on, it is likely that they would have been able to articulate general differences among them. That their discussions of their composing processes and experiences with the Web indicated little if any awareness of the Web as home to multiple genres suggests both a lack of attention to the issue in their classes and a general sense among the students of the Web as a monolithic, "genre-free" medium.

Student Writing Processes and Emerging Notions of Web Genres: The Impact of Print Genres on Student Conceptions of Web Sites

The writing processes of the six student writers reflect, to varying degrees, their understanding of the possible structures of Web documents, the need to provide navigation support for readers, the expanded range of illustrations that can be used in Web documents, and emerging conventions for page design. Along with interactivity, database integration, and communication tools, which were not addressed by the students in this study, these issues are likely to make strong contributions to emerging genres among Web documents. For the six students in this study, who had not been confronted by these issues in print-genre academic writing assignments, the need to consider them significantly complicated their composing processes. In many cases, faced with unfamiliar challenges, the students drew on their experiences as readers and writers of print genres to create their sites.

The Shape of Web Documents: Student Efforts to Create Appropriate Site Structures

The structures of the student Web sites varied in size and complexity. The two students in the speech communication course adopted a relatively straightforward interlinked structure consisting of six pages. The other students produced sites with combined structures that incorporated linear, interlinked, and hierarchical elements (see table 1).

With one exception, the sites exhibited the influence of print genres that students had worked with prior to taking the courses for which they created their Web sites. The two sites created by Jessica and Reid, the speech communication students, strongly resembled an academic essay, with an introduction (home page), three or four main points (related pages), and a works cited list (bibliography page). Ellen's site, a lengthy treatment of Emily Dickinson and her work, was organized in a linear structure that closely resembled—and was in many ways intended to be read as—an academic essay. And both graduate students, Callie and Paul, modeled their sites—in each case a collection of nonfiction essays and vignettes—on literary anthologies. Only one student, Kathy, created a site that had little resemblance to print genres, most likely because she was working on a type of site that has no print analogue—a commercial site for a small business (see figure 6).

In their interviews, the students indicated that their experiences as readers and writers of print genres had played a significant role in their

TABLE **1**

Structure and Page Lengths of Student Web Sites

Writer	Structure	Pages	Typical Page Length (screens)	Longest Page
Jessica	Interlinked	6	2	2
Reid	Interlinked	6	5	10
Ellen	Combined (strong linear influence with some hierarchy)	28	1 to 2	3
Kathy	Combined (strong interlinked influence with some hierarchy)	20	2	5
Callie	Combined (interlinked and linear elements)	32	1	4
Paul	Combined (interlinked and linear elements)	24	1	2

Figure 6: Site structure for Kathy's WhatchaThinking.com Web site (M = presence of side menu).

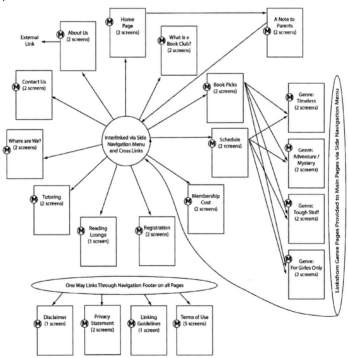

decisions about the structure of their sites. When asked why he had not considered breaking up his longest page, which required the reader to scroll ten times to view its complete content, Reid responded, "You know, it actually never crossed my mind." He suspected that he hadn't considered breaking up the page because his assignment had specified a minimum of five pages, including a home page, three content pages, and a bibliography page. "I think I had a very linear thought process instead of being Web page minded," he said. "In the future, I'd like to put it on another server and then I'll break it up into smaller pages."

Ellen, whose sites about the life and work of Emily Dickinson used a combined structure that had a strong linear component, had initially planned to create a site that echoed Dickinson's idea of "circumference, or the open-ended circular pattern that characterizes most of her poetry." Ellen adopted a linear structure, however, to address the demands of a complex site. "I had too much information and too many pages to keep it all ordered in my head," she observed. "I decided to go about building a linear structure first and then adding in a more circular dimension, but I ran out of time."

Callie and Paul created Web sites that served essentially as collections of their nonfiction essays. This required them to create a structure within which their essays could be housed and devise structures for the essays themselves. Both the overall structures of their Web sites and the structures they adopted for their essays were influenced by print genres. The overall sites were structured in a manner similar to a book-length collection of essays and to literary journals. Both sites used a cover—or opening page—that linked to a secondary page that linked to the essays. Callie used both an introduction and a table of contents, while Paul used only an introduction. The essays themselves were structured linearly, although both writers made an effort to chunk the essays into smaller sections and to link to related pages that functioned, particularly in Callie's case, as sidebars.

The challenges of adapting her writing to the Web affected Callie's project significantly. Initially, she had hoped to adapt a collection of nonfiction essays she had been working on for her MFA degree. She eventually chose, however, to create new essays that were more appropriate for reading on the Web. "As the essays stand, they are too verbose for an Internet read," she said. "So after some discussion with my professor, I was able to change gears and ultimately decided to create a 'parent' essay for the entire portfolio that would work well with a vignette setup—that

TABLE **2**

Navigation Tools on Student Web Sites

Writer	Menu	Footer	Header	Table of Contents	Next/Back Links	Text Links	Image Links
Jessica	X					X	X
Reid		X					
Ellen	X				X	X	X
Kathy	X	X				X	
Callie		X	X	X	X	X	X
Paul	X	X			X	X	X

is, several short stories that fit together but could be read independently of each other."

Helping Readers Move through Web Documents: Navigation Tools

The influence of students' experience as readers of Web sites was particularly evident in their choice and placement of navigation tools. The authors of the speech communication course Web sites, which were also the smallest and least complex sites, tended to rely on a single primary navigation tool. Ellen and Kathy used two primary tools each: menus and either a footer or a set of next/back links. Callie and Paul, the most experienced writers in the group, used the widest range of navigation tools. Callie was the only writer in the group to use a separate table of contents page, which showed the strong influence of print genres on the development of her site. A summary of the navigation tools used by the students is found in table 2.

In several cases, and in a manner similar to that through which writers learn print genres, the students noted that their decisions about which type or types of navigation tools to provide were influenced by their experiences navigating Web sites. Jessica created a navigation menu that appeared on the left side of each page on her site because she wanted to help readers move through her site easily. "That's my number one pet peeve," she said about navigating Web sites. "A good Web site has either a navigation bar or some sort of sequenced progression. Some sites lend themselves well to looking at this page first and this page second. So either that, a next and a back button, or some sort of navigation bar on the side or the top."

Like Jessica, Kathy included a side menu and links to the pages on her site. She also used a navigation footer (see figure 7). She based her decisions largely—but not completely—on her preferences as a reader of Web sites: "I used a side menu on my site as a primary navigation tool for

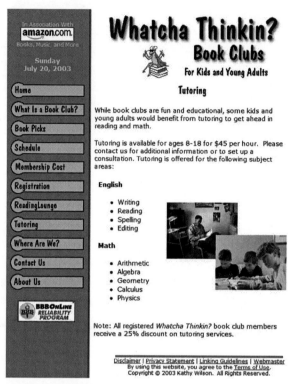

Figure 7: A side menu, footer, and links support navigation on the WhatchaThinkin? Web site.

one simple reason: I prefer this type of tool on sites I visit. I make a lot of purchases and obtain a lot of information from Web sites. I have always found a sidebar preferable to any other type [of navigation tool]. My only reason for including a footer navigation system is because I have talked to others who prefer this (weird people out there, let me tell ya)."

Callie and Paul, who were enrolled in the graduate Web writing workshop, considered two navigation issues not addressed by the undergraduate writers: whether a site should surprise readers and whether Web developers should use navigation tools to direct readers toward particular parts of the site. Callie, who used navigation headers and footers, reflected on her goal of surprising, but not bewildering, her readers: "I appreciate sites that intend the reader to get lost a little and experience something unique or nonlinear. But, ultimately, I want my readers to be able to get in *where* they want and get out *when* they want. I decided to put in both a "let me guide you" and "table of contents" path to give the reader those options. I also provided vignette links at the top of the page for all other vignettes besides the one the reader is in. Then at the bottom of the page, I provided some general links (such as home, back, table of contents, etc.). Some of the pictures are linked and ultimately I would like all pictures to link to another page with some information on it."

Paul, who used a side menu, a footer, and links to support navigation, addressed the issue of constraining readers' navigation choices: "I had a little fun with the navigation in the sense that I organized the choices one had in exploring the site. There were certain pages where you could only go one way and other pages where you could go either one of two ways. I did that because I wanted to direct, to some extent, the reader's attention to stuff I put up. It might have been a little selfish, but if I went to the trouble of putting something somewhere, it's because I want the reader to see it."

More than Words Alone: Illustrations and Captions

Although all of the students used illustrations on their sites, their reasons for doing so varied. Reid, concerned that his history page, which includes a 2,400-word essay he had written for another course, would be intimidating to readers, used four photographs and two logos solely "to break up the text." Other writers used images to establish a relationship with their readers, provide information not available through the text on the pages, and support navigation to other pages on their sites. Ellen used scanned images of her own artwork to establish a mood that carried across her site (see figure 8), while Kathy selected images that carried a clear message about the importance of children becoming engaged readers. Kathy observed, "As long as [images] are not so big that they keep pages from pulling up quickly, I see them as a powerful way to implant ideas into the surfer's mind. In a sort of 'set the mood' kind of way, I believe they say a lot about you" (see figure 9).

Paul and Callie used images to establish a relationship with readers and to add information that would be difficult or impossible to convey through text alone. Paul's site used photographs and scanned images of paintings to display the landscape through which Lewis and Clark traveled and the handwritten journals kept by the two explorers. He also used line drawings to explain some of the complexities associated with bicycling (see figure 10). Callie used photographs of family members and settings in Kentucky to illustrate her essays (see figure 11).

In a clear departure from print conventions, the students largely avoided the use of captions. Reid explained that he did not use captions for

Historical Context: Women in the 19th Century

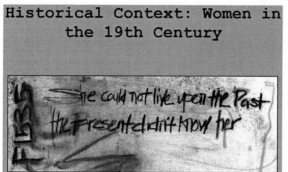

Figure 8: Ellen used images to establish a mood that carried across her site.

Figure 9: Kathy used images to stress the importance of children becoming involved readers.

Join a *Whatcha Thinkin?* Book Club and watch book groups become an exciting and fun way to spend time with your friends.

Figure 10: Paul used images to convey information about complex concepts in his essay "Keeping Time."

Figure 11: The image in the margins serves as a link to a sidebar about "the real Sue Ellen."

'Tucky | Humidity | Heart Attack | Readin' and Writin' | Cheated

The Sue Ellens Are Comin'

My brother-in-law, Moe-the first in-law victim to join our clan-calls every female in our large family, "Sue Ellen." This includes my sister Sara, which is his wife, his 3 year old daughter Annie, me, my other three sisters--Lucy, Nancy, and Deb, and of course my mom, the real Sue Ellen.

Before I moved to Colorado, I watched Sara and Moe's four kids a couple days a week. They have three boys and a "Sue Ellen." She would let me dress little Sue Ellen on the days I came early in the morning. It was always a treat to make sure little Sue Ellen had on a cute jumper, tights, and matching barrettes.

Sometimes Moe would get home from work before my sister did. Moe is one of those people who always wears a sarcastic half smile on his face, so when he is actually smiling he looks like the Joker from Batman. On those days, his first words through the door were always, "Hi little Sue Ellen." Then Annie, his daughter, would come toddling the images on his history of contemporary Christian music page because he didn't want to add more text to a text-heavy page. Asked whether he might have used captions if he'd broken the page up into several linked pages, he said, "I don't know if captions are unnecessary for Web pages in general." He observed that ALT tags—labels that appear when an image cannot be viewed or when a mouse hovers over it—served a function similar to captions and that he'd grown to expect writers to use them: "As far as the ALT tags go, if you really want to see what's there you can. And the funny thing about that is that I've been to Web sites since that don't have the ALT tag and it drives me nuts."

Reid's and Jessica's use of ALT tags reflect a requirement to do so by their instructor. In their interviews, they indicated that they were unaware of the TITLE tag, which is intended to serve a function similar to a caption (in contrast to the ALT tag, which is intended as a brief label for the image). The students in the undergraduate and graduate writing courses had been made aware of this distinction. Ellen and Kathy chose to use neither ALT nor TITLE tags, while Callie and Paul used both. Paul was the only writer in the group to use captions on his site. Although he tended to use the TITLE tag with the majority of his images, he also used captions for the images in his essay "Keeping Time," which displayed four line drawings that illustrated epicycloidal curves (see figure 10 above).

Approaching the Reader: Page Design

The students involved in the three classes discussed in this chapter found varying degrees of guidance regarding page design, in the sense of being able to consider established genre conventions. Jessica, Reid, and Ellen, who created sites that essentially served as academic essays, found themselves faced with a wide range of design choices—and differences in the design of their respective sites reflect that range. Kathy, who developed a Web site for her small business, used the designs of sites that offered similar services to guide her decisions. Callie and Paul adopted designs heavily influenced by two print genres—essay collections and literary magazines.

The most striking differences in design among the student sites are found on the home pages (see figures 12–17). The home pages of Jessica's propaganda site, Reid's contemporary Christian music site, and Kathy's WhatchaThinkin? site have the same layout of other pages on their respective sites. Jessica uses a title and side menu to frame the main content of the site. Paul uses a title and footer as part of a sandwich in

Figure 12: The home page of Jessica's propaganda site.

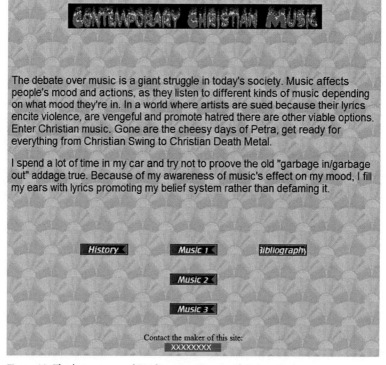

Figure 13: The home page of Reid's contemporary Christian music site.

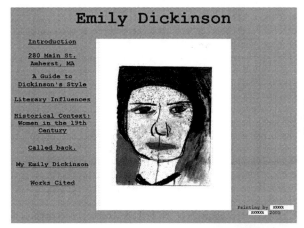

Figure 14: The home page of Ellen's Emily Dickinson site

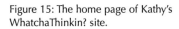

Figure 15: The home page of Kathy's WhatchaThinkin? site.

Figure 16: The home page of Callie's Kentucky Tangents site.

Figure 17: The home page of Paul's Exploring Lewis and Clark site.

which body text serves as the filling. Kathy uses a title, side menu, and footer to frame the content on her site. Ellen's Emily Dickinson site home page serves largely as a table of contents for the site. The title and a set of links formatted in a manner similar to the side menu used on other pages in the site frame an image Ellen created for the site. Callie and Paul's home pages function in a manner similar to the cover of a book. Readers can enter the site only after clicking on the main image on the home page. The linked images bring readers to introductions on the two sites.

Pages within the students' sites reflected a variety of design philosophies and interests. Ellen, who created many of the images used on her site, noted that she "spent a lot of time on page design because it was my first time working with visual materials and I really enjoyed being able to use color and pictures in coordination with text." Paul, in contrast, indicated that the design of his site "was kept purposely simple." He created a template for his pages and used a linked cascading style sheet to establish "a sense of unity" on the site—"and also to keep from biting off more than I could chew."

The ability to experiment with design was of interest to all of the writers in the study. Kathy explained that decisions about page design were critical elements in her composing process. "Web sites must take appearances seriously," she observed. "Competing with thousands of other sites that may offer similar information, the appearance of the words on the page became a huge factor."

CONCLUSIONS

As the six students wrote for the Web, they found themselves addressing four issues that they had not had to deal with in significant depth—and in some cases not at all—while composing the standard academic essays they had written for other courses: document structure (or shape), navigation tools, illustrations, and page design. As they addressed these issues, they reflected on their experiences reading (and in two cases developing sites for) the Web, located and analyzed Web sites similar to those they were creating, sought guidance from their instructors, and drew on their experiences as readers and writers of print genres.

Faced with a medium in which genres are very much in a process of emergence, without the historically established conventions of print genres, the students turned to other Web sites for ideas about site structure, navigation, and design. Most of them also borrowed heavily from other Web sites, obtaining HTML code, cascading style sheet definitions, scripts of various kinds, and illustrations such as photos and artwork that were relevant to their topics. They also borrowed from print genres. Ellen's Web site about Emily Dickinson, for example, was structured in a manner similar to a longer academic essay, while Callie and Paul's collections of nonfiction essays and vignettes echoed the genre conventions of book-length collection of essays and literary journals. Similarly, echoing the page-turning function of print documents, Ellen, Callie, and Paul each used next-page and previous-page links in their sites. Callie went even further, using a table of contents—a navigation tool familiar to readers through its frequent use in print genres—to help readers find their way through her site.

In some ways, the comparative lack of genre conventions for Web documents simplified the writers' task. Because there is more latitude to structure and design a site, and because a wide range of digital illustrations can be used on the Web, the six writers felt more freedom to experiment with their sites. Callie's observation that she found the idea of working on the Web "liberating" was echoed by other students. The idea that the conventions associated with print genres might be left behind without being replaced by analogous conventions for Web documents—even as many of them drew on print-genre conventions—seemed to foster a sense of experimentation and innovation among the students.

At the same time, that comparative lack of genre conventions worked against the students, complicating their ideas and forcing them to reinvent solutions that have been found by other writers. All of the students struggled to some extent with decisions about how to structure their sites and design individual pages. And, unlike writers of print documents, where navigation decisions are often limited to the use of footnotes, endnotes, or marginal glosses, all of them spent a significant amount of time thinking about the relative merits of menus, headers, footers, and previous/next buttons.

For writing instructors, these issues raise a number of concerns. When asked in an interview about the extent to which she had encouraged her students to think about writing for the Web as a process that differed from writing for print genres, the instructor of the intermediate Web development class explained that she had taken care to encourage them to think about writing first and design issues second, even though this meant that their sites might not be as technically proficient or as well designed as they might be had they focused primarily on coding and design. "I encouraged them to take their writing seriously and *then* take that into their Web design," she said. "But they definitely had to think about that writing in a way different than they had for any class before."

Debates about the merits of focusing on coding first and writing second or vice versa have their analogues in discussions of visual rhetoric and document design. It is likely that instructors of writing courses who assign creating Web sites might profit from examining those discussions. It is also likely that such instructors can benefit from considering the literature, including the essays in this collection, about genre and writing instruction. If instructors inform their assignments with an understanding of the Web as a home to multiple genres, those assignments are more likely to attend to issues concerning organizational structure, page design, navigational tools, and the use of digital illustrations. Clearly, we are far from arriving at a consensus about the conventions associated with Web genres—or, for that matter, about precisely which Web genres have emerged. However, if instructors emphasize the emergent nature of genres on the Web, student writers are more likely to appreciate the range of choices they can make as they compose Web documents.

12
WHAT WE'VE LEARNED
Implications for Classroom Practice

Anne Herrington and Charles Moran

In our first chapter, as you may remember, we laid out what we saw as the territory: the evolution and present state of genre theory as it is applied to the teaching of writing. We located ourselves in what Aviva Freedman and others call the "North American" school of genre theorists. We wrote that first chapter as part of the book's prospectus, well before we had read the chapters that now form the body of the book. Our basic understanding of the field, and our position in that field, have not changed since that time. But our understandings of both theory and application have deepened and shifted as we read the chapter drafts and corresponded with the authors about these drafts. In this last chapter, we describe what we have learned through the dialogues that we have had with our chapter authors. In a sense, we have experienced the processes that many of our authors chronicle in their chapters, as they and their students negotiate their understandings around a classroom genre. As editors of this volume, we began with our own understandings, which were the product of our prior experience as scholars and as teachers. Through discourse with others, our understandings have evolved, as our thinking has been influenced, inflected, by the thinking of others.

As we have read through the chapter drafts, we have been impressed by the careful and thoughtful teaching that the authors describe. The teachers we meet in this book are thoughtful and reflective about the kinds of writing they assign and about the ways in which they will approach this writing in their classrooms. We have been impressed, too, with the range of genres that have found their way into these classrooms. The academic genres assigned by the teachers have a tremendous range and resist easy categorization by discipline. Karen St. Clair, in psychology, asks for an oral presentation with an accompanying one-page handout; Mike Edwards, in writing, asks for a researched persuasive essay as a Web site; Elizabeth Petroff, in comparative literature, asks for spiritual autobiographies; Rochelle Kapp and Bongi Bangeni, in language development, ask for an argument tailored for readers in the social sciences; David Hibbett, a biologist, asks for a mini-review aimed at nonspecialist science readers; David Eastzer, another biologist, asks for a flyer, a science in the media journal, and a case study as his students work toward a larger project; John Williams, a historian, asks for an essay.

Through reading the book's chapters as they have evolved, we have learned how closely connected the genres chosen by the teachers are to their teaching goals, which are a function of their disciplines, certainly, but also of their institutions, the position of their course in the curriculum, and their own sense of what their students most need. So David Hibbett, working with upper-level science majors and graduate students, wants his students, as professionals in training, to be able to write a "mini-review" that explains a crux in their discipline to "a general audience who might not know the fungi he knew well." David Eastzer, working in the same discipline but with students in a general-education science course, wants his students to be informed citizens, able to read and understand reports of scientific research in the popular media. So the genres that he assigns are less connected to his discipline. The difference between these two science teachers' goals, and the genres in which they ask their students to write, can be understood in terms of the difference between a specialist course and a nonspecialist general-education course.

What we see in Eastzer's course is a balancing of specialist and nonspecialist goals, goals that that Russell and Yanez (2003) show can often be in tension in a general-education course. We see a similar balancing in the general-education courses of Petroff and St. Clair. Elizabeth Petroff, in comparative literature, wants her general-education students to come to a deeper understanding of their own lives as well as to become better readers of autobiography, and these goals have led her to focus her course on the reading and writing of spiritual autobiography. Karen St. Clair, in psychology, wants her general-education students to improve their ability to analyze and evaluate "complex contemporary issues in psychology" and to express their views in writing and speaking; this goal leads her to assign the oral presentation of an article in psychology accompanied by a handout.

First-year writing teachers, such as Kapp and Bangeni, McKee and Edwards, Kynard, and Peagler and Yancey, are teaching in courses whose institutional mission is, to some degree, to prepare students for academic writing in the rest of their curriculum. All want their first-year students to have a critical understanding of, and the ability to produce, the kinds of writing required of them in their subsequent coursework. And, as we see, their understanding of this academic discourse varies a good deal. Because of this variation, their teaching goals for their students are different, and the difference brings about differences in genre: Kapp and Bangeni teach toward a critical approach to the argumentative essay in the social sciences; McKee and Edwards teach toward their students' ability to write on the Web; and Kynard wants her students to rethink and understand the research paper that they have previously learned to write. Peagler and Yancey include the resumé in their English 102 course as a way of fulfilling their own goals for their students' learning: to teach that all writing is situated and rhetorical, and to engage their students in reflective identity formation. Common to all of these first-year writing teachers, though, is an interest in students becoming more self-aware as writers and thinkers and more confident in their critical abilities, traits that are typically valued across many disciplines.

Though we have been naming genres in the paragraphs above, in our work with the chapter authors we have learned that these general labels say very little about the kind of texts that students are being ask to write in specific classes. By looking at teachers' intentions and practices in specific classes, we can see how they inflect genres with particular purposes. At the more abstract levels, genre knowledge exists as social knowledge that we carry in our heads and that varies depending on our past experiences and social interactions. As teachers, we then enact this knowledge in specific ways, depending on our intentions in a particular class. Thus, to take an obvious example from this collection, to say that Carmen Kynard assigns a "research paper" does little to explain what she asks her students to do. It is only through understanding her practice in the classroom that we can see that she is asking students for something quite different from the "typical" research paper, as she scaffolds her students' practice in drawing on their own knowledge and in writing in a range of voices. Reading about her practice enables us to consider alternatives to our own conceptions of this genre and our practice of teaching it. In this instance, Kynard's goals led her to teach against the dominant conventions for a research paper. In the instance of Kapp and Bangeni, their goals for their students, while similar in some ways to Kynard's, led in a different direction. They want their students to see the validity of their own views and voices, but for them, the focus is on helping their students do so within the realm of conventions of academic discourse. Thus they teach academic argument as it manifests itself in the social sciences.

We find it interesting—and are pleased, given our own theoretical position—that none of these teachers teaches form alone. For these authors, form is almost always connected to, or grows out of, personal and social purpose. When we look at the teachers' statements about their purposes for their students' writing, we see some surprising connections. Most striking to us is a connection between Peagler and Yancey's goals for their students' resumé writing and Petroff's goals for her students as they compose their spiritual autobiographies. Both are teaching genres that function in the world, but in very different ways. The resumé feels to us like a species of Britton's "transactional" writing—writing that does the work of the world; while the spiritual autobiography feels to us like a species of "expressive" writing. Yet, both teachers of these different genres inflect their teaching of these genres with a personal purpose for the student writers related to self-understanding and self-shaping. Peagler and Yancey see composing a resumé as an activity that stimulates reflection on one's past life and projection of one's future. Petroff sees both writing and reading spiritual autobiography as contributing to deeper self-understanding and, for some, healing. Reading both Peagler/Yancey and Petroff, we hear clear echoes of Britton, from Harding, on the "spectator" function of language, where through the telling one steps aside from the world to reflect on and reshape one's experiences. Petroff defines autobiography as a "search for self-knowledge and a desire to place ourselves in the world." It is through this writing that one creates the positioning of self in relation to others, linking personal and social functions. In other courses, the personal and social are intertwined as learning the ways of a given discipline. As Beaufort and Williams write, "Genres really are the vehicles of social action for those in a discourse community." In learning to write in genres of a given discipline, students are "doing" history or "doing" biology.

We have learned as well that talking about genres at this high level of abstraction—"the analytical essay" or "argument in the social sciences" or "the academic Web essay," and in this way talking only of forms and/ or the teacher's intentions—does not help us see how students "learn" genre. What is most interesting to us in these chapters, because it teaches us about how students acquire genre knowledge, are moments when we can see negotiations taking place in the interaction between teacher and student—specific interactions situated in a specific classroom. Here we draw on the vocabulary of activity theory and look at activity systems (e.g., the classroom or the institution), genre systems (the institution's, the discipline's), and genre sets (the student's, the teacher's) (Bazerman and Prior 2004, 309–19; Bawarshi 2003, 112–44). What we almost universally see in these chapters is that a teacher brings his or her genre set into the classroom via the syllabus, the assignment, and informal interaction with students. This genre set will be a function of the teacher's past experience, individual institution, and his or her location within that institution, as well as the teacher's learning goals for students. The students bring their own genre set with them—chiefly, with the exceptions shown in Palmquist's and Edwards and McKee's chapters, a set composed of academic genres they have previously experienced in their schooling. And then the negotiation begins, or not. The fruit of negotiation is the student's finished piece of writing, which will vary substantially from student to student, the variance a function of the difference among the genre sets that students bring to their writing, the nature of the negotiations, and their intentions in the specific situation. John Williams points to the limitation of situations where there is little interaction or negotiation. In reflecting retrospectively on his experience assigning a single end-of-semester essay in a large lecture course, he concludes that his learning goals for students were not realized. He points to the fact that the large class was not conducive to discussing the assignment and that the assignment did not occasion the same opportunity for practice and interaction between student and teacher as would have some short writings early in the semester.

A clear instance of this negotiation is visible in the accounts of David Eastzer's general-education Science in Society class, where Jonathan and Carson bring their very different genre sets with them into the classroom and, as Mary Soliday writes in chapter 4, these writers "used this knowledge to conform to, yet also depart from, David's instructions when they organized their work." And in Carmen Kynard's classroom we see a conflict between her students' genre sets, and in particular their understanding of the almost, for them, automated "research paper," and the kinds of writing that she wants her students to do. In a subsequent semester, to bring this conflict in understandings out for negotiation, she began by asking students to reflect on their prior research experiences in order to learn their internalized conception of this genre, "research paper."

Another instance of this negotiation occurs in a first-year writing course taught in computer-equipped classrooms, where Mike Edwards and Heidi McKee ask their students, in different ways, to write "papers" on the Web. Edwards wants academic essays that have been "migrated" to the Web; McKee will accept "native" Web sites. Both teachers' expectations are more visibly unclear than other teachers in our chapters, more visibly unclear because they are working in a new medium with academic genres that are, for the moment, not clearly defined. The students in this course bring to their academic Web composing their own experience of the Web, which is chiefly of nonacademic Web sites and is therefore to some degree unfamiliar to their teachers. The result, at least in Edwards's class, is, as he writes, clearly visible "disjunctions created by our differing expectations about the conventions of essays and the World Wide Web." McKee's student Jennifer draws on her experience of the "bio profile" Web site; after the fact, McKee reflects that she finds herself missing the "little essay." The Web sites produced by the students in Mike Palmquist's study show the influence on these sites of print genres, such as the anthology. The one student, Kathy, whose site was not visibly influenced by print genres was influenced by her research into what she deemed "business Web sites"—a case of a student looking for models while she composes.

As we look at the chapters from this perspective, focusing on the negotiations that take place around genre, it begins to become clear that these negotiations are facilitated by informal interactions between teacher and student. The teacher presents his or her sense of the appropriate genre to students in a syllabus and in an assignment, but these documents are not adequate for the student to discover and understand precisely "what the teacher wants." In the informal interaction that is part of class discussion or teacher responses to questions in lecture, the teacher can make expectations more explicit. Further, in discussion and other exchanges, both students and teachers can learn and change their understandings of a given genre. As Edwards and McKee demonstrate, the interaction can be two-way and can include what we learn from reading our students' work. And, behind the careful work of a teacher like Elizabeth Petroff lie decades of this interaction, as her past students have helped shape her present sense of what spiritual autobiography can be.

In Mary Soliday's chapter, one of her focus students, Dawn, describes how she came to understand David Eastzer's expectations—not through the syllabus alone, or through David's careful scaffolding through reading and writing, but through informal classroom interaction. "Well, we did a few examples—like in class...we would come to class [and] he'd give us an article [to] read and put up some sample questions on the board and then we would take like fifteen minutes to write out what we thought and then we would go over it. And he would say, 'You know, this is the kind of writing you need to do for the question.'" Soliday distinguishes between the substantial "explicit maps for genres" that David supplied to his students and the implicit teaching he did "through the repeated social situations he created in his classroom—for example, through class discussions, lectures, and impromptu writing." And Rachel remembers a moment during a class interaction with David when she and, she believes, her classmates as well, came to understand what was an essential point for David: that questions in science might not have clear answers. This understanding would have a formative effect on the academic writing that Rachel and her classmates would do in this class—visible in intellectual stance, voice, and perhaps structure.

In David Hibbett's upper-level science course, although in his assignment he seemed to Anne Geller to have "suggested a fairly rigid textual structure," what he wanted wasn't "clear" to his students, who drew on their own genre sets as they tried to understand it. Was it "creative writing"? Was it like the research paper? Geller writes that, "it wasn't until the writing workshops that David could articulate the central motive for writing a mini-review." Geller continues, "It was the collaborative environment of David's classroom that made negotiation of genre a possibility." In this course, students gave presentations and planned classes. In Geller's view, this sharing of authority helped them "practice the expert stance they would need to have in their mini-reviews." These writing workshops reminded David of "'lab meetings,' times when all who work in a lab get together with the PI (principal investigator) to talk about and negotiate projects, experiments, successes, challenges, and pending publications." In this interactive context, David's students Caitlin and Ewa are able to draw on their very different academic genre sets as they move toward what David understands as the mini-review in science. As Geller notes, "We often forget the power of this type of conversation, perhaps because it is so difficult to fit into a semester's discipline-specific teaching."

In our introduction, we indicated our own discomfort with what has been identified as the Sydney School genre approach, primarily because of what seems to us its prescriptiveness. Not surprisingly, none of the contributors to our collection identify directly with this approach either. What we do see, though, is a variant genre approach, particularly in the courses taught by Kapp and Bangeni, Peagler and Yancey, and Petroff. From these, we learn how a genre approach can be enacted in ways that are flexible and that invite students to take on more authority as users of that genre. In all three of these courses, a primary goal is teaching and learning a specific genre, but that is not the sole purpose: the genre is taught as having both personal and social purposes—to advance one's understanding of a given issue, to present oneself to others for a job, to shape an understanding of one's own life in a way that might serve a similar purpose for readers. In these courses, models are used not as exemplars to be slavishly imitated but as illustrations to evaluate and use as guides for one's own writing. Further, in all three courses there is a good deal of interaction and negotiation wherein students' views are respected: interactions between teacher and students, between student and students, and between reading and writing.

In characterizing their "genre approach," both Kapp and Bangeni and Peagler and Yancey differentiate their approach from ones they see as solely instrumental. In doing so, they identify key aspects of the pedagogy of many of the teachers in this collection. As Kapp and Bangeni write, "If students are to become critical members of, and contributors to, the discourse, rather than instrumental producers, they have to be allowed the time and space to engage with the messy process of exploring (through talking, reading, and writing) who they are (and who they are becoming) in relation to the authoritative voices in the field." Peagler and Yancey link their approach to what Russel Durst identifies as "reflective instrumentalism." Peagler and Yancey write that they "resist an instrumental approach that, we believe, is at odds with student growth and development as well as with what we know about writing. The addition of 'reflective' to such instrumentalism, in our case, means that writing is useful, that it is conceptual and theoretical, that it allows both faculty and students to learn through reflection and in the exercise of writing." Time and space, exploratory talk, reading and writing, critical reflection on a genre and one's own position in using that genre, students as learners with some authority, an openness to learning and change on the part of both the student and teacher, and something key to an understanding of genre as social—writing as useful: we see aspects of many of these traits in the practice of the teachers in this collection. Further, regardless of whether learning a specific genre is a primary or subordinate goal of a course, we see affirmed in all of these chapters the importance of some scaffolding of learning. This scaffolding might take the form of sequencing writing activities, of integrating reading and writing activities, of workshops, or of drafting and revising.

Finally, we have learned, though we knew it before, how important talk among teachers is to the quality of teaching and learning. This teacher-talk makes us more conscious of the pedagogical choices we make, and therefore more able to set goals, develop strategies, and assess the results. The talk we've seen in these chapters happens in a number of locations. It takes place between teachers in the context of a writing or WAC program, linking a specialist in writing with a specialist in another discipline. We can imagine, and often hear directly in these chapters, the talk between Anne Beaufort and John Williams; Mary Soliday and her graduate students and David Eastzer; Anne Geller and David Hibbett; Heidi McKee and Mike Edwards; and Chris Anson, Deanna Dannels, and Karen St. Clair. Each of these chapters is the result of a structured project of reflective teaching. Together these chapters constitute a powerful argument for the inclusion into the teacher's workday of structured occasions for teacher-talk.

We have experienced this talk among teachers directly as we have read and responded to the chapter authors. As the drafts of the chapters progressed to their final form, we believe that we have seen reflection on, and revision of, teaching practice on the part of the chapter authors. Many of the teachers in our chapters say that "next time" they will do things a little differently, which strongly suggests to us that they have learned as they have reflected on their practice. Karen St. Clair, the teacher in chapter 9, vows that next time she will "provide a lot more guidance to students," and, reading between her lines, this guidance will come in group and one-to-one discussion. In reflecting on his experience, John Williams resolves that he will include shorter and more frequent writing throughout the semester.

This talk about teaching has affected us, as it has our chapter authors. Through the conversations we have had with the chapter authors, both of us have been moved to reflect on and talk with each other about our own teaching practice in ways that have been useful, even formative. The book stands, then, as an argument for genre theory as an important locus for talk, reading, and writing about pedagogical theory as it is individually applied in particular classrooms, with particular students. The book stands as well, by implication, as an argument for practices both in our teaching and in our professional lives that create spaces for this talk, this conversation, this social action.

REFERENCES

AAHE 2003. Scholarship of Teaching and Learning Initiative. http://www.aahe. org/.

Achebe, Chinua. 1975. *Morning Yet on Creation Day*. London: Heinemann.

Allende, Isabel. 1994. *Paula*. Translated by Margaret Sayers Peden. New York: Harper and Row.

Angélil-Carter, Shelley. 2002. *Stolen Language? Plagiarism in Writing*. New York: Longman.

Angelo, Thomas A. 1991. Ten Easy Pieces: Assessing Higher Learning in Four Dimensions. In *Classroom Research: Early Lessons From Success*, edited by Thomas A. Angelo, 17–31. San Francisco: Jossey-Bass.

Angelo, Thomas A., and Patricia K. Cross. 1993. *Classroom Assessment Techniques: A Handbook for College Teachers*. 2nd ed. San Francisco: Jossey-Bass.

Anson, Chris M., and Dannels, Deanna. P. 2004. Writing and Speaking in Conditional Rhetorical Space. In *Classroom Spaces and Writing Instruction*, edited by Ed Nagelhout and Carol Rutz, 55–70. Cresskill, NJ: Hampton.

Applebee, Arthur. 1974. *Tradition and Reform in the Teaching of English: A History*. Urbana, IL: NCTE.

Aristotle. 1954. *The Rhetoric and Poetics of Aristotle*. Translated by Ingraham Bywater and W. Rhys Roberts. New York: Random House.

Arms, George. 1943. The Research Paper. *College English* 5, 19-26.

AsianAvenue. 2003. Terms of Service (May). http://www.asianavenue.com/Terms of Service.

Askari, Emlia. 2002. Germs Develop a Deadly Defense: Drug Resistance to New Class of Antibiotic. *Detroit Free Press*, November 12.

Austin, Wendy Warren. 2001. Hypertext Research Papers: Pedagogical Strategies and Possibilities. *Kairos* 6.2. http://english.ttu.edu/kairos/6.2/coverWeb/ hypertext/jonesbowieaustin/index.htm.

Axelrod, Rise, and Charles Cooper. 2001. *The St. Martin's Guide to Writing*. 6th ed. Boston: Bedford/St. Martin's.

Bakhtin, M. M. 1986. The Problem of Speech Genres. In *Speech Genres and Other Late Essays*, translated by Vern W. McGee, 60–102. Austin: University of Texas Press.

Ballenger, Bruce. 1994. *The Curious Researcher: A Guide to Writing Research Papers*. Boston: Allyn and Bacon.

Bartholomae, David. 1985. Inventing the University. In *When a Student Can't Write*, edited by Mike Rose, 134–65. New York: Guilford.

Bauman, Marcy Lassota. 1999. The Evolution of Internet Genres. *Computers and Composition* 16.2: 269–82.

Bawarshi, Anis. 2003. *Genre and the Invention of the Writer: Reconsidering the Place of Invention in Composition.* Logan: Utah State University Press.

Bazerman, Charles. 1981. *The Informed Writer.* Boston: Houghton Mifflin.

———. 1988. *Shaping Written Knowledge: The Genre and Activity of the Experimental Article in Science.* Madison: University of Wisconsin Press.

———. 1997. The Life of Genre, the Life in the Classroom. In *Genre and Writing: Issues, Arguments, Alternatives,* edited by Wendy Bishop and Hans Ostrom, 19–26. Portsmouth, NH: Heinemann.

Bazerman, Charles, and Paul Prior, eds. 2004. *What Writing Does and How It Does It: An Introduction to Analyzing Texts and Textual Practices.* Mahwah, NJ: Lawrence Erlbaum.

Beaufort, Anne. 1999. *Writing in the Real World: Making the Transition from School to Work.* New York: Teachers College Press.

———. Forthcoming. Developmental Gains of a History Major: A Case for Theory-Building. *Research in the Teaching of English.*

Berkenkotter, Carol, and Thomas Huckin. 1995. *Genre Knowledge in Disciplinary Communication.* Hillsdale, NJ: Lawrence Erlbaum.

Berlin, James. 1987. *Rhetoric and Reality.* Carbondale: Southern Illinois University Press.

Biko. Steve. 1987. *I Write What I Like.* Cape Town: David Phillip.

Bizzell, Patricia. 2002. The Intellectual Work of "Mixed" Forms of Academic Discourses. In Schroeder, Fox, and Bizzell 2002, 1–10.

Black Elk, Nicholas. 1932. *Black Elk Speaks: Being the Life Story of a Holy Man of the Ogalala Sioux as Told to John G. Neihardt.* New York: W. Morrow.

Bohan, Chara Haeussler, and O. L. Davis, Jr. 1998. Historical Constructions: How Social Studies Student Teachers' Historical Thinking Is Reflected in Their Writing of History. *Theory and Research in Social Education* 26.2: 173–97.

Bolter, Jay David. 1991. *Writing Space: The Computer, Hypertext, and the History of Writing.* Hillsdale, NJ: Lawrence Erlbaum.

———. 1993. Alone and Together in the Electronic Bazaar. *Computers and Composition* 10: 5–18.

———. 2001. *Writing Space: Computers, Hypertext, and the Remediation of Print.* 2nd ed. Mahwah, NJ: Lawrence Erlbaum.

Bolter, Jay David, and Richard Grusin. 1999. *Remediation: Understanding New Media.* Cambridge: MIT Press.

Booth, Wayne, Gregory Colomb, and Joseph Williams. 1995. *The Craft of Research.* Chicago: University of Chicago Press.

Boseley, Sarah. 2002. Setback in Superbug Battle: Patient Shows Resistance to New Class of Antibiotic. *Guardian,* December 7.

Brent, Doug. 1997. Rhetorics of the Web: Implications for Teachers of Literacy. *Kairos* 2.1. http://english.ttu.edu/kairos/2.1/features/brent/bridge.html.

Britt, Anne M., Jean-Francois Rouet, Mara C. Georgi, and Charles A. Perfetti. 1994. Learning from History Texts: From Causal Analysis to Argument Models. In Leinhardt, Beck, and Stainton 1994, 47–84.

Britton, James. 1970. *Language and Learning*. Harmondsworth: Penguin.

———. 1986. Talking to Learn. In *Language, the Learner, and the School*, edited by Douglas Barnes, James Britton, and Mike Torbe, 91–130. Harmondsworth: Penguin.

Britton, James, Tony Burgess, Nancy Martin, Alice McCleod, and Harold Rosen. 1975. *The Development of Writing Abilities (11–18)*. London: Macmillan.

Brooke, Robert. 1991. *Writing and a Sense of Self*. Urbana, IL: NCTE.

———. 1994. *Small Groups in Writing Workshops: Invitations to a Writer's Life*. Urbana, IL: NCTE.

Bruffee, Kenneth. 1984. Collaborative Learning and the "Conversation of Mankind." *College English* 46.7: 635–52.

Bunyan, John. 1962. *Grace Abounding to the Chief of Sinners*. Edited by Roger Sharrock. Oxford: Clarendon.

Burbules, Nicholas C. 1998. Rhetorics of the Web: Hyperreading and Critical Literacy. In Snyder 1998, 102–22.

Burke, Kenneth. 1969. *Rhetoric of Motives*. Berkeley: University of California Press.

Bush, Vanevar. 1945. As We May Think. *Atlantic Monthly* 176.1: 101–08.

———. 1967. Memex Revisited. In *Science Is Not Enough*, edited by Vanevar Bush, 1967, 75–101. New York: William Morrow.

California Polytechnic University. 2003. Medieval assignment. http://cla.calpoly.edu/~dschwart/engl512/512oral.html.

Cardinal, Marie. 1983. *The Words to Say It*. Translated by Pat Goodheart. Cambridge, MA: Van Vactor and Goodheart.

Chapman, David W. 1999. A Luddite in Cyberland, or, How to Avoid Being Snared by the Web. *Computers and Composition* 16.2: 247–52.

Clark, Romy, and Roz Ivanič. 1997. *The Politics of Writing*. London: Routledge.

Coe, Richard. 1994. Teaching Genre as a Process. In Freedman and Medway 1994b, 157–69. Portsmouth, NH: Boynton/Cook.

Comprone, Joseph. 1993. Generic Constraints and Expressive Motives. In *Professional Communication: The Social Perspective*, edited by Nancy Blyer and Charlotte Thralls, 92–109. Newbury Park, CA: Sage.

Conklin, J. 1987. Hypertext: An Introduction and Survey. *Computer* 20.9: 17–41.

Connors, Robert J. 1981. The Rise and Fall of the Modes of Discourse. *College Composition and Communication* 32: 444–55.

Conway, Jill Ker. 1998. *When Memory Speaks*. New York: Vintage.

Cooper, Marilyn. 1999. Postmodern Pedagogy in Electronic Conversations. In Hawisher and Selfe 1999a, 140–60.

Cope, Bill, and Mary Kalantzis. 1993a. Introduction: How a Genre Approach to Literacy Can Transform the Way Writing Is Taught. In Cope and Kalantzis 1993c, 1–21.

———. 1993b. The Power of Literacy and the Literacy of Power. In Cope and Kalantzis 1993c, 63–89.

————, eds. 1993c. *The Powers of Literacy: A Genre Approach to Teaching Writing.* London: Falmer.

Crowley, Sharon, and Debra Hawhee. 1999. *Ancient Rhetorics for Contemporary Students.* 2nd. ed. Boston: Allyn and Bacon.

Crowston, Kevin, and Marie Williams. 2000. Reproduced and Emergent Genres of Communication on the World Wide Web. *Information Society* 16.3: 201–15.

Davis, Robert, and Mark Shadle. 2000. "Building a Mystery": Alternative Research Writing and the Academic Act of Seeking. *College Composition and Communication* 51: 417–46.

de Casíol, María González, and Mary C. Dyson. 2002. Identifying Graphic Conventions for Genre Definition in Web Sites. *Digital Creativity* 13.3: 165–81.

de Jesus, Carolina Maria. 1962. *Child of the Dark.* Translated by David St. Clair. New York: Dutton.

Delpit, Lisa. 1988. The Silenced Dialogue: Power and Pedagogy in Educating Other People's Children. *Harvard Educational Review* 58: 280–98.

————. 1995. *Other People's Children: Cultural Conflict in the Classroom.* New York: New Press.

Dertouzos, Michael L. 1997. *What Will Be: How the New World of Information Will Change Our Lives.* San Francisco: HarperEdge.

Devitt, Amy J. 1993. Generalizing about Genre: New Conceptions of an Old Concept. *College Composition and Communication* 44: 573–86.

————. 2000. The Developing Discipline of Composition: From Text Linguistics to Genre Theory. In *History, Reflection, and Narrative: The Professionalizing of Composition, 1963–1983,* edited by Mary Rosner, Beth Boehm, and Debra Journet 177-186. Stamford, CT: Ablex.

Dewar, James A. 1998. The Information Age and the Printing Press: Looking Backward to See Ahead. The RAND Corporation. Document P-8014. http://www.rand.org/publications/P/P8014.

DeWitt, Scott Lloyd. 1999. Defining Links. In DeWitt and Strasma 1999, 117–54.

DeWitt, Scott Lloyd, and Kip Strasma, eds. 1999. *Contexts, Intertexts, and Hypertexts.* Cresskill, NJ: Hampton.

Dias, Patrick. 1994. Initiating Students into Genres of Discipline-Based Reading and Writing. In Freedman and Medway 1994b, 193–206.

Dias, Patrick, Aviva Freedman, Peter Medway, and Anthony Pare. 1999. *Worlds Apart.* Mahwah, NJ: Lawrence Erlbaum.

Dillon, Andrew, and Barbara A. Gushrowski. 2000.Genres and the Web: Is the Personal Home Page the First Uniquely Digital Genre? *Journal of the American Society for Information Science* 51.2: 202–5.

DiPardo, Anne. 1993. *A Kind of Passport: A Basic Writing Adjunct Program and the Challenge of Student Diversity.* Urbana, IL: NCTE.

Dixon, John. 1967. *Growth through English: A Report Based on the Dartmouth Seminar, 1966.* London: Oxford University Press.

Douglas, Jane Yellowlees. 1998. Will the Most Reflexive Relativist Please Stand Up: Hypertext, Argument, and Relativism. In Snyder 1998, 144–62.

Douglass, Frederick. 2000. *Narrative of the Life of Frederick Douglass, an American Slave* and *Harriet Jacobs, Incidents in the Life of a Slave Girl, Written by Herself.* New York: Modern Library.

DuBois, W. E. B. 1996. *The Souls of Black Folk.* New York: Modern Library.

Durst, Russel K. 1999. *Collision Course: Conflict, Negotiation, and Learning in College Composition.* Urbana, IL: NCTE.

Eakins, John. 1999. *How Our Lives Become Stories,* Ithaca: Cornell University Press.

Eberhart-Phillips, Jason. 2000. *Outbreak Alert: Responding to the Increasing Threat of Infectious Diseases.* Oakland: New Harbinger.

Eisenstein, Elizabeth L. 1979. *The Printing Press as an Agent of Change: Communications and Cultural Transformations in Early Modern Europe.* New York: Cambridge University Press.

Elbow, Peter. 1973. *Writing without Teachers.* New York: Oxford University Press.

———. 2000. The Spirit and the Letter of the Writing Program. Writing Program Orientation. University of Massachusetts, Amherst.

Elbow, Peter, and Pat Belanoff. 1995. *A Community of Writers.* 2nd ed. New York: McGraw-Hill.

Emig, Janet. 1977. Writing as a Mode of Learning. *College Composition and Communication* 28: 122-128

Erickson, Carolly. 1998. *Arc of the Arrow: Writing Your Spiritual Autobiography.* New York: Pocket.

Ewald, Paul W. 2000. *Plague Time: How Stealth Infections Cause Cancers, Heart Disease, and Other Deadly Ailments.* New York: Free Press.

Fakundiny, Lydia. 1991. On Approaching the Essay. In *The Art of the Essay,* edited by Lydia Fakundiny, 1–19. Boston: Houghton Mifflin.

Fishman, Stephen M., and Lucille McCarthy. 2000. *Unplayed Tapes: A Personal History of Collaborative Teacher Research.* Urbana, IL: NCTE.

Foner, Eric. 2002. *Who Owns History? Rethinking the Past in a Changing World.* New York: Hill and Wang.

Foss, Megan. 1999. Love Letters. *Creative Non-Fiction* 9: 13–33.

Frank, Anne. 1952. *The Diary of a Young Girl.* Translated by B. M. Mooyaart. Garden City, NY: Doubleday.

Freedman, Aviva. 1994. "Do as I Say": The Relationship between Teaching and Learning New Genres. In Freedman and Medway 1994a, 191–210.

———. 1995. The What, Where, When, Why, and How of Classroom Genres. In *Reconceiving Writing, Rethinking Writing Instruction,* edited by Joseph Petraglia, 121–44. Mahwah, NJ: Lawrence Erlbaum.

Freedman, Aviva. 1993. Show and Tell? The Role of Explicit Teaching in the Learning of New Genres. *Research in the Teaching of English* 27, 222-251

Freedman, Aviva, and Peter Medway, eds. 1994a. *Genre and the New Rhetoric.* London: Taylor and Francis.

————, eds. 1994b . *Learning and Teaching Genre.* Portsmouth, NH: Boynton/ Cook.

————. 1994c. Locating Genre Studies: Antecedents and Prospects. In Freedman and Medway 1994a, 1–20.

————. 1994d. New Views of Genre and Their Implications for Education. In Freedman and Medway 1994b, 1–22.

Freisinger, Randall. 1980. Cross-Disciplinary Writing Workshops: Theory and Practice. *College English* 42: 154–66.

Frye, Northrop. 1957. *Anatomy of Criticism.* Princeton: Princeton University Press.

Fulwiler, Toby. 1979. Journal-Writing across the Curriculum. In *Classroom Practices in Teaching English, 1979–1980: How to Handle the Paper Load,* edited by Gene Stanford, 15–22. Urbana, IL: NCTE.

————, ed. 1987. *The Journal Book.* Portsmouth, NH: Boynton/Cook.

Gawande, Atul. 2002. Cold Comfort. *New Yorker,* March 11, 42–47.

Gee, James. 1990. *Social Linguistics and Literacies: Ideologies in Discourses.* London: Falmer.

Gere, Anne Ruggles. 1990. Talking in Writing Groups. In *Perspectives on Talk and Learning,* edited by Susan Hynds and Donald L. Rubin, 115–28. Urbana, IL: NCTE.

Giltrow, Janet, and Michele Valiquette. 1994. Genres and Knowledge: Students Writing in the Disciplines. In Freedman and Medway 1994b, 47–62.

Gilyard, Keith. 1991. *Voices of the Self: A Study of Language Competence.* Detroit: Wayne State University Press.

Glassick, Charles E., Mary Taylor Huber, and Gene I. Maeroff. 1997. *Scholarship Assessed: Evaluation of the Professoriate.* San Francisco: Jossey-Bass.

Golson, Emily. 1999. Cognition, Meaning, and Creativity: On Reading Student Hypertexts. In DeWitt and Strasma 1999, 155–75.

Goodman, David. 1999. *Fault Lines: Journeys into the New South Africa.* Berkeley: University of California Press.

Graves, Donald. 1983. *Writing: Teachers and Children at Work.* Exeter, NH: Heinemann.

Greene, Stuart. 1993. The Role of Task in the Development of Academic Thinking through Reading and Writing in a College History Course. *Research in the Teaching of English* 27.1: 46–75.

————. 2001. The Question of Authenticity: Teaching Writing in a First-Year College History of Science Class. *Research in the Teaching of English* 35: 525–69.

Gregory, Dick. 1964. *Nigger.* New York: Dutton.

Haas, Christina. 1994. Learning to Read Biology: One Student's Rhetorical Development in College. *Written Communication* 11.1: 43–84.

Hairston, Maxine. 1982. The Winds of Change: Thomas Kuhn and the Revolution in the Teaching of Writing. *College Composition and Communication* 33: 76-88

Hallden, Ola. 1994. On the Paradox of Understanding History in an Educational Setting. In Leinhardt, Beck, and Stainton, 27–46.

Halliday, M. A. K.. 1985. *An Introduction to Functional Grammar.* Baltimore: Edward Arnold.

Harr, Jonathan. 1995. *A Civil Action.* New York: Random House.

Harris, Muriel. 1979. Contradictory Perceptions of Rules of Writing. *College Composition and Communication* 30: 218–20.

Harvey, Gordon. 1994. Presence in the Essay. *College English* 56.6: 642–54.

Hawisher, Gail E., and Cynthia L. Selfe, eds. 1999a. *Passions, Pedagogies, and 21st Century Technologies.* Logan: Utah State University Press.

———. 1999b. The Passions that Mark Us: Teaching, Texts, and Technologies. In Hawisher and Selfe 1999a, 1–12.

Hawisher, Gail E., and Patricia A. Sullivan. 1999. Fleeting Images: Women Visually Writing the Web. In Hawisher and Selfe 1999a, 268–91.

Heilker, Paul. 1996. *The Essay: Theory and Pedagogy for an Active Form.* Urbana, IL: NCTE.

Herrington, Anne. 1985. Writing in Academic Settings: A Study of the Contexts for Writing in Two College Chemical Engineering Courses. *Research in the Teaching of English* 19: 331–61.

Herrington, Anne, and Marcia Curtis. 2000. *Persons in Process: Four Stories of Writing and Personal Development in College.* Urbana, IL: NCTE.

Herrington, Anne, and Charles Moran, eds. 1992. *Writing, Teaching, and Learning in the Disciplines.* New York: Modern Language Association.

Hesse, Douglas. 1999. Saving a Place for Essayistic Literacy. In Hawisher and Selfe 1999a, 34–48.

Hibbett, David S. 2002. Plant-Fungal Interactions: When Good Relationships Go Bad. *Nature* 419: 345–46.

Collins, Patricia Hill. 1990. *Black Feminist Thought: Knowledge, Consciousness, and the Politics of Empowerment.* New York: Routledge.

Holdstein, Deborah H. 1996. Power, Genre, and Technology. *College Composition and Communication* 47.2: 279–84.

Jacobs, Harriet. 2000. *Incidents in the Life of a Slave Girl, Written by Herself* and *Narrative of the Life of Frederick Douglass, an American Slave.* New York: Modern Library.

Jamieson, Kathleen Hall, and Karlyn Khors Campbell. 1982. Rhetorical Hybrids: Fusions of Generic Elements. *Quarterly Journal of Speech* 68: 146–57.

Johns, Ann M. 1997. *Text, Role, and Context: Developing Academic Literacies.* Cambridge: Cambridge University Press.

———. 2002a. Destabilizing and Enriching Novice Students' Genre Theories. In Johns 2002b, 237–46.

———, ed. 2002b. *Genre in the Classroom: Multiple Perspectives.* Hillsdale, NJ: Lawrence Erlbaum.

Jolliffe, David. 1996. Twelve Readers Reading: Exemplary Responses, Thorny Problems. *Assessing Writing* 3.2: 221–33.

Jones, Billie. 2001. From Linear Text to Hypertext: A Cyber Odyssey Worth Taking? *Kairos* 6.2. http://english.ttu.edu/kairos/6.2/coverWeb/hypertext/jonesbowieaustin/index.htm.

Joyce, Michael. 1995. *Of Two Minds: Hypertext Pedagogy and Poetics.* Ann Arbor: University of Michigan Press.

Kaplan, Nancy. 1995. E-Literacies: Politexts, Hypertexts, and Other Cultural Formations in the Late Age of Print. *Computer-Mediated Communication Magazine* 2.3. http://www.ibiblio.org/cmc/mag/1995/mar/kaplan.html.

Kapp, Rochelle. 2000. "With English You Can Go Everywhere": An Analysis of the Role and Status of English at a Former DET School. *Journal of Education* 25: 227–59.

Karlen, Arno. 1995. *Man and Microbes: Disease and Plagues in History and Modern Times.* New York: Putnam.

Killoran, John B. 2002. Under Constriction: Colonization and Synthetic Institutionalization of Web Space. *Computers and Composition* 19: 19–37.

Kitzhaber, Albert R. 1990. *Rhetoric in American Colleges, 1850–1900.* Dallas: Southern Methodist University Press.

Kogawa, Joy. 1994. *Obasan.* New York: Anchor.

Kolb, David. 1994. Socrates in the Labyrinth. In Landow 1994a, 323–44.

Kress, Gunther. 1999a. English at the Crossroads: Rethinking Curricula of Communication in the Context of the Turn to the Visual. In Hawisher and Selfe 1999a, 66–89.

———. 1999b. Genre and the Changing Contexts for English Language Arts. *Language Arts* 76: 461–69.

Kress, Gunther, and Terry Threadgold. 1988. Towards a Social Theory of Genre. *Southern Review* 21: 215–43.

Kress, Gunther, and Theo van Leeuwen. 1996. *Reading Images: The Grammar of Visual Design.* London: Routledge.

Krog, Antjie. 1999. *Country of My Skull: Guilt, Sorrow, and the Limits of Forgiveness in the New South Africa.* New York: Times Books.

Landow, George. 1991. The Rhetoric of Hypermedia: Some Rules for Authors. In *Hypermedia and Literary Studies*, edited by Paul Delany and George Landow, 81–103. Cambridge: MIT Press.

———, ed. 1994a. *Hypert/Text/Theory.* Baltimore: Johns Hopkins University Press.

———. 1994b. What's a Critic to Do? Critical Theory in the Age of Hypertext. In Landow 1994a, 1–48.

———. 1997. *Hypertext 2.0.* Baltimore: Johns Hopkins University Press.

Langer, Judith A. 1984. The Effects of Available Information on Responses to School Writing Tasks. *Research in the Teaching of English* 18.1: 27–44.

———. 1992. Speaking of Knowing: Conceptions of Understanding in Academic Disciplines. In Herrington and Moran 1992, 69–85.

Lanham, Richard. 1991. *A Handlist of Rhetorical Terms.* Berkeley: University of California Press.

———. 1993. *The Electronic Word: Democracy, Technology, and the Arts.* Chicago: University of Chicago Press.

Lankshear, Colin, and Knobel, Michele. 2000. Strategies, Tactics, and the Politics of Literacy. Plenary address, Third National Conference on Academic Texts, Puebla, Mexico April 15, 2000. htttp://www.geocities.com/Athens/Academy/1160/strategies.

Larson, Richard. 1982. The "Research Paper" in the Writing Course: A Non-Form of Writing. *College English* 44: 811–16.

Lave, Jean, and Etienne Wenger. 1991. *Situated Learning: Legitimate Peripheral Participation.* Cambridge: Cambridge University Press.

Leinhardt, Gaea, Isabel Beck, and Catherine Stainton, eds. 1994. *Teaching and Learning History.* Hillsdale, NJ: Lawrence Erlbaum.

Leinhardt, Gaea, and Kathleen McCarthy Young. 1996. Two Texts, Three Readers: Distance and Expertise in Reading History. *Cognition and Instruction* 14.4: 441–86.

Lejeune, Philippe. 1989. *On Autobiography.* Edited by Paul John Eakin. Translated by Katherine Leary. Minneapolis: University of Minnesota Press.

Lemke, Jay L. 1998. Multiplying Meaning: Visual and Verbal Semiotics in Scientific Text. In *Reading Science: Critical and Functional Perspectives on Discourses of Science,* edited by James Martin and Robert Veel, 87–113. London: Routledge.

———. 2002a. Multimedia Genres for Science Education and Scientific Literacy. In *Developing Advanced Literacy in First and Second Languages,* edited by Mary Schleppegrell and Cecelia Colombi, 21–44. Mahwah, NJ: Lawrence Erlbaum.

———. 2002b. Travels in Hypermodality. *Visual Communication* 1.3: 299–325.

Leverenz, Carrie. 1997. Talk *Is* Writing: Style in Computer-Mediated Discourse. In *Elements of Alternate Style: Essays on Writing and Revision,* edited by Wendy Bishop 1997, 131–39. Portsmouth, NH: Boynton/Cook.

Levi, Carlo. 1970. *Christ Stopped at Eboli.* Translated by Frances Frenaye. New York: Farrar, Straus, and Giroux.

Levi, Primo. 1993. *Survival in Auschwitz: The Nazi Assault on Humanity.* Translated by Stuart Woolf. New York: Collier.

Lewis, Karron G., and J. Povlacs Lunde, eds. 2001. *Face to Face: A Sourcebook of Individual Consultation Techniques for Faculty/Instructional Developers.* 2nd ed. Stillwater, OK: New Forums.

Long, Laura Lai. 2002. Full (dis)Course Meal: Some Words on Hybrid/Alternative Discourses. In Schroeder, Fox and Bizzell 2002, 139-154.

Luke, Allan. 1994. Series editor's preface to Freedman and Medway 1994a, vii–xi.

———. 1996. Genres of Power? Literacy Education and the Production of Capital. In *Literacy and Society,* edited by Ruqaiya Hasan and Geoff Williams, 308–38. London: Longman.

Macken, Mary, and Diana Slade. 1993. Assessment: A Foundation for Effective Learning in the School Context. In Cope and Kalantzis 1993c, 203–30.

Macken-Horarik, Mary. 2002. "Something to Shoot For": A Systemic Functional Approach to Teaching Genre in Secondary School Science. In Johns 2002b, 17–42.

Macrorie, Ken. 1970. *Uptaught.* New York: Hayden.

Madhubuti, Haki. 1990. *Black Men: Obsolete, Single, Dangerous? The Afrikan American Family in Transition: Essays in Discovery, Solution, and Hope.* Chicago: Third World.

Maimon, Elaine P., Gerald L. Belcher, Gail W. Hearn, Barbara F. Nodine, and Finbarr W. O'Connor. 1981. *Writing in the Arts and Sciences.* Cambridge, MA: Winthrop.

Makine, Andrei. 1997. *Dreams of My Russian Summers.* Translated by Geoffrey Strachan. New York: Penguin.

Malinowitz, Harriet. 1998. A Feminist Critique of Writing-in-the-Disciplines. In *Feminism and Composition Studies,* edited by Susan Jarratt and Lynn Worsham, 291–312. New York: Modern Language Association.

Marable, Manning. 1991. *Reform and Rebellion: The Second Reconstruction in Black America, 1945–1990.* Jackson: University Press of Mississippi.

Marable, Manning, and Leith Mullings. 1999. *Let Nobody Turn Us Around.* Lanham, MD: Rowman and Littlefield.

Marsella, Joy. 1992. How Students Handle Writing Assignments: A Study of Eighteen Responses in Six Disciplines. In Herrington and Moran 1992, 174–88.

Marshall, James. 1994. Of What Does Skill in Writing Really Consist? The Political Life of the Writing Process Movement. In *Taking Stock: The Writing Process Movement in the '90's,* edited by Lad Tobin and Thomas Newkirk, 45–55. Portsmouth, NH: Boynton/Cook.

Martin, J. R. 1993. A Contextual Theory of Language. In Cope and Kalantzis 1993c, 116–36.

Mauriello, Nicholas, Gian S. Pagnucci, and Tammy Winner. 1999. Reading between the Code: The Teaching of HTML and the Displacement of Writing Instruction. *Computers and Composition* 16.3: 409–19.

Miller, Carolyn 1984. Genre as Social Action. *Quarterly Journal of Speech* 70: 151–67

———. 1994. Rhetorical Community: The Cultural Basis of Genre. In Freedman and Medway 1994a, 67–78.

Moffett, James. 1981. *The Active Voice.* Portsmouth, NH: Boynton/Cook.

Moran, Charles, and Anne Herrington. 2002. Evaluating Academic Hypertexts. In *Teaching Writing with Computers,* edited by Pamela Takayoshi and Brian Huot, 247–57. Boston: Houghton Mifflin.

Morrison, Toni. 1970. *The Bluest Eye.* New York: Holt, Rinehart, and Winston.

Mountford, Roxanne. 2001. On Gender and Rhetorical Space. *Rhetoric Society Quarterly* 31.1: 41–71.

Murray, Donald. 1968. *A Writer Teaches Writing.* Boston: Houghton Mifflin.

———. 1982. The Listening Eye: Reflections on the Writing Conference. In *Learning by Teaching,* 157–63. Portsmouth, NH: Boynton/Cook.

Myers, Greg. 1990. *Writing Biology: Texts in the Social Construction of Scientific Knowledge.* Madison: University of Wisconsin Press.

———. 1991. Stories and Styles in Two Molecular Biology Review Articles. In *Textual Dynamics of the Professions: Historical and Contemporary Studies of Writing in Professional Communities,* edited by Charles Bazerman and James Paradis, 45–75. Madison: University of Wisconsin Press.

Negroponte, Nicholas. 1995. *Being Digital.* New York: Knopf.

Nelson, Ted. 1983. *Literary Machines.* Bloomington: Indiana University Press.

Ngugi wa Thiong'o. 1986. *Decolonising the Mind: The Politics of Language in African Literature.* Portsmouth, NH: Heinemann.

Nguyen, Lucy, and Joel Halpern. 1960. *The Far East Comes Near.* Amherst: University of Massachusetts Press.

Nielsen, Jakob. 1996. Top Ten Mistakes in Web Design. *Jakob Nielsen's Alertbox* (May). http://useit.com/alertbox/9605.html.

———. 1997. Changes in Web Usability since 1994. *Jakob Nielsen's Alertbox,* December. http://useit.com/alertbox/9712a.html.

North Carolina State University. 2003a. Design Fundamentals. http://www2.chass.ncsu.edu/cwsp/seminar_reports/toplikar_ex.html.

———. 2003b. First-Year Inquiry. http://www.ncsu.edu/firstyearinquiry.

Norton, David, Beverly Zimmerman, and Neil Lindeman. 1999. Developing Hyperphoric Grammar to Teach Collaborative Hypertexts. In DeWitt and Strasma 1999, 177–202.

N.W.A. 1989. Fuck tha Police. By Ice Cube and MC Ren. *Straight Outta Compton.* Priority.

Olney, James. 1998. *Memory and Narrative.* Chicago: University of Chicago Press.

Paxton, Richard J. 1999. A Deafening Silence: History Textbooks and the Students Who Read Them. *Review of Educational Research* 69.3: 315–39.

Perelman, Chaim, and Lucie Olbrechts-Tyteca. 1969. *The New Rhetoric.* Translated by John Wilkinson and Purcell Weaver. Notre Dame: University of Notre Dame Press.

Petroff, Elizabeth A. 1986. *Medieval Women's Visionary Literature.* New York: Oxford University Press.

Plato. 1995. *Phaedrus.* Translated by Alexander Nehamus and Paul Woodruff. Indianapolis: Hackett.

Powell, Malea. 2002. Listening to Ghosts: An Alternative (Non)argument. In Schroeder, Fox, and Bizzell 2002, 11–22.

Prior, Paul. 1998. *Writing/Disciplinarity.* Mahwah, NJ: Lawrence Erlbaum.

Ramphele, Mamphela. 1995. *A Life.* Cape Town: David Phillip.

Reddy, Michael J. 1979. The Conduit Metaphor: A Case of Frame Conflict in Our Language about Language. In *Metaphor and Thought,* edited by Andrew Ortony, 164–201. Cambridge: Cambridge University Press.

Rho, Young J., and T. D. Gedeon. 2000. Academic Articles on the Web: Readings, Patterns, and Formats. *International Journal of Human-Computer Interaction* 12.2: 219–40.

Rice, R. Eugene. 1996. *Making a Place for the New American Scholar.* Washington, DC: American Association for Higher Education.

Robinson, Cedric. 2000. *Black Marxism: The Making of the Black Radical Tradition.* Chapel Hill: University of North Carolina Press.

Rodriguez, Richard. 1983. *Hunger of Memory: The Education of Richard Rodriguez.* New York: Bantam.

Romano, Tom. 2000. *Blending Genre, Altering Style: Writing Multi-Genre Papers.* Portsmouth, NH: Boynton/Cook.

Russell, David R. 1991. *Writing in the Academic Disciplines, 1870–1990: A Curricular History.* Carbondale: Southern Illinois University Press.

———. 1997. Rethinking Genre in School and Society. *Written Communication* 14: 504–55.

Russell, David R., and Arturo Yan ez. 2003. "Big Picture People Rarely Become Historians": Genre Systems and the Contradictions of General Education. In *Writing Selves/Writing Societies,* edited by Charles Bazerman and David R. Russell, 331–62. http://wac.colostate.edu/books/selves_societies.

Rymer, Jone. 1988. Scientific Composing Processes: How Eminent Scientists Write Journal Articles. In *Advances in Writing Research,* Vol. 2: *Writing in Academic Disciplines,* edited by David Joliffe 211-250. Norwood, NJ: Ablex.

Schön, Donald A. 1987. *Educating the Reflective Practitioner.* San Francisco: Jossey-Bass.

Schroeder, Christopher, Helen Fox, and Patricia Bizzell, eds. 2002. *AltDis: Alternative Discourses and the Academy.* Portsmouth, NH: Boynton/Cook.

Schryer, Catherine F. 1994. The Lab vs. the Clinic: Sites of Competing Genres. In Freedman and Medway 1994a, 105–24.

Scott, Mary. 2002. Cracking the Codes Anew: Writing about Literature in England. In *Writing and Learning in Cross-National Perspective: Transitions from Secondary School to Higher Education,* edited by David Foster and David Russell, 88–133. Urbana, IL: NCTE.

Shaughnessy, Mina P. 1977. *Errors and Expectations.* New York: Oxford.

Siddler, Michelle. 2002. Web Research and Genres in Online Databases: When the Glossy Page Disappears. *Computers and Composition* 19.1: 57–70.

Simpson, Alyson. 2003. Textbook assignment. http://www.edfac.usyd.edu.au/ staff/simpsona/ 2003unitoutlines/Undergrad/EDUP4012Multi.html.

Slatin, John M. 1990. Reading Hypertext: Order and Coherence in a New Medium. *College English* 52.8: 870–83.

Slevin, James F. 1988. Genre Theory, Academic Discourse, and Writing within Disciplines. In *Audits of Meaning,* edited by Louise Z. Smith, 3–16. Portsmouth, NH: Boynton/Cook.

Smith, Sidonie, and Julia Watson. 2001. *Reading Autobiography: A Guide for Interpreting Life Narratives.* Minneapolis: University of Minnesota Press.

Smitherman, Geneva. 2000. *Talkin That Talk: Language, Culture, and Education in African America*. New York: Routledge.

Snyder, Ilana, ed. 1998. *Page to Screen: Taking Literacy into the Electronic Era*. Sydney: Allen and Unwin.

Some, Malidoma Patrice. 1995. *Of Water and the Spirit*. New York: Penguin.

Spooner, Michael, and Kathleen Yancey. 1996. Postings on a Genre of Email. *College Composition and Communication* 47.2: 252–78.

Stockton, Sharon. 1995. Writing History: Narrating the Subject of Time. *Written Communication* 12.1: 47–73.

Storey, William Kelleher. 1999. *Writing History: A Guide for Students*. New York: Oxford University Press.

Swales, John, and Margaret Luebs. 2002. Genre Analysis and the Advanced Second Language Writer. In *Discourse Studies in Composition*, edited by Ellen Barton and Gail Stygall, 135–54. Cresskill, NJ: Hampton.

Tan, Amy. 1991. Mother Tongue. In *Best American Essays*, edited by Joyce Carol Oates and Robert Atwan, 196–202. Boston: Ticknor and Fields.

Thesen, Lucia. 1997. Voices, Discourse, and Transition: In Search of New Categories in EAP. *Tesol Quarterly* 31.3: 487–511.

Thornton, Robert. 1988. Culture: A Contemporary Definition. In *South African Keywords*, edited by Emile Boonzaier and John Sharp, 17–28. Cape Town: David Phillip.

Tosh, John. 1984. *The Pursuit of History: Aims, Methods, and New Directions in the Study of Modern History*. New York: Longman.

Toulmin, Stephen E. 1958. *The Uses of Argument*. New York: Cambridge University Press.

Trimbur, John. 2002. *The Call to Write*. Brief 2nd. ed. New York: Longman.

University of Massachusetts Writing Program. 2002. Course goals. *Syllabus for English 112*. http://writingprogram.hfa.umass.edu/for_students/112/sylla-bus.html.

Vaughan, Misha W., and Andrew Dillon. 2000. Learning the Shape of Information: A Longitudinal Study of Web-News Reading. *Proceedings of the Fifth ACM Conference on Digital Libraries*, San Antonio, Texas, 236–237. New York: ACM.

Walker, Kristin. 2002. Theoretical Foundations for Website Design Courses. *Technical Communication Quarterly* 11.1: 61–83.

Walters, Margaret Bennett. 1992. Robert Zoellner's "Talk-Write Pedagogy": An Instrumental Concept for Today. *Rhetoric Review* 10: 239–43.

Walvoord, Barbara, and Lucille P. McCarthy. 1990. *Thinking and Writing in College*. Urbana, IL: NCTE.

Watt, Ian. 1957. *The Rise of the Novel: Studies in Defoe, Richardson, and Fielding*. Berkeley: University of California Press.

Watters, Carolyn, and Michael A. Shepherd. 1997. The Digital Broadsheet: An Evolving Genre. *Proceedings of the 30th Annual Hawaii International Conference on System Sciences*, 22–29. Los Alamitos: IEEE Computer Society.

Watts, David G. 1972. *The Learning of History.* London: Routledge and Kegan Paul.

Weinstein, Fred. 1990. *History and Theory after the Fall.* Chicago: University of Chicago Press.

Wellek, René, and Austin Warren. 1942. *Theory of Literature.* New York: Harcourt.

Wickliff, Greg, and Kathleen Blake Yancey. 2001. The Perils of Creating a Class Web Site: It Was the Best of Times, It Was the . . . *Computers and Composition* 18.2: 177–86.

Williams, Joseph, and Gregory Colomb. 1993. The Case for Explicit Teaching: Why What You Don't Know Won't Help You. *Research in the Teaching of English* 27: 252–64.

Williams, Sean D. 2001. Part 2: Toward an Integrated Composition Pedagogy in Hypertext. *Computers and Composition* 18.2: 123–35.

Wineburg, Samuel S. 1991a. Historical Problem Solving: A Study of the Cognitive Processes Used in the Evaluation of Documentary and Pictorial Evidence. *Journal of Educational Psychology* 83.1: 73–87.

———. 1991b. On the Reading of Historical Texts: Notes on the Breach between School and Academy. *American Educational Research Journal* 28.3: 495–519.

———. 1994. The Cognitive Representation of Historical Texts. In Leinhardt, Beck, and Stainton 1994, 85–135.

———.2001. *Historical Thinking and Other Unnatural Acts: Charting the Future of Teaching the Past.* Philadelphia: Temple University Press.

Wynter, Sylvia. 1981. "In Quest of Matthew Bondsman: Some Cultural Notes on the Jamesian Journey." *Urgent Tasks* 12, 54

Wysocki, Anne Frances. 2001. Impossibly Distinct: On Form/Content and Word/ Image in Two Pieces of Computer-Based Interactive Multimedia. *Computers and Composition* 18: 137–62.

Yahoo. 2003. Yahoo Privacy (May). http://privacy.yahoo.com/privacy/us/print. html.

Yancey, Kathleen Blake. 1998. *Reflection in the Writing Classroom.* Logan: Utah State University Press.

———. 2001. A Matter of Design: The Uses of Writing, Speech, and the Visual in Learning across the Curriculum. Plenary address, Conference on Writing across the Curriculum: Writing, Teaching, and Learning in New Contexts, Bloomington, IN, June 1.

———. 2004. *Teaching Literature as Reflective Practice.* Urbana, IL: NCTE.

Young, Kathleen McCarthy, and Gaea Leinhardt. 1998. Writing from Primary Documents: A Way of Knowing in History. *Written Communication* 15.1: 25–68.

Zoellner, Robert. 1969. Talk-Write: A Behavioral Pedagogy for Composition. *College English* 30: 267–320.

CONTRIBUTORS

ANNE HERRINGTON is professor and chair of English at the University of Massachusetts at Amherst. She is also a former director of the writing program. With Charles Moran, she co-edited *Writing, Teaching, and Learning in the Disciplines* (MLA, 1992). She and Marcia Curtis co-authored *Persons in Process: Four Stories of Writing and Personal Development in College* (NCTE, 2000), for which they received NCTE's David Russell Award for Distinguished Research in the Teaching of Writing.

CHARLES MORAN is professor of English, emeritus, at the University of Massachusetts at Amherst. With Anne Herrington, he co-edited *Writing, Teaching, and Learning in the Disciplines* (MLA, 1992). With Gail Hawisher, Paul LeBlanc, and Cynthia Selfe he co-authored *Computers and the Teaching of Writing in American Higher Education, 1979-1994: A History* (Ablex, 1996). He has served as director of the university writing program and as site director of the Western Massachusetts Writing Project, and has published articles in a range of professional journals.

CHRIS ANSON is professor of English and director of the Campus Writing and Speaking Program at North Carolina State University, where he helps faculty in nine colleges to integrate writing and speaking into all courses. He has published twelve books and fifty articles and book chapters, and has spoken or consulted at colleges and universities across the U.S. He is current president of the Council of Writing Program Administrators.

BONGI BANGENI is lecturer in language development at the University of Cape Town. Her research interests lie in the area of ESL writing and identity, multi-lingualism in higher education, and language attitudes. Her work also includes consulting at the institution=s writing center.

ANNE BEAUFORT is associate professor of writing and rhetoric at Stony Brook University. She is the author of *Writing in the Real World: Making the Transition from School to Work* (1999 Teachers College Press), an ethnography of writers learning to write in new discourse communities and new genres. Her most recent research, a portion of which was published in *Research in the Teaching of English* (Nov. 2004) chronicles one student=s writing in two academic discourse communities (fresh-man composition and history) and in engineering.

DEANNA P. DANNELS is associate professor of communication and the assistant director of the Campus Writing and Speaking Program at North Carolina State University. Her research explores theoretical frameworks for communication across the curriculum and protocols for implementing and assessing communication within the disciplines. She has published in the fields of communication, composition, education, and technical communication. She is the guest editor of a special issue of *Communication Education* (1/05) focused on oral genres in the disciplines.

MIKE EDWARDS is a Ph.D. candidate at the University of Massachusetts at Amherst. He co-edited *The Original Text-Wrestling Book* (Kendall-Hunt, 2001), and writes regularly about composition, class, technology, and other topics at http://www.vitia.org. He is currently working on a dissertation on economics, computers, and writing.

ANNE ELLEN GELLER has been since 1999 director of the writing center and writing program at Clark University, in Worcester, Massachusetts, where she also teaches writing classes, including a literacy class that incorporates community engagement. As part of a Carnegie Corporation funded initiative, she has, for the past two years, worked with high school literacy coaches consulting across the disciplines in the Worcester Public Schools. She has been a co-chair of the 2004 and 2005 International Writing Centers Association summer institutes.

ROCHELLE KAPP is senior lecturer in language development in the Centre for Higher Education Development at the University of Cape Town. Her Ph.D. was on the politics of English in black township schools. She has published in the areas of literacy studies, English as a second language, and multilingualism in secondary and higher education contexts. She has recently completed a research fellowship hosted by the Five College African Scholars= Program in Amherst, Massachusetts.

CARMEN KYNARD is instructor at Medgar Evers College of the City University of New York. She teaches first year composition and "The Spoken Word in African American Written Texts" as well as education department courses. She is a Ph.D. candidate at New York University, completing her dissertation, "Runnin Wit The Rabbits But Huntin Wit the Dogs: Race, Literacy, and Composition Studies, 1969-1977." This comp newjack says that when she grows up, she wants to be a teacher.

HEIDI A. MCKEE is a doctoral student in English at the University of Massachusetts at Amherst. Her work has appeared in *College Composition and Communication, Computers and Composition, Computers and Composition Online,* and *Pedagogy.* With Danielle Nicole DeVoss, she is currently co-editing the collection *Digital Writing Research: Technologies, Methodologies, and Ethical Issues.*

MIKE PALMQUIST is professor of English and University Distinguished Teaching Scholar at Colorado State University. His scholarly interests include writing across the curriculum, the effects of computer and network technologies on writing instruction, and the use of hypertext/hypermedia in instructional settings. He is the 2004 recipient of the Charles Moran Award for Distinguished Contributions to the Field.

T. Shane Peagler is a graduate of the University of North Carolina at Charlotte and a former faculty member at Clemson University. He is currently pursuing a variety of interests in writing, editing, architecture and management in Greenville, South Carolina, where he lives happily with his wife, Dennise, and his two cats, Maddie and Cleo.

Elizabeth Petroff is professor of comparative literature at the University of Massachusetts at Amherst, the author of three books on medieval women writers, author of numerous articles on medieval saints and mystics, autobiography and biography, and myths of the feminine, and of translations from Latin and Italian. Her current research and teaching interests are reading and writing autobiography and myths about women in ancient literatures.

Karen St. Clair, assistant director of North Carolina State University=s Faculty Center for Teaching and Learning, provides formative teaching evaluation services and graduate student teaching assistant programming. In addition, she teaches "Psychological Controversies" for a freshman, critical thinking-based program. Through both roles, she engages in the scholarship of teaching and learning by collaborating with other campus service units and presenting at teaching and learning conferences.

Mary Soliday is associate professor of English at the City College of New York where she is also a City University of New York Writing Across the Curriculum coordinator. She is the author of *The Politics of Remediation* (University of Pittsburgh Press, 2002), which received the CCCC 2004 Outstanding Book Award. She has contributed many articles on composition teaching and research to edited collections and professional journals.

Kathleen Blake Yancey is R. Roy Pearce Professor of English at Clemson University. Chair of the Conference on College Composition and Communication and past president of the Council of Writing Program Administrators, she directs the Pearce Center for Professional Communication. She has edited, co-edited, or authored 8 books, most recently *Teaching Literature as Reflective Practice* (NCTE, 2004). Her current projects include the *Portraits of Composition* research and *Electronic Portfolios: Interfaces for Learning.*

John A. Williams received his Ph.D. from the University of Wisconsin in 1957. He has been in the history department at SUNY Stony Brook since 1968, where he has taught African, Indian, and British Empire history. His books include Politics of the New Zealand Maori (1969), and Classroom in Conflict: Teaching Controversial Subjects in a Diverse Society (1994).

INDEX